Eighth Edition

Form A

Inside Writing

A Writer's Workbook

William Salomone
Palomar College

Stephen McDonald
Palomar College

Martin Japtok
Palomar College

CENGAGE
Learning

Australia • Brazil • Mexico • Singapore • United Kingdom • United States

CENGAGE
Learning

**Inside Writing: A Writer's Workbook, Form A,
Eighth Edition**
William Salomone, Stephen McDonald,
Martin Japtok

Product Director: Monica Eckman

Developmental Studies Product Manager:
    Annie Todd

Content Developer: Margaret Manos

Content Coordinator: Elizabeth Rice

Product Assistant: Luria Rittenberg

Media Developer: Christian Biagetti

Marketing Manager: Lydia Lestar

Rights Acquisitions Specialist: Ann Hoffman

Manufacturing Planner: Betsy Donaghey

Art and Design Direction, Production
    Management, and Composition:
    Cenveo® Publisher Services

Cover Image: Gettyimages.com

For product information and technology assistance, contact us at
Cengage Learning Customer & Sales Support, 1-800-354-9706

For permission to use material from this text or product,
submit all requests online at **www.cengage.com/permissions.**
Further permissions questions can be emailed to
permissionrequest@cengage.com.

Library of Congress Control Number: 2013946062

ISBN-13: 978-1-285-44354-6

ISBN-10: 1-285-44354-3

Cengage Learning
200 First Stamford Place, 4th Floor
Stamford, CT 06902
USA

Cengage Learning is a leading provider of customized learning solutions with office locations around the globe, including Singapore, the United Kingdom, Australia, Mexico, Brazil and Japan. Locate your local office at **international.cengage.com/region.**

Cengage Learning products are represented in Canada by
Nelson Education, Ltd.

For your course and learning solutions, visit **www.cengage.com.**

Purchase any of our products at your local college store
or at our preferred online store **www.cengagebrain.com.**

Instructors: Please visit **login.cengage.com** and log in to access instructor-specific resources.

Printed in the United states of America
2 3 4 5 17 16 15 14

To Rosemary, Marlyle, and Nagadya

Contents

Chapter Five   Using Punctuation and Capitalization   281

Preface

Inside Writing was constructed on the premise that there is really only one reason for learning the essential rules of English grammar—to become better writers. In this text, we constantly stress that all college students are writers and that the aim of any college writing course—developmental or otherwise—is to improve writing. To this purpose, *Inside Writing* has been created with clear and simple organization, a friendly, nonthreatening tone, thorough integration of grammar sections with writing sections, and unique thematic exercises.

The Reason for This Text

We are all aware of widespread disagreement about what should be presented in a first-semester developmental writing course. *Inside Writing* was written to address the resulting diversity of course content with a union of grammar and writing instruction. In it, we teach basic grammar and sentence structure, yet we also provide extensive practice in sentence combining and paragraph writing.

Moving beyond a Traditional Approach. The traditional approach to developmental writing has been to review the rules of grammar, punctuation, and usage and then to test the students' understanding of those rules through a series of chapter tests. However, as research and experience have demonstrated, there is no necessary correlation between the study of grammar and the development of competent writers. As a result, many English departments have restructured their developmental courses to focus on the process of writing, developing courses that have very little in common with each other from one campus to the next. Today, some developmental writing instructors teach the traditional exercises in grammar, others focus on journal and expressive writing, others emphasize sentence combining, and still others teach the writing of paragraphs and short essays.

Using an Integrated Approach. Inside Writing responds to this spectrum of course content by integrating grammar instruction and writing practice. Certainly the practice of writing is important in a first-semester developmental class. Yet the study of traditional grammar, punctuation, and usage is also important because it provides a fundamental knowledge of sentence structure—knowledge that writers need not only to revise their own writing but also to discuss their writing with others. The writing practices in this text are specifically designed to support, not merely to supplement, the grammar instruction. As soon as students have mastered a particular grammatical principle, they are asked to put their knowledge into practice in the writing sections of each chapter. This immediate reinforcement makes it more likely that students will improve their writing as well as retain the rules of grammar, usage, and mechanics.

Text Organization and Features

Inside Writing is presented in five chapters and an appendix. Each chapter consists of five sections that cover major principles of basic grammar, sentence construction, and paragraph writing. The appendix provides a review of common ESL issues. Throughout the text, the instruction is kept as simple as possible, giving the students only the information that is absolutely essential.

- Each chapter's grammar instruction is broken into three sections so that the students are not presented with too much at once.

- Each of the three grammar sections includes various practices and ends with several exercises that give the students an opportunity to apply the concepts and rules they have learned.

- Each chapter is followed by a practice test covering the material presented in the first three sections of the chapter, and the text closes with a practice final examination.

- The fourth section of each chapter presents both instruction and exercises in sentence combining, based on the specific concepts and rules covered in the three grammar sections. For example, in the chapter covering participial phrases and adjective clauses, the sentence combining section instructs the students to combine sentences by using participial phrases and adjective clauses.

- The fifth section of each chapter includes instruction in writing paragraphs and essays and a choice of several writing assignments, again designed to reinforce the grammar sections of the chapter by leading students to employ in their own writing the rules for sentence structure they have studied.

- The appendix, "Working with ESL Issues," discusses common challenges faced by the ESL writer, including the correct use of count and noncount nouns, articles, subjects and verbs, and adjectives.

- At the end of the text, answers to the practices—but not to the exercises—are provided. These answers allow the students to check their understanding of the material as they read the text. The extensive exercises without answers permit the instructor to determine where more explanation or study is needed.

- Many of the practices and exercises develop thematic ideas or contain a variety of cultural, mythological, and historical allusions. Some exercises, for example, explain the origin of the names of our weekdays, tell the story of the Native American character Woodpecker, or illustrate common urban legends. In addition, individual sentences within practices and exercises often provoke questions and discussion when they refer to characters and events from history, mythology, or contemporary culture. This feature of *Inside Writing* encourages developmental writing students to look beyond grammar, mechanics, and punctuation. It reminds them—or it allows us as instructors to remind them—that the educated writer has command of much more than the correct use of the comma.

Connecting Concepts and Writing Practice. To emphasize further the connection between the writing assignments and the grammar exercises, the writing assignment in each chapter is modeled by three thematic exercises within the grammar sections of the chapter. For instance, in Chapter 3, Exercises 1D, 2D, and 3C are paragraphs that use examples to support a statement made in a topic sentence. The writing practice section then extends this groundwork by presenting instruction in the writing of a similar expository paragraph or essay.

In each writing assignment, the students are introduced gradually to the writing process and encouraged to improve their writing through prewriting and careful revision. They are also introduced to the basic concepts of academic writing—thesis statements, topic sentences, unity, specificity, completeness, order, and coherence. However, the main purpose of the writing instruction is to give the students an opportunity to use their new knowledge of grammar and sentence structure to communicate their own thoughts and ideas.

Changes to This Edition

We have improved the Eighth Edition of *Inside Writing* in several areas:

■ Over 50 percent of practices and exercises are new.

■ New thematic exercises that function not only as a way to test the students' comprehension of grammar, punctuation, or usage principles but also as an example of the writing assignment introduced in the chapter have been added throughout the text.

■ All thematic practices and exercises are now presented as complete paragraphs rather than as separate numbered sentences to emphasize the connection between the study of grammar, punctuation, and usage and the process of writing, revising, and editing.

■ Exercises are included that ask students to find and bring to class from their own readings (such as magazines, newspapers, books, or websites) sentences that illustrate the concept under review.

■ Chapter Six has been removed from the text to allow instructors more time to review and complete all material in the first five chapters. It will, however, be available online for instructors to use if they wish to do so.

■ Chapter tests are now formatted so that instructors can test only the material in the chapter under study, bypassing the review questions from earlier chapters.

■ As with all previous editions, we have included literary, historical, and cultural allusions as well as references to popular culture to interest both the instructor and the student. For example, in just the first three sections of Chapter 1 are allusions to Pandora, Benjamin Franklin, Hafiz, the Black Eyed Peas, Toni Morrison, Kanye West, Emily Dickinson, Yo-Yo Ma, Persephone, Steve Jobs, Thor, Oedipus, Pablo Neruda, the *Brave New World*, Mother Teresa, Kobe Bryant, Mozart, and Taylor Swift. Later in the text, one will find many more allusions, including references to Mahatma Gandhi, women in ancient Egypt, samurai, and the popular HBO series *Game of Thrones*.

Many instructors use these allusions as part of their classes, asking students if they know what they refer to, or, if a joke is involved, whether or not they get the joke. Here's an example from page 3: "Pandora stared curiously at the box in her hand." Instructors can use this sentence as they would any other sentence in the practice (underlining nouns), or they can stop for a moment and ask if anyone knows whether Pandora opened that box—or if she should open the box. A few students at this level will have heard of Pandora, but not many. Those who can answer the question teach the other students a little about mythology. Not all the allusions are serious. Some are ironic or humorous: "When Mr. Nosferatu came over for dinner last night, he kept staring at my fiancée's neck" or "My favorite Mae West quotation is this one: 'When I'm good, I'm very good, but when I'm bad, I'm better.'" The point is that such allusions provide a depth of content and a lighthearted tone that go beyond the rote recitation of practices and exercises.

An Exceptional Support Package

The Instructor's Manual, accessible on the instructor companion site at login.cengage.com, provides suggestions for how to use the text, answers to the exercises, diagnostic and achievement tests, a series of five chapter tests and five alternate chapter tests, a final examination, answers to the tests and final examination, additional writing assignments, and model paragraphs. With this material, the instructor can use a traditional lecture approach, working through each chapter and then testing the students together, or the instructor can allow the students to work through the book at their own pace, dealing with the students' questions individually and giving students tests as they complete each chapter.

In addition, the material omitted from this edition of the text—Chapter Six, "Choosing the Right Words and Spelling Them Correctly"—will be available on the instructor companion site for those instructors who prefer to teach it.

This text is available in an alternate version, "Form B," which includes reading selections, for added teaching flexibility in the second semester.

Acknowledgments

We thank all our friends and colleagues in the English Department at Palomar College, particularly to those of you who have used *Inside Writing* and so generously offered your support and suggestions.

We extend our thanks to the staff at Cengage Learning, including Annie Todd, Product Manager; Lydia Lestar, Marketing Manager; Elizabeth Rice, Content Coordinator; Luria Rittenberg, Product Assistant; Tania Andrabi, Production Project Manager; and Margaret Manos, who so ably assisted us throughout the revision.

We are very grateful to the following professors who provided valuable input for this revision:

Mary Findley	*Vermont Technical College,* Randolph, VT
Dianne Krob	*Rose State College,* Midwest City, OK
Richard Hishmeh	*Palomar College,* San Marcos, CA
Mary McWilliams	*Palomar College,* San Marcos, CA
Jon Panish	*Palomar College,* San Marcos, CA
Melissa Barrett	*Portland Community College, Clark Community College* Portland, OR
Karen Abele	*Sauk Valley Community College,* Dixon, IL
Margie Dernaika	*Southwest Tennessee Community College,* Memphis, TN
Joel Boehner	*Bethel College,* Mishawaka, CA
Michael Boyd	*Illinois Central College,* East Peoria, IL
Judy Covington	*Trident Technical College,* North Charleston, SC

Finally, of course, we thank our families and friends for their patience and support as we once again worked late into the night.

William Salomone
Stephen McDonald
Martin Japtok

Naming the Parts

Let's face it. Few people find grammar a fascinating subject, and few study it of their own free will. Most people study grammar only when they are absolutely required to do so. Many seem to feel that grammar is either endlessly complicated or not important to their daily lives.

The problem is not that people fail to appreciate the importance of writing. The ability to express oneself clearly on paper is generally recognized as an important advantage. Those who can communicate their ideas and feelings effectively have a much greater chance to develop themselves, not only professionally but personally as well.

Perhaps the negative attitude toward grammar is due in part to the suspicion that studying grammar has little to do with learning how to write. This suspicion is not at all unreasonable—a knowledge of grammar by itself will not make anyone a better writer. To become a better writer, a person should study *writing* and practice it frequently. In addition, anyone wishing to become a better writer will also have to read regularly, just as anyone wishing to be a musician has to listen to music.

However, the study of writing is much easier if one understands grammar (just as becoming a musician is helped by learning something about the technical aspects of music). Certainly a person can learn to write well without knowing exactly how sentences are put together or what the various parts are called. But most competent writers do know these things because such knowledge enables them not only to develop their skills more easily but also to analyze their writing and discuss it with others.

Doctors, for example, don't necessarily have to know the names of the tools they use (stethoscope, scalpel, sutures), nor do mechanics have to know the names of their tools (wrench, screwdriver, ratchet). But it would be hard to find competent doctors or mechanics who are not thoroughly familiar with the tools of their trades, for it is much more difficult to master any important skill and also more difficult to discuss that skill without such knowledge.

The terms and concepts you encounter in this chapter are familiar to most of you, but probably not familiar enough. It is not good enough to have a vague idea of what a linking verb is or a general notion of what a prepositional phrase is. You should know *precisely* what these terms mean. This chapter and subsequent chapters present only what is basic and necessary to the study of grammar, but it is essential that you learn *all* of what is presented.

A sound understanding of grammar, like a brick wall, must be built one level at a time. You cannot miss a level and go on to the next. If you master each level as it is presented, you will find that grammar is neither as difficult nor as complicated as you may have thought. You will also find, as you work through the writing sections of the text, that by applying your knowledge of grammar you can greatly improve your writing skills.

Subjects and Verbs

Of all the terms presented in this chapter, perhaps the most important are **SUBJECT** and **VERB**, for subjects and verbs are the foundation of every sentence. Sentences come in many forms, and the structures may become quite complex, but they all have one thing in common: <u>Every sentence must contain a SUBJECT and a VERB.</u> Like most grammatical rules, this one is based on simple logic. After all, without a subject you have nothing to write about, and without a verb you have nothing to say about your subject.

Subjects: Nouns and Pronouns

Before you can find the subject of a sentence, you need to be able to identify nouns and pronouns because the subjects of sentences will always be nouns or pronouns (or, occasionally, other words or groups of words that function as subjects). You probably know the definition of a noun: **A noun names a person, place, thing, or idea.**

---

noun

A noun names a person, place, thing, or idea.

This definition works perfectly well for most nouns, especially for those that name concrete things we can *see, hear, smell, taste,* or *touch.* Using this definition, most people can identify words such as *door, road,* or *tulip* as nouns.

EXAMPLES

      N   N   N
Paula reads her favorite **book** whenever she goes to the **beach**.

      N   N   N
My **brother** likes to watch **football** on television.

Unfortunately, when it comes to identifying <u>ideas</u> as nouns, many people have trouble. Part of this problem is that nouns name even more than ideas. They name **emotions, qualities, conditions,** and many other **abstractions or concepts.** Abstract nouns such as *fear, courage, happiness,* and *trouble* do not name persons, places, or things, but they <u>are</u> nouns.

Following are a few examples of nouns, arranged by category. Add nouns of your own to each category.

Persons	*Places*	*Things*	*Ideas*
Paula	New York	spaghetti	sincerity
engineer	beach	book	anger
woman	India	sun	democracy
artist	town	bicycle	intelligence
_____	_____	_____	_____
_____	_____	_____	_____
_____	_____	_____	_____

☯ PRACTICE   Place an "N" above all the nouns in the following sentences.

             N   *N*   *N*   *N*

1. Brad asked Jennifer to look in the mirror at her hair.

2. Harebrained is the name of a new salon in our city.

3. Pandora stared curiously at the box in her hand.

4. Humpty hoped the men near the wall would solve his problem.

5. Barack Obama gave a confident speech at his inauguration.

To help you identify <u>all</u> nouns, remember these points:

1. Nouns can be classified as **proper nouns** and **common nouns**. **Proper nouns** name specific persons, places, things, and ideas. The first letter in each of these nouns is capitalized (Manuelita, Missouri, Mazda, Marxism). **Common nouns** name more general categories. The first letter of a common noun is not capitalized (man, mansion, moss, marriage).

2. **A, an,** and **the** are noun markers. A noun will always follow one of these words, though not necessarily immediately. There might be other words between **a, an,** and **the** and the noun.

☯ EXAMPLES

                   N   N
The young police officer was given a new car.

             N   N   N   N
The final point of the lecture addressed an inconsistency in the last report.

3. If you are unsure whether or not a word is a noun, ask yourself if it <u>could be introduced with **a, an,** or **the.**</u>

☯ EXAMPLE

               N   N   N
My granddaughter asked for my opinion of her new outfit.

4. Words that end in -**ment**, -**ism**, -**ness**, -**ence**, -**ance**, and -**tion** are usually nouns.

⑥⑨ **EXAMPLE**

         N   N

Her **criticism** of my **performance** made me very unhappy.

---

⑥⑨ **PRACTICE**   Place an "N" above all the nouns in the following sentences.

        N   *N*   *N*   *N*

1. Relationships between gods and goddesses can create many problems.

2. Hades and Persephone had a volatile marriage.

3. In spring Persephone surfaced on the coast of Greece.

4. Her husband missed her as she enjoyed the cool breezes of the Aegean Sea.

5. In autumn she packed her clothes and descended to her home in the underworld.

6. Alice stared in amazement at the cat with the enormous grin.

7. Love and tolerance are not usually characteristics of racism and prejudice.

8. The success of his experiment came as no shock to Benjamin Franklin.

9. The tiny decorative candle cast a thin light that did little to improve the depressing condition of the room.

10. Hafiz was a poet of the fourteenth century who combined wit, humor, eroticism, and a deep reverence for the sacred.

A pronoun takes the place of a noun. The "pro" in *pronoun* comes from the Latin word meaning "for." Thus, a <u>pronoun</u> is a word that in some way stands "for a noun." Pronouns perform this task in a variety of ways. Often, a pronoun will allow you to refer to a noun without having to repeat the noun. For instance, notice how the word *John* is awkwardly repeated in the following sentence:

<u>John</u> put on <u>John's</u> coat before <u>John</u> left for <u>John's</u> job.

Pronouns allow you to avoid the repetition:

John put on <u>his</u> coat before <u>he</u> left for <u>his</u> job.

pronoun
A pronoun takes the place of a noun.

In later chapters we will discuss the use of pronouns and the differences among the various types. For now, you simply need to be able to recognize pronouns in a sentence. The following list includes the most common pronouns. Read over this list several times until you are familiar with these words.

Personal Pronouns

I	we	you	he	she	they	it
me	us	your	him	her	them	its
my	our	yours	his	hers	their	
mine	ours				theirs	

Indefinite Pronouns

some	everyone	anyone	someone	no one
all	everything	anything	something	nothing
many	everybody	anybody	somebody	nobody
each				
one				
none				

Reflexive/Intensive Pronouns

myself	ourselves
yourself	yourselves
himself	themselves
herself	
itself	

Relative Pronouns

who, whom, whose
which
that

Demonstrative Pronouns

that	this
those	these

Interrogative Pronouns

who, whom, whose
which
what

PRACTICE

Place an "N" above all nouns and a "Pro" above all pronouns in the following sentences.

1. Erik noticed their boat was drifting toward the falls, so he dropped its anchor.

(N above Erik, Pro above their, N above falls, Pro above he, Pro above its, N above anchor)

2. Each of us should know whose entry on Facebook started the rumor.

3. The winners on *Survivor* all developed a taste for insects.

4. Whom did Richard Nixon visit when he went to China in 1972?

5. My account on Twitter is not working on your smartphone.

6. Does anyone know what the term "junk bond" means?

7. The Black Eyed Peas have had dozens of hits, and my brother has all of them on his iPhone.

8. Many of the veterans of Korea and Vietnam are assisting those who return from Iraq and Afghanistan with injuries.

9. I read the novel *Beloved,* by Toni Morrison, by myself, but I understood it much better after my sister explained it to me.

10. Some claim that Kanye West is a great rapper, but my mother has always preferred Tupac Shakur.

PRACTICE

In the following sentences, write nouns and pronouns of your own choice as indicated.

          N   N   Pro   N

1. The _*sailor*_ on the _*pier*_ stared at _*his*_ _*pipe*_ .

       N   Pro   N   Pro   N

2. _____ will share _____ _____ with _____ _____.

       N   Pro   N   Pro

3. _____ asked _____ to be quiet while _____ shot _____ free throw.

       N   N   Pro   N

4. _____ liked the _____ that _____ bought at the _____.

       N   Pro   N

5. _____ searched _____ backpack to find a _____ because

      Pro   N   Pro

_____ _____ had cut _____ foot.

Verbs

Once you can identify nouns and pronouns, the next step is to learn to identify verbs. Although some people have trouble recognizing these words, you should be able to identify them if you learn the following definition and the few points after it: **A verb either shows action or links the subject to another word.**

> **verb**
>
> A verb either shows action or links the subject to another word.

As you can see, this definition identifies two types of verbs. Some are "action" verbs (they tell what the subject is <u>doing</u>), and others are "linking" verbs (they tell what the subject is <u>being</u>). This distinction leads to the first point that will help you recognize verbs.

Action Verbs and Linking Verbs

One way to recognize verbs is to know that some verbs can do more than simply express an action. Some verbs are action verbs; others are linking verbs.

ACTION VERBS

Action verbs are usually easy to identify. Consider the following sentence:

> The deer leaped gracefully over the stone wall.

If you ask yourself what the **action** of the sentence is, the answer is obviously *leaped*. Therefore, *leaped* is the verb.

EXAMPLES OF ACTION VERBS *run, read, go, write, think, forgive, wait, laugh*

PRACTICE Underline the action verbs in the following sentences.

1. Rihanna <u>ran</u> across the stage.

2. The samurai cut the block of wood in two with his sword.

3. Taylor Swift wore a red dress on the talk show.

4. During the French and Indian War, Native Americans fought both on the French and British sides.

5. Napoleon's army invaded Spain.

LINKING VERBS

Linking verbs are sometimes more difficult to recognize than action verbs. Look for the verb in the following sentence:

> Helen **is** a woman of integrity.

Notice that the sentence expresses no real action. The verb *is* simply links the word *woman* to the word *Helen*.

EXAMPLES OF LINKING VERBS forms of *be*: am, is, are, was, were, be, being, been

forms of *become, seem, look, appear, smell, taste, feel, sound, grow, remain*

Linking verbs can link three types of words to a subject.

1. They can link nouns to the subject:

   Hank <u>became</u> a hero to his team. (*Hero* is linked to *Hank*.)

2. They can link pronouns to the subject:

   Cheryl <u>was</u> someone from another planet. (*Someone* is linked to *Cheryl*.)

3. They can link adjectives (descriptive words) to the subject:

   The sky <u>was</u> cloudy all day. (*Cloudy* is linked to *sky*.)

PRACTICE   Underline the linking verbs in the following sentences.

1. The pizza from the restaurant around the corner <u>tastes</u> good.

2. Steve Jobs was the cofounder of a major American company.

3. She felt important when she received the presidential medal.

4. The touchscreen becomes dull after extended usage.

5. Marilyn Monroe and JFK were famous in the 1960s.

Verb Tense

Another way to identify verbs is to know that they appear in different forms to show the time when the action or linking takes place. These forms are called *tenses*. The simplest tenses are present, past, and future.

Present		Past	
I walk	we walk	I walked	we walked
you walk	you walk	you walked	you walked
he, she, it walks	they walk	he, she, it walked	they walked

Future	
I will walk	we will walk
you will walk	you will walk
he, she, it will walk	they will walk

Note that the verb *walk* can be written as *walked* to show past tense and as *will walk* to show future tense. When a verb adds "d" or "ed" to form the past tense, it is called a **regular verb.**

Other verbs change their forms more drastically to show past tense. For example, the verb *eat* becomes *ate,* and *fly* becomes *flew.* Verbs like these, which do not add "d" or "ed" to form the past tense, are called **irregular verbs.** Practice in irregular verbs is accessible on the Instructor Companion Website. For now, to help you identify verbs, remember this point: <u>Verbs change their forms to show tense.</u>

◎◎ PRACTICE　In the following sentences, first underline the verb and then write the tense (present, past, or future) in the space provided.

present **1.** She <u>watches</u> news on CNN and the Fox channel.

_____ **2.** E.T. wanted to go home.

_____ **3.** Evelyn's toy poodle will not obey.

_____ **4.** George Washington Carver made plastics, cosmetics, and even a form of gasoline from peanuts.

_____ **5.** Yo-Yo Ma often plays tango music by Astor Piazzolla.

Helping Verbs and Main Verbs

<u>A third way to identify verbs is to know that the verb of a sentence is often more than one word.</u> The **MAIN VERB** of a sentence may be preceded by one or more **HELPING VERBS** to show time, condition, or circumstances. The helping verbs allow us the flexibility to communicate a wide variety of ideas and attitudes. For example, note how adding a helping verb changes the following sentences:

I *run* indicates that an action is happening or happens repeatedly.

I *will run* indicates that an action is not occurring now but will occur in the future.

I *should run* indicates an attitude toward the action.

The **COMPLETE VERB** of a sentence, then, includes a **MAIN VERB** and any **HELPING VERBS.** The complete verb can contain as many as three helping verbs.

◎◎ EXAMPLES

　　　　MV
He *writes.*

　　HV　　MV
He *has written.*

　　HV　HV　　MV
He *has been writing.*

　　HV　　HV　　HV　　MV
He *might have been writing.*

You can be sure that you have identified all of the helping verbs in a complete verb simply by learning the helping verbs. There are not very many of them.

These words are **always** helping verbs:

can	may	could
will	must	would
shall	might	should

These words are sometimes helping verbs and sometimes main verbs:

Forms of have	*Forms of* do	*Forms of* be		
have	do	am	was	be
has	does	is	were	being
had	did	are		been

In the following examples, note that the same word can be a helping verb in one sentence and a main verb in another:

EXAMPLES

            MV
Anna **had** thirty pairs of shoes.

        HV   MV
Jordan **had** thought about the problem for years.

        MV
She **did** well on her chemistry quiz.

        HV MV
Natalia **did** go to the game after all.

        MV
The bus **was** never on time.

     HV   MV
He **was** planning to leave in the morning.

When you are trying to identify the complete verb of a sentence, remember that any helping verbs will always come before the main verb; however, other words may occur between the helping verb(s) and the main verb. For instance, you will often find words such as *not, never, ever, already,* or *just* between the helping verb and the main verb. Also, in questions you will often find the subject between the helping verb and the main verb.

EXAMPLES

HV   S   MV
Will the telephone company raise its prices?

    S   HV   MV
Nobody has **ever** proved the existence of the Loch Ness Monster.

PRACTICE   In the spaces provided, identify the underlined words as main verbs (MV) or helping verbs (HV).

_MV_   **1.** The cowboy <u>is</u> a popular figure in American folklore.

_____   **2.** Early cowboys in the Southwest <u>had</u> the Spanish title of *vaquero*.

_____   **3.** Soon American pronunciation <u>had</u> changed vaquero to *buckeroo*.

_____   **4.** Buckeroos <u>were</u> not called cowboys until the 1820s.

_____   **5.** Cowboys <u>were</u> mostly simple ranch hands.

_____   **6.** They <u>did</u> many physically demanding jobs on the ranch.

_____   **7.** However, they <u>did</u> not drive cattle across country until the late 1860s.

_____   **8.** Texans had <u>been</u> raising cattle for many years before that.

_____   **9.** But their problem had always <u>been</u> the distance between Texas and the markets to the north and east.

_____   **10.** In response, the cowboys <u>would</u> move hundreds of thousands of cattle across the country from Texas to the railheads in Kansas and Nebraska.

PRACTICE   **A.** In the following sentences, place "HV" over all helping verbs and "MV" over all main verbs.

                  HV MV

1. Kobe Bryant is playing at the top of his game today.

2. In his novel *Brave New World*, Aldous Huxley has foreseen many of today's realities.

3. Thor was swinging his hammer in all directions.

4. Could you memorize all of the linking verbs?

5. The man with the take-out boxes should have offered his leftovers to that homeless person.

B. In the following sentences, write helping verbs and main verbs of your own choice as indicated.

                        MV

6. John Lee Hooker _played_ some blues for his friends.

                  MV   MV

7. Wyatt Earp _____ the revolver and _____ it to Doc Holliday.

                HV   MV

8. Penelope _____ _____ patiently for Odysseus for twenty years.

       HV   MV   MV

9. _____ Shakespeare _____ the tragedy that I _____ for him?

                  HV   MV

10. George Gershwin _____ _____ to a lot of African American

                  MV

music before he _____ *Porgy and Bess.*

Verbals

A fourth way to identify verbs is to recognize what they are not. Some verb forms do not actually function as verbs. These are called **VERBALS.** One of the most important verbals is the **INFINITIVE,** which usually begins with the word *to* (*to write, to be, to see*). The infinitive cannot serve as the verb of a sentence because it cannot express the time of the action or linking. *I wrote* communicates a clear idea, but *I to write* does not.

    Another common verbal is the "-ing" form of the verb when it occurs without a helping verb (*running, flying, being*). When an "-ing" form without a helping verb is used as an adjective, it is called a **PRESENT PARTICIPLE.** When it is used as a noun, it is called a **GERUND.**

☯ EXAMPLES

    MV   Verbal

I **hope to pass** this test.

    HV   MV

I **should pass** this test.

         Verbal   MV

The birds **flying** from tree to tree **chased** the cat from their nest.

         HV   MV

The birds **were flying** from tree to tree.

  Verbal MV

Jogging is good cardiovascular exercise.

  MV

I **jog** for the cardiovascular benefits of the exercise.

PRACTICE In the following sentences, write "HV" above all helping verbs, "MV" above all main verbs, and "Verbal" above all verbals.

        HV   *MV*   *Verbal*
1. San Diego has not been an easy place to buy a house in recent years.

2. Texting furiously, the student never noticed the other people in the classroom.

3. To illustrate Meryl Streep's talent, Penelope will describe her comedic, musical, and dramatic performances.

4. The photographer had taken a picture of Mother Teresa attending a sick man.

5. The old lady stirring the broth of bat wings and spider legs might agree to give you a taste.

PRACTICE Place "HV" above all helping verbs and "MV" above all main verbs in the following sentences. Draw a line through any verbals.

        HV *MV*
1. Paul had intended ~~to reach~~ Damascus before dark.

2. Brent and Bruce were discussing Bill Gates's attempts to alleviate world famine and disease.

3. Does Oedipus really want to marry Jocasta?

4. Mozart had a marvelous ability for creating melodies.

5. The anthropologist must have seen the full moon rising exactly between the two Anasazi ruins.

6. Rodin was looking for the right material to make a new sculpture.

7. To impress Beyonce, JZ decided to do two hundred push-ups every morning.

8. Becoming increasingly angry, the movie critic wondered how many sequels a movie could have.

9. Josita has been trying for years to find the long-lost city of *El Dorado*.

10. When writing poetry, Pablo Neruda needed silence.

Identifying Subjects and Verbs

Finding the Subject

Most sentences contain several nouns and pronouns used in a variety of ways. One of the most important ways is as the subject of a verb. In order to identify which of the nouns or pronouns in a sentence is the subject, you need to identify the complete verb first. After identifying the verb, it is easy to find the subject by asking yourself "Who or what   (verb)   ?"

EXAMPLE

                    S   HV   MV
The **man** in the green hat **was following** a suspicious-looking stranger.

The complete verb in this sentence is *was following*, and when you ask yourself "Who or what was following?" the answer is "the man." Therefore, *man* is the subject.

Remember, most sentences contain several nouns and pronouns, but not all nouns and pronouns are subjects.

EXAMPLE

                    S   MV
The **people** from the **house** down the **street** often borrow our **tools**.

This sentence contains four nouns, but only *people* is the subject. The other nouns in this sentence are different types of **objects**. The noun *tools* is called a **direct object** because it receives the action of the verb *borrow*. The nouns *house* and *street* are called **objects of prepositions**. Direct objects will be discussed in Chapter Four. Objects of prepositions will be discussed later in this chapter. For now, just remember that not all nouns and pronouns are subjects.

PRACTICE

In the following sentences, place an "HV" above any helping verbs, an "MV" above the main verbs, and an "S" above the subjects.

          S   HV MV
1. Al Capone was sent to Alcatraz Federal Penitentiary in 1932.

2. The famous prison sits in the middle of San Francisco Bay.

3. Escaping prisoners would drown in the cold waters of the bay.

4. Over the years, several men were shot while trying to escape.

5. After only twenty-nine years as a prison, Alcatraz was closed in 1963.

Subject Modifiers

Words that modify or describe nouns or pronouns should not be included when you identify the subject.

EXAMPLE

        S   MV
The red wheelbarrow is in the yard.

The subject is *wheelbarrow,* not *the red wheelbarrow.*
   Remember that the possessive forms of nouns and pronouns are also used to describe or modify nouns, so do not include them in the subject either.

EXAMPLES

         S   MV
My brother's suitcase is very worn.

      S   MV
His textbook was expensive.

The subjects are simply *suitcase* and *textbook,* not *my brother's suitcase* or *his textbook.*

Verb Modifiers

Just as words that describe or modify the subject are not considered part of the subject, words that describe or modify the verb are not considered part of the verb. Watch for such modifiers because they will often occur between helping verbs and main verbs and may be easily mistaken for helping verbs. Notice that in the following sentence the words *not* and *unfairly* are modifiers and, therefore, not part of the complete verb.

EXAMPLE

  S   HV   MV
Parents should **not unfairly** criticize their children.

Some common verb modifiers are *not, never, almost, just, completely, sometimes, always, often,* and *certainly.*

PRACTICE

Place "HV" over helping verbs, "MV" over main verbs, and "S" over the subjects of the following sentences.

       S   HV   MV
1. The demonstrator in the park was slowly waving a very big sign.

2. The sign had not been rained on but was still difficult to read.

3. The demonstrator had often protested against banks.

4. Wendy had unfortunately lost her house in a foreclosure proceeding.

5. Since then, Wendy has been quietly living in an apartment.

Multiple Subjects and Verbs

Sentences may contain more than one subject and more than one verb.

◎◎ **EXAMPLES**

       S   MV
Fred petted the dog.

       S   S   MV
Fred and Mary petted the dog.

       S   S   MV   MV
Fred and Mary petted the dog and scratched its ears.

       S   MV   S   MV
Fred petted the dog, and Mary scratched its ears.

       S   S   MV   S MV
Fred and Mary petted the dog before they fed it.

◎◎ **PRACTICE**

Place "HV" over helping verbs, "MV" over main verbs, and "S" over subjects in the following sentences.

                           S   MV

1. In 1775, British General Lord Dunmore offered freedom to African

    Americans on Southern plantations.

2. Many African Americans took his offer and fought on the side of the British.

3. After the Revolutionary War had ended, the British transported many of

    these African Americans to Canada.

4. Some years later, many African Americans were brought on British ships to

    Sierra Leone, West Africa, where they settled.

5. Their descendants are still living in Sierra Leone.

Special Situations

SUBJECT UNDERSTOOD

When a sentence is a command (or a request worded as a polite command), the pronoun *you* is understood as the subject. *You* is the only understood subject.

◎◎ **EXAMPLES**

       MV
Shut the door. (Subject is *you* understood.)

MV
Please **give** this book to your sister. (**Subject** is *you* understood.)

VERB BEFORE SUBJECT

In some sentences, such as in questions, the verb comes before the subject.

⊚⊚ **EXAMPLE**

MV   S
Is your **mother** home?

The verb also comes before the subject in sentences beginning with *there* or *here*, as well as in some other constructions.

⊚⊚ **EXAMPLES**

MV   S
There **is** a **bug** in my soup.

MV   S
Here **is** another **bowl** of soup.

MV   S
Over the hill **rode** the **cavalry**.

MV   S
On the front porch **was** a **basket** with a baby in it.

⊚⊚ **PRACTICE**

Place "HV" over helping verbs, "MV" over main verbs, and "S" over subjects in the following sentences. Verbals and verb modifiers should not be included in the complete verb.

     MV
1. Help the man across the street.

2. Somewhere on the planet dreams the next great inventor.

3. Does her new smartphone have a decent camera?

4. There were many Egyptians helping to remove President Mubarak after he

had ruled for thirty years.

5. Enter the security code.

⊚⊚ **PRACTICE**

Underline all subjects once and complete verbs twice in the following sentences. Remember that the complete verb contains the main verb and all helping verbs and that verbals and verb modifiers should not be included in the complete verb.

1. <u>You</u> certainly <u>wear</u> those baggy shorts with style.

2. Sonny could have treated the injured dog better.

3. Neil Armstrong might have hesitated before taking that first step.

4. The glue on postage stamps in Israel is certified to be kosher.

5. Will the person in the back row close his cell phone?

6. Godzilla was looking forward to his vacation in Jurassic Park.

7. Tell the marketing department to stop those disgusting duck ads.

8. My daughter loves her iPod Touch, but I would prefer to own an iPad.

9. There must have been two thousand people at the concert.

10. The little mermaid looked at Aladdin and winked.

PRACTICE Write sentences of your own that follow the suggested patterns. Identify each subject (S), helping verb (HV), and main verb (MV).

1. A statement with one subject and two main verbs (S-MV-MV):

   A large black cat hopped off the fence

   and crept into our yard.

2. A statement with a subject and two main verbs (S-MV-MV):

   _____

   _____

3. A statement with one subject, one helping verb, and one main verb (S-HV-MV):

   _____

   _____

4. A question with one helping verb, one subject, and one main verb (HV-S-MV):

   _____

   _____

5. A command that begins with a main verb (MV):

_____

_____

6. A statement that starts with "Here" and is followed by a main verb and a subject ("Here" MV-S):

_____

_____

7. A statement with two subjects and one main verb (S-S-MV):

_____

_____

8. A statement with one subject, one helping verb, and one main verb followed by "after" and another subject and another main verb (S-HV-MV "after" S-MV):

_____

_____

9. A statement with a subject, a helping verb, a main verb followed by ", and" and another subject, helping verb, and main verb (S-HV-MV ", and" S-HV-MV):

_____

_____

10. A statement with a subject and a main verb followed by "although" and another subject and main verb (S-MV "although" S-MV):

_____

_____

Section One Review

1. A **noun** names a person, place, thing, or idea.

   a. **Proper nouns** name specific persons, places, things, or ideas. They begin with a capital letter. **Common nouns** name more general categories and are not capitalized.

   b. **A, an,** and **the** are noun markers. A noun always follows one of these words.

   c. If you are unsure whether or not a word is a noun, ask yourself if it could be introduced with **a, an,** or **the.**

   d. Words that end in -**ment**, -**ism**, -**ness**, -**ence**, -**ance**, and -**tion** are usually nouns.

2. A **pronoun** takes the place of a noun.

3. A **verb** either shows **action** or **links** the subject to another word.

4. Verbs appear in different **tenses** to show the time when the action or linking takes place.

5. The **complete verb** includes a **main verb** and any **helping verbs.**

6. **Verbals** are verb forms that do not function as verbs.

   a. The **infinitive** is a verbal that begins with the word *to*.

   b. The "-ing" form of the verb without a helping verb is called a **present participle** if it is used as an adjective.

   c. The "-ing" form of the verb without a helping verb is called a **gerund** if it is used as a noun.

7. To identify the **subject** of any sentence, first find the verb. Then ask, "Who or what (verb)?"

8. **Subject modifiers** describe or modify the subject. They should not be included when you identify the subject.

9. **Verb modifiers** describe or modify verbs. They are not considered part of the verb.

10. Sentences may contain **multiple subjects** and **multiple verbs.**

11. When a sentence is a command (or a request worded as a polite command), the pronoun *you* is understood as the subject. *You* is the only understood subject.

12. In some sentences the verb comes before the subject.

Exercise 1A

Listen to or watch the news, or read a magazine, newspaper, or book. Write down ten sentences that you find. Identify which news program, magazine, newspaper, or book you used. After writing down the sentences, underline the subject or subjects of each sentence once and the complete verbs twice.

1. _____

   _____

2. _____

   _____

3. _____

   _____

4. _____

   _____

5. _____

   _____

6. _____

   _____

7. _____

   _____

8. _____

   _____

9. _____

   _____

10. _____

    _____

Exercise 1B

In the spaces provided, indicate whether the underlined word is a subject (write "S"), a helping verb (write "HV"), or a main verb (write "MV"). If it is none of these, leave the space blank.

_MV_ **1.** Naoko has <u>found</u> her bracelet.

_____ **2.** Messi has been a wonderful player for Barcelona but <u>has</u> not shown his full talent when playing for Argentina.

_____ **3.** Octavio Paz <u>was</u> an important Mexican poet and essayist who received the Nobel Prize in Literature in 1990.

_____ **4.** Having played baseball, Eric thought that <u>volleyball</u> would be easy for him.

_____ **5.** Is the Cheesecake Factory really the best <u>place</u> to eat cheesecake?

_____ **6.** A camel has two humps, but a <u>dromedary</u> has only one.

_____ **7.** Like the <u>Egyptians</u>, the Mayas built pyramids.

_____ **8.** Some of the olive trees in the Garden of Gethsemane <u>are</u> over two thousand years old.

_____ **9.** In 1872 Susan B. Anthony <u>was</u> arrested for voting in the presidential election.

_____ **10.** When people vote, does <u>that</u> make a country a democracy?

_____ **11.** Why did Martin Luther <u>translate</u> the Bible into German?

_____ **12.** When Mahatma Gandhi was asked what he thought of Western civilization, he answered that he thought it <u>would</u> be a good idea.

_____ **13.** If you go to the Thai restaurant down the street, you should definitely <u>try</u> the Phad Thai.

_____ **14.** The Chernobyl nuclear power plant <u>suffered</u> a major meltdown in 1986.

_____ **15.** Native American burial sites <u>have</u> usually been considered holy and should not be tampered with.

Exercise 1C

A. Underline all subjects once and complete verbs twice in the following paragraph. Remember that a sentence may have more than one subject and more than one verb.

1. <u>Indiana Jones</u> <u><u>was</u></u> not entirely a fictional character. **2.** In fact, *Raiders of the Lost Ark* was written in part about a real person. **3.** Vendyl Jones is the head of the Institute for Judaic-Christian studies. **4.** The writer of the story had met Jones on an archeological dig. **5.** Do you remember the gigantic rolling boulder in the movie? **6.** The real-life Vendyl Jones and his assistants escaped from a booby-trap of four gigantic bouncing boulders. **7.** One assistant was almost crushed by the boulders, but he survived by jumping off a cliff. **8.** Before he finds the lost Ark, Jones wants to find the ashes of the Red Heifer. **9.** According to one of the Dead Sea Scrolls, the Ark is buried near those ashes. **10.** Jones is using the Dead Sea Scrolls and has already found twenty of the reference points leading to the Red Heifer.

B. Write sentences of your own that follow the suggested patterns. Identify each subject (S), helping verb (HV), and main verb (MV).

11. A statement with two subjects and one main verb (S-S-MV):

The baseball player and his agent decided to

meet for lunch.

12. A question that begins with "Where" followed by a helping verb, a subject, and a main verb ("Where" HV-S-MV):

_____

_____

13. A command that begins with a main verb (MV):

_____

_____

Exercise 1C

continued

14. A statement with two subjects, a helping verb, and a main verb (S-S-HV-MV):

_____

_____

15. A statement with a subject and main verb followed by ", so" and another subject and main verb (S-MV ", so" S-MV):

_____

_____

Exercise 1D

In the following paragraph, underline all subjects once and complete verbs twice.

1. When confronted with new and unfamiliar foods, many <u>people</u> <u>are</u> afraid to try new things. **2.** Either they will refuse to take a single bite of the food, or they will try a bite too small to determine whether they like it. **3.** One reason for those typical reactions is that we often consider the foods from our childhood to be "normal." **4.** This belief is reinforced when we see people around us eating the same foods. **5.** If familiar foods are "normal," then foods unfamiliar to us are "strange," and we react with suspicion toward them. **6.** However, the belief that some food is normal and some is "strange" is determined by our culture. **7.** Some cultures consider it "normal" to eat animal intestines and blood; others do not. **8.** Raw fish or raw meats are part of the regular diet in some places. **9.** However, people from other places find it unpleasant to eat uncooked meats or fish. **10.** Some cultures use insects as foods; others do not. **11.** If one grows up eating insects, that practice will not appear strange, and one will think it funny that other people will not eat them. **12.** Therefore, when confronted with new and "strange" foods, it helps to remember that one person's "strange" food is another person's ordinary diet. **13.** Besides, if we refuse to try new foods, we might miss the chance to taste something really delicious.

Modifiers

Although subjects and verbs form the basis of any sentence, most sentences also contain many other words that serve a variety of purposes. One such group of words includes the modifiers, which limit, describe, intensify, or otherwise alter the meaning of other words. The word *modify* simply means "change." Notice how the modifiers change the meaning in each of the following sentences.

EXAMPLE

The dictator had **total** power.

The dictator had **great** power.

The dictator had **little** power.

The dictator had **no** power.

As you can see, the word *power* is significantly changed by the different modifiers in these sentences.

Although modifiers can change the meaning of words in many different ways, there are basically only two types of modifiers, **ADJECTIVES** and **ADVERBS.** You will be able to identify both types of modifiers more easily if you remember these three points:

1. Sentences often contain more than one modifier.

EXAMPLE

The **new** moon rose **slowly** over the desert.

In this example, the word *new* modifies *moon;* it describes the specific phase of the moon. The word *slowly* modifies *rose;* it describes the speed with which the moon rose.

2. Two or more modifiers can be used to modify the same word.

EXAMPLE

The moon rose **slowly** and **dramatically** over the desert.

In this example the words *slowly* and *dramatically* both modify *rose. Slowly* describes the speed, and *dramatically* describes the manner in which the moon rose.

3. All modifiers must modify *something.* You should be able to identify the specific word that is being modified as well as the modifier itself.

EXAMPLE

Slowly the **new** moon rose over the desert.

In this example, notice that the word *slowly* still modifies *rose,* though the two words are not close to each other. The arrows point from the modifiers to the words being modified.

◎◎ PRACTICE Draw an arrow from the underlined modifier to the word it modifies.

1. Merchants <u>once</u> sold <u>pink</u> ducklings at Easter.

2. The pizza was <u>cold</u> and <u>salty</u>.

3. Rafiki <u>rarely</u> uses <u>his</u> <u>new</u> skateboard.

4. The <u>expanded</u> version of the song was <u>extremely</u> <u>long</u>.

5. The <u>corn</u> tortilla had <u>fresh</u> cilantro and <u>sliced</u> radishes on it.

Adjectives

An adjective modifies a noun or a pronoun. In English, most adjectives precede the noun they modify.

> **adjective**
> An adjective modifies a noun or a pronoun.

◎◎ EXAMPLE

Adj ⤷   Adj ⤷
The **young** eagle perched on the **rocky** cliff.

In this example, the word *young* **modifies** *eagle,* and the word *rocky* **modifies** *cliff*.

Although most adjectives precede the noun or pronoun they modify, they may also follow the noun or pronoun and be connected to it by a linking verb.

◎◎ EXAMPLE

Adj   Adj
Poisonous plants are **dangerous**.

In this example, the word *poisonous* describes the noun *plants*. Notice that it **precedes** the noun. However, the word *dangerous* also describes the noun *plants*. It is **linked** to the noun by the linking verb *are*. Both *poisonous* and *dangerous* are adjectives that modify the noun *plants*.

Many different types of words can be adjectives, as long as they **modify** a noun or pronoun. Most adjectives answer the questions **which? what kind?** or **how many?** Here are the most common types of adjectives.

1. Descriptive words

◎◎ EXAMPLES

I own a **blue** suit.

That is an **ugly** wound.

2. Possessive nouns and pronouns

🌀 EXAMPLE   I parked **my** motorcycle next to **John's** car.

3. Limiting words and numbers

🌀 EXAMPLES   **Some** people see **every** movie that comes out.

Two accidents have happened on **this** street.

4. Nouns that modify other nouns

🌀 EXAMPLE   The **basketball** game was held in the **neighborhood** gym.

🌀 PRACTICE   **A.** In the following sentences, circle all adjectives and draw an arrow to the noun or pronoun each adjective modifies.

1. Strange cats have appeared on our front lawn recently.

2. The team's orange uniforms are unique.

3. Our two turtledoves keep fighting with that stupid partridge in the

pear tree.

4. My fancy new espresso maker has many buttons with unknown uses.

5. Emily Dickinson wrote many excellent poems, yet she asked her sister

to burn them.

B. Add two adjectives of your own to each of the following sentences.

6. The *new* dance floor was full of *excited* people.

7. The jogger felt uneasy when he was jogging alone in the desert.

8. The water in the pool was colder than the boy had expected.

9. The dessert was displayed on the table.

10. Students who learn about recipes for food begin to feel hungry.

Adverbs

An adverb modifies a verb, adjective, or another adverb. Adverbs are sometimes more difficult to recognize than adjectives because they can be used to modify three different types of words—verbs, adjectives, and other adverbs. They can either precede or follow the words they modify and are sometimes placed farther away from the words they modify than are adjectives.

> **adverb**
> An adverb modifies a verb, adjective, or another adverb.

EXAMPLES

          V   Adv

The president walked across the room **quickly**.
(adverb modifying a verb)

                   Adv   Adj

The president seemed **unusually** nervous.
(adverb modifying an adjective)

                Adv   Adv

The president left **very** quickly after the press conference.
(adverb modifying an adverb)

Because adverbs are often formed by adding "ly" to adjectives such as *quick* or *usual,* many adverbs end in "ly" (*quickly* and *usually*). However, you cannot always use this ending as a way of identifying adverbs because some words that end in "ly" are <u>not</u> adverbs and because some adverbs do <u>not</u> end in "ly," as the following list of common adverbs illustrates:

already	never	often	soon	too
also	not	quite	still	very
always	now	seldom	then	well

Here are two ways to help you identify adverbs:

1. <u>Find the word that is being modified.</u> If it is a verb, adjective, or adverb, then the modifier is an adverb.

EXAMPLES

                      V

Thelma **seriously** injured her finger during the tennis match.

                            Adj

My brother and I have **completely** different attitudes toward Spam.

                  Adv

Tuan **almost** always arrives on time for work.

2. <u>Look for words that answer the questions **when? where? how?** or **to what extent?**</u>

EXAMPLES

My grandparents **often** bring gifts when they visit. (**when?**)

The turnips were grown **locally**. (**where?**)

Rachel **carefully** removed the paint from the antique desk. (**how?**)

Homer is **widely** known as a trainer in a flea circus. (**to what extent?**)

NOTE: Adverbs are **not** considered part of the complete verb, even if they come between the helping verb and the main verb. (See page 29 for a list of common adverbs that come between the helping verb and the main verb.)

EXAMPLE

HV Adv MV
He has **not** failed to do his duty.

PRACTICE

A. In the following sentences, circle all adverbs and draw an arrow to the word that each adverb modifies.

1. The detective (quietly) stepped into the corridor and (slowly) raised his revolver.

2. The bachelorette instinctively knew that she had a very small chance of finding love on a reality show.

3. The patient's pulse accelerated quickly when the doctor slowly approached.

4. The studio immediately scheduled a sequel to the awful movie even though it did not make a lot of money.

5. The quarterback was rather surprised when his team won decisively.

B. Add one adverb of your own to each of the following sentences.

6. The full moon moved *slowly* across the sky.

7. Michael argued that soccer was a more interesting sport than baseball, but Jamie disagreed.

8. Surfers were excited when they heard that winds were blowing.

9. Although she avoided the traffic, she missed the show.

10. The doctor performed the surgery, and she was satisfied with the outcome.

Comparative and Superlative Forms

Adjectives and adverbs are often used to compare two or more people or things. **The comparative form is used to compare two people or things. The superlative form is used to compare three or more people or things.**

EXAMPLES

(comparative)   He is **happier** than I am.

(superlative)   He is the **happiest** man in town.

Writing Comparatives

Use the following guidelines for most adjectives and adverbs.

- Add *-er* to adjectives and adverbs of one syllable.

green	greener
soon	sooner

- Use the word *more* before adjectives and adverbs of two or more syllables.

tedious	more tedious
swiftly	more swiftly

- If a two-syllable adjective ends in *-y* (but not in *-ly*), change the *y* to *i* and add *-er*.

crispy	crispier
sunny	sunnier

Writing Superlatives

Use the following guidelines for most adjectives and adverbs.

- Add *-est* to adjectives and adverbs of one syllable.

green	greenest
soon	soonest

- Use the word *most* before adjectives and adverbs of two or more syllables.

tedious	most tedious
swiftly	most swiftly

- If a two-syllable adjective ends in *-y* (but not in *-ly*), change the *y* to *i* and add *-est*.

crispy	crispiest
sunny	sunniest

☾☾ PRACTICE   Write the comparative and superlative form of each of the following words.

    1. quiet   _____   _____

    2. slow   _____   _____

    3. pretty   _____   _____

    4. deceitful   _____   _____

    5. rapidly   _____   _____

    6. easy   _____   _____

    7. convenient   _____   _____

    8. far   _____   _____

    9. slowly   _____   _____

    10. effective   _____   _____

Using Adjectives and Adverbs Correctly

    1. <u>Do not use an adjective when you need an adverb.</u>

☾☾ EXAMPLES

(incorrect)	He does not speak very **clear**.
(correct)	He does not speak very **clearly**.
(incorrect)	He breathes **deep** whenever he is worried.
(correct)	He breathes **deeply** whenever he is worried.

    2. <u>Distinguish between *good* and *well, bad* and *badly, real* and *really.*</u> The words *good, bad,* and *real* are always adjectives. The words *badly* and *really* are always adverbs. The word *well* is usually an adverb, although it is used as an adjective to describe someone's health.

☾☾ EXAMPLES

(incorrect)	He sells a lot of novels because he writes **good**.
(correct)	He sells a lot of novels because he writes **well**. (The adverb *well* modifies the verb *writes*.)

| (incorrect) | Joey says he feels fine, but he does not look **good** to me. |
| (correct) | Joey says he feels fine, but he does not look **well** to me. (The adjective *well* describes the health of *Joey*.) |

| (incorrect) | April felt **badly** when she accidentally insulted her friend. |
| (correct) | April felt **bad** when she accidentally insulted her friend. (The adjective *bad* modifies the noun *April*.) |

| (incorrect) | Slim says that it's **real** hot in Phoenix today. |
| (correct) | Slim says that it's **really** hot in Phoenix today. (**The adverb** *really* modifies the adjective *hot*.) |

3. <u>Avoid doubling the comparative or superlative form.</u> Do not use *more* with an *-er* form or *most* with an *-est* form.

EXAMPLES

| (incorrect) | Michael is **more taller** than Oscar. |
| (correct) | Michael is **taller** than Oscar. |

| (incorrect) | Sabrina is the **most smartest** student in the class. |
| (correct) | Sabrina is the **smartest** person in the class. |

4. <u>Avoid using the superlative when you are comparing only two persons or things.</u>

EXAMPLES

| (incorrect) | His Toyota seems to be the **fastest** of the two cars. |
| (correct) | His Toyota seems to be the **faster** of the two cars. |

5. <u>Use *than*, not *then*, in comparisons.</u>

EXAMPLES

| (incorrect) | Melissa is taller **then** her older sister. |
| (correct) | Melissa is taller **than** her older sister. |

PRACTICE   Correct any errors in the use of adjectives and adverbs (or in the use of *then* and *than*) in the following sentences.

1. The car looked ~~more~~ better without rims ~~then~~ *than* with them.

2. When gas prices reached the most high average ever, she thought that

   buying an SUV was the worse mistake she had ever made.

3. Under Cyrus the Great, the ancient Persian Empire reached its most great expansion.

4. One can dance good to techno music, but it can also be real repetitive.

5. Of the two, which is the most popular, Facebook or MySpace?

6. The pizza tasted badly, but it was not worst then the beer that came with it.

7. The speakers were more louder, but their sound quality was worst.

8. In some outlet stores, the prices are not less cheaper then in normal stores.

9. Even though the opera star did not sing very good, the audience applauded loud after she had finished her aria.

10. He texted fastest than his sister, but she spelled the most correct.

Section Two Review

1. **Modifiers** limit, describe, intensify, or otherwise alter the meaning of other words.

   a. Sentences often contain more than one modifier.

   b. Two or more modifiers can be used to modify the same word.

   c. All modifiers must modify *something*.

2. An **adjective** modifies a noun or a pronoun.

3. Most adjectives answer the questions which? what kind? or how many?

4. Common types of adjectives are the following:

   a. Descriptive words

   b. Possessive nouns and pronouns

   c. Limiting words and numbers

   d. Nouns that modify other nouns

5. An **adverb** modifies a verb, adjective, or another adverb.

6. There are two ways to identify adverbs:

   a. Find the word that is being modified. If it is a verb, an adjective, or an adverb, then the modifier is an adverb.

   b. Look for words that answer the questions when? where? how? or to what extent?

7. The **comparative form** is used to compare two people or things.

8. The **superlative form** is used to compare three or more people or things.

9. Use adjectives and adverbs correctly.

   a. Do not use an adjective when you need an adverb.

   b. Distinguish between *good* and *well, bad* and *badly, real* and *really.*

   c. Avoid doubling the comparative or superlative form.

   d. Avoid using the superlative when you are comparing only two persons or things.

   e. Use *than*, not *then*, in comparisons.

Exercise 2A

Take a magazine (such as *Time, U.S. News and World Report, National Geographic, Harper's,* etc.) and find five sentences that contain at least one adjective, five that contain at least one adverb, and five that have both at least one adjective and at least one adverb.

Sentences with at least one adjective (underline the adjectives):

1.

2.

3.

4.

5.

Sentences with at least one adverb (underline the adverbs):

1.

2.

3.

4.

5.

Sentences with at least one adjective and one adverb (underline and label each one):

1.

2.

3.

4.

5.

A. In the following sentences, identify all adjectives by writing "Adj" above them, and identify all adverbs by writing "Adv" above them.

                 Adj   *Adv*

1. He wanted to be a famous author, but he did not like to read books.

2. She wanted to be a pop star, but she never listened to music carefully.

3. He slowly nodded as the soft country music played in the diner.

4. Herman Melville's most famous book is *Moby Dick*, but he wrote many others.

5. Beethoven's last symphony was also the first symphony to use a choir.

B. Add one adjective and one adverb to each of the following sentences. Do not use the same adjective or adverb more than once.

   colonial   *often*

6. In America, American trappers and hunters lived among Native Americans.
      ^   ^

7. The president limped to the stage and spoke to the people of the country.

8. The barista steamed the milk, poured the espresso, and served the coffee drink.

9. People assume that they can predict personality based on appearance.

10. People are incorrect in their assumptions.

C. Correct any errors in the use of adjectives and adverbs (or in the use of *then* and *than*) in the following sentences.

            very   *well*

11. Monica was ~~real~~ happy when she performed ~~good~~ in the college play.

12. Is Chris Rock funnier then Jim Carrey?

13. The band always plays too loud; it is louder then an airplane taking off.

14. Working in a fast-food restaurant was the worse job of my life; it was even worst than cleaning the floors in a grocery store.

15. He is snoring so loud that I can't understand you, no matter how clear you speak.

Exercise 2C

In the following paragraph, write "Adj" above all adjectives and "Adv" above all adverbs. Underline all subjects once and all verbs twice.

     Adv   *Adj*
1. People often ignore the information on a common coin.   **2.** Our commonest coin, the lowly penny, is an especially good example.   **3.** The right profile of Abraham Lincoln appears on one side of the coin.   **4.** Above his head is the sometimes controversial sentence "IN GOD WE TRUST."   **5.** "LIBERTY" can easily be seen to the left of Lincoln.   **6.** Near Mr. Lincoln's tie is the coin's date.   **7.** A capital letter below the date precisely indicates which city minted the coin.   **8.** The famous Lincoln Memorial appears on the reverse side, and "E PLURIBUS UNUM" is minutely embossed above it.   **9.** This widely familiar phrase means "from many, one."   **10.** Interestingly, Benjamin Franklin strongly objected to the phrase.   **11.** He favored an alternate quotation: "Rebellion to Tyrants Is Obedience to God."   **12.** "UNITED STATES OF AMERICA" is clearly written in large letters across the top.   **13.** In even larger letters "ONE CENT" occurs under the memorial.   **14.** America was severely short of copper during World War II, so the penny of 1943 was made of zinc-coated steel.   **15.** Today's pennies are always made of copper-coated zinc.

Exercise 2D

In the following paragraph, identify each of the underlined words as noun (N), pronoun (Pro), verb (V), adjective (Adj), or adverb (Adv).

1. In ancient Egypt, women [N] enjoyed a better [Adj] status than women in many other ancient societies.

2. Property in ancient Egypt generally passed down through the female line. **3.** Partially because of this property law, Egyptian women had economic freedoms that women in other ancient societies did not. **4.** Women also had access to schooling and to civil and political rights.

5. Those Egyptian women who learned to read, write, and who also had mathematical skills could sometimes become business women. **6.** Egyptian women who were the wives of the pharaoh were responsible for managing the production of cloth in the kingdom. **7.** Some worked as midwives, and others successfully owned shops. **8.** There were also women musicians, and some women found employment as dancers. **9.** Even though most pharaohs were men, three women ascended to the throne in ancient Egypt. **10.** The most famous of these female pharaohs is Hatshepsut. **11.** She ruled Egypt for over two decades, from about 1500 BC to 1447 BC

12. However, men usually occupied the position of pharaoh. **13.** As a result, even the female pharaoh Hatshepsut was depicted with a false beard and with masculine clothes. **14.** Some statues of male pharaohs and their queens also show the pharaoh and his queen as being the same height and stature, implying a degree of equality. **15.** As archeologists, linguists, and other scholars continue to explore the Egyptian past, we may still learn more about how women and men interacted in ancient Egypt.

Connectors

The final group of words consists of the connectors. These are signals that indicate the relationship of one part of a sentence to another. The two types of connectors are **conjunctions** and **prepositions.**

Conjunctions

A conjunction joins two parts of a sentence. The word *conjunction* is derived from two Latin words meaning "to join with." The definition is easy to remember if you know that the word *junction* in English refers to the place where two roads come together.

> ### conjunction
> A conjunction joins two parts of a sentence.

The two types of conjunctions are **coordinating** and **subordinating.** In Chapter Two we will discuss the subordinating conjunctions. You will find it much easier to distinguish between the two types if you memorize the coordinating conjunctions now.

The **coordinating conjunctions** are *and, but, or, nor, for, yet,* and *so.*

NOTE: An easy way to learn the coordinating conjunctions is to remember that their first letters can spell **BOYSFAN:** (<u>B</u>ut <u>O</u>r <u>Y</u>et <u>S</u>o <u>F</u>or <u>A</u>nd <u>N</u>or).

Coordinating conjunctions join elements of the sentence that are <u>equal</u> or <u>parallel</u>. For instance, they may join two subjects, two verbs, two adjectives, or two parallel groups of words.

EXAMPLE

    S Conj S   MV Conj   MV
Ernie **and** Bert often disagree **but** never fight.

In this example, the first conjunction joins two subjects, and the second joins two verbs.

EXAMPLE

    S   MV   Adj   Conj   Adj   Conj   MV
Susan often felt awkward **or** uncomfortable **yet** never showed it.

In this example, the first conjunction joins two adjectives, and the second joins two verbs.

Coordinating conjunctions may even be used to join two entire sentences, each with its own subject and verb.

EXAMPLE

S HV MV   S   MV

The rain had fallen steadily all week long. The river was close to overflowing.

S HV MV   Conj   S   MV

The rain had fallen steadily all week long, **so** the river was close to overflowing.

Notice that the coordinating conjunctions have different meanings and that changing the conjunction can significantly change the meaning of a sentence. *A person should never drink **and** drive* communicates a very different idea from *A person should never drink **or** drive.*

■ The conjunction *and* indicates **addition.**

EXAMPLE

Jules **and** Jim loved the same woman.

■ The conjunctions *but* and *yet* indicate **contrast.**

EXAMPLES

She wanted to go **but** didn't have the money.

I liked Brian, **yet** I didn't really trust him.

■ The conjunctions *or* and *nor* indicate **alternatives.**

EXAMPLES

You can borrow the my cell phone **or** my laptop

He felt that he could neither go **nor** stay.

■ The conjunction *for* indicates **cause.**

EXAMPLE

The plants died, **for** they had not been watered.

■ The conjunction *so* indicates **result.**

EXAMPLE

Her brother lost his job, **so** he had to find another.

PRACTICE

A. In the following sentences, circle all coordinating conjunctions. Underline all subjects once and all complete verbs twice.

1. The water ⓞⓡ the fire will threaten the nuclear plant.

2. There are many good actors, but most of them never win an Oscar.

3. There are also many good musicians, and most of them never become

   famous or earn much money.

4. Aisha did not like tuna, nor did she enjoy anchovies.

5. John did enjoy them, so he ordered a pizza with anchovies and capers.

B. In the following sentences, add coordinating conjunctions that show the relationship indicated in parentheses.

6. We could go to Cancun, ____*or*____ we could fly to Hawaii, but we can't

   do both. (alternatives)

7. The student felt intimidated by grammar, _____ she had no reason to be worried. (contrast)

8. I have a lot of chemistry homework tonight, _____ I have to prepare for my English test. (addition)

9. In Canada, both French and English are spoken, _____ both French and English settlers arrived in the seventeenth century. (cause)

10. Cesar Chavez was concerned about the conditions of Mexican American farm workers, _____ he organized the National Farm Workers Association. (result)

Prepositions

> ### preposition
> A preposition relates a noun or pronoun to some other word in the sentence.

A preposition relates a noun or a pronoun to some other word in the sentence. Prepositions usually indicate a relationship of **place** (*in, near*), **direction** (*toward, from*), **time** (*after, until*), or **condition** (*of, without*).

EXAMPLE

      Prep
The boy ran **to** the store.

  Notice how the preposition *to* shows the relationship (direction) between *ran* and *store*. If you change prepositions, you change the relationship.

EXAMPLES

      Prep
The boy ran **from** the store.

      Prep
The boy ran **into** the store.

      Prep
The boy ran **by** the store.

Here are some of the most common prepositions:

about	because of	during	near	to
above	before	except	of	toward
across	behind	for	on	under
after	below	from	onto	until
among	beneath	in	over	up
around	beside	in spite of	past	upon
as	between	into	through	with
at	by	like	till	without

NOTE: *For* can be used as a coordinating conjunction, but it is most commonly used as a preposition. *To* can also be used as part of an infinitive, in which case it is not a preposition.

◉◉ PRACTICE

Write "Prep" above the prepositions in the following sentences.

1. Yi-huan was *Prep* in a good mood because she knew *Prep* about her friend's arrival.

2. For her hard work, Sonia received a present from her mother.

3. Marcus was under pressure, but he knew he would pass the test with flying colors.

4. When René Descartes thought about himself, he felt like shouting.

5. During one of his therapy sessions, Sigmund Freud forgot to bring his pipe, and he was surprised at his psychologist's interpretation of that event.

Prepositional Phrases

The word *preposition* is derived from two Latin words meaning "to put in front." The two parts of the word (pre + position) indicate how prepositions usually function. They are almost always used as the first words in **prepositional phrases.**

> **prepositional phrase**
> Preposition + Object (noun or pronoun) = Prepositional Phrase.

    A prepositional phrase consists of a preposition plus a noun or a pronoun, called the object of the preposition. This object is almost always the last word of the prepositional phrase. Between the preposition and its object, the prepositional phrase may also contain adjectives, adverbs, or conjunctions. A preposition may have more than one object.

EXAMPLES

Prep   Obj
after a short **lunch**

Prep   Obj   Obj
with his very good **friend** and his **brother**

Prep Obj   Obj
to you and **her**

     Prep   Obj
through the long and dismal **night**

Although prepositions themselves are considered connectors, prepositional <u>phrases</u> actually act as modifiers. They may function as adjectives, modifying a noun or pronoun, or they may function as adverbs, modifying a verb.

EXAMPLES

The cat (**from next door**) caught a gopher.

The burglar jumped (**from the window**).

In the first example, the prepositional phrase functions as an adjective, modifying the noun *cat,* and in the second example, the prepositional phrase functions as an adverb, modifying the verb *jumped.*

NOTE: If you can recognize prepositional phrases, you will be able to identify subjects and verbs more easily **because neither the subject nor the verb of a sentence can be part of a prepositional phrase.**

In the following sentence it is difficult at first glance to determine which of the many nouns is the subject.

EXAMPLES

In a cave near the village, a member of the archaeological team found a stone ax from an ancient civilization.

If you first eliminate the prepositional phrases, however, the true subject becomes apparent.

EXAMPLES

                                  S
(In a cave) (near the village), a member (of the archaeological team)

   MV
found a stone ax (from an ancient civilization).

PRACTICE

Place parentheses around the prepositional phrases and write "Prep" above all prepositions and "Obj" above the objects of the prepositions.

                          Prep   *Obj*   *Prep*   *Obj*
1. Francis Scott Key wrote the words (to the national anthem)(of our country.)

2. However, the music itself came from a popular drinking song.

3. Francis Scott Key witnessed the British bombardment of Fort McHenry in 1814.

4. He was inspired by the sight of the American flag flying over the fort.

5. During the attack, he composed the first stanza of "The Star-Spangled Banner" on the back of an envelope.

6. The next day Key was told that his poem would go well with a tune that was popular in many taverns.

7. The original tune, called "Anacreon in Heaven," was probably written by John Stafford Smith in 1780.

8. Anacreon was a Greek poet who wrote about wine, song, love, and revelry.

9. "The Star-Spangled Banner" was sung at official ceremonies for many years.

10. In spite of its popularity, it was not declared the official national anthem until March 3, 1931.

Section Three Review

1. A **conjunction** joins two parts of a sentence.

2. The **coordinating conjunctions** are *and, but, or, nor, for, yet,* and *so*.

3. A **preposition** relates a noun or pronoun to some other word in the sentence.

4. A **prepositional phrase** consists of a **preposition** plus a noun or a pronoun, called the **object of the preposition.**

5. Neither the subject nor the verb of a sentence can be part of a prepositional phrase.

Exercise 3A

Prepositional phrases are all around us, and we use them constantly. Since they are so important (and so helpful in determining what cannot be a subject), it is useful to be able to recognize them easily. Pay attention to your everyday conversation with people and write down ten sentences that you used or heard somebody use that contain at least one prepositional phrase. Find prepositional phrases using different prepositions. There should be at least six different prepositions in the ten sentences you write down below.

1.

2.

3.

4.

5.

6.

7.

8.

9.

10.

Exercise 3B

A. Combine each pair of sentences into one sentence. Use the coordinating conjunction indicated in parentheses.

1. (addition)
   Alice Walker is a well-known African American novelist.
   Amy Tan is a respected Asian American writer.

   Alice Walker is a well-known African American novelist, and Amy Tan

   is a respected Asian American writer.

2. (contrast)
   Joan was prepared to give up her chicken sandwich.
   She was not willing to surrender her dessert.

3. (cause)
   Glaciers are melting.
   Human energy output is increasing.

4. (alternative)
   The Patriots could win again.
   They could lose to the 49ers.

5. (alternative)
   Napoleon did not like the winter in Moscow.
   He also did not like the summer in St. Helena.

---

continued

> **6.** (result)
> Mozart found it boring to write down the music he had composed in his head.
> He entertained himself doing other things while writing music.

_____

_____

B. In the following paragraph, change each underlined *and* to a coordinating conjunction that expresses the relationship between the ideas in the sentence. If the *and* does not need to be changed, do nothing to it.

                                                        but

  1. The Greeks tried to convince Achilles to fight, ~~and~~ he refused to leave his tent.

2. Achilles could stay in his tent, <u>and</u> he could get off his cot and be a hero. **3.** Achilles was quite proud, <u>and</u> he decided to fight the Trojans. **4.** Secretly, Achilles was worried, <u>and</u> his ankle was irritating him. **5.** To make him invulnerable, Achilles's mother had dipped him in the River Styx, <u>and</u> she had missed his ankle. **6.** Achilles killed many Trojans, <u>and</u> then he killed the Trojan hero Hector. **7.** Paris, the brother of Hector, wanted revenge, <u>and</u> he shot Achilles in the heel. **8.** With Achilles dead, the Greeks seemed defeated, <u>and</u> then they came upon the idea of a large wooden horse.

Exercise 3C

Place all prepositional phrases in parentheses and circle all conjunctions. For additional practice, underline all subjects once and all complete verbs twice.

1. <u>Ahmed</u> (and) ten other soccer <u>players</u> <u><u>drove</u></u> (to the game).

2. When they arrived at the field, the other team was already waiting for them.

3. The Coldplay concert had started, and people in the audience were glad, since the opening act had been terrible.

4. After fifteen years, the tattoo parlor closed, but a tattoo removal clinic opened in its place.

5. Too much tooth whitener is bad for you.

6. The Inca Empire was one of the most impressive civilizations on the American continents.

7. Its center was in the country that people call Peru today.

8. By the way, do you know where Surinam is?

9. Benjamin Franklin tended to get up at dawn and to go to bed at dusk.

10. Pho is a delicious Vietnamese soup with rice noodles and many other ingredients.

11. Nairobi is the capital of Kenya, a country in East Africa.

12. During the Great Depression, some poor people jumped on railway freight cars to get from one place to another.

13. Until the 1950s, trains were the most common and important means of transportation.

14. That is why many old train stations are large and impressive buildings.

15. When automobiles became affordable, train systems declined throughout the United States, but on the East Coast, trains are still widely used.

Exercise 3D

In the following sentences, identify each of the underlined words as noun (N), pronoun (Pro), verb (V), adjective (Adj), adverb (Adv), conjunction (Conj), or preposition (Prep).

1. According to many Native American legends, the <u>animal</u> [*Adj*] character Woodpecker was instrumental <u>in</u> [*Prep*] bringing fire to the earth. **2.** Long ago, when there was no fire, the chief of the animal people <u>devised</u> a plan to enter the sky country and bring back some <u>fire</u>. **3.** <u>He</u> told the animal people to make bows <u>and</u> arrows to shoot at the sky. **4.** When they hit the sky, they <u>would</u> make a chain <u>of</u> arrows down to the earth. **5.** They would <u>then</u> climb the chain to the sky and steal <u>some</u> fire. **6.** Unfortunately, <u>none</u> of <u>them</u> succeeded in hitting the sky with their arrows. **7.** Then <u>Woodpecker</u> <u>began</u> to work. **8.** He made a bow <u>from</u> the rib of Elk and arrows from the <u>serviceberry</u> bush. **9.** He <u>used</u> feathers from Golden Eagle and Bald Eagle and <u>arrowheads</u> from Flint Rock. **10.** When the animal people met <u>again</u>, they all laughed at Woodpecker, saying he could <u>not</u> hit the sky with his arrows. **11.** However, <u>their</u> own arrows fell short of the sky, <u>so</u> the chief asked Woodpecker to try. **12.** When Woodpecker shot his <u>first</u> arrow, it hit the sky. **13.** Then <u>each</u> following arrow stuck in the neck of the preceding arrow until there was a chain of arrows down to the earth. **14.** One by one, <u>they</u> all ran <u>swiftly</u> up the chain of arrows to the sky. **15.** After each one <u>had</u> stolen some fire, they raced to the arrow chain, chased by the sky people, <u>but</u> the chain had broken. **16.** To escape, each bird took an animal to the earth on <u>its</u> <u>back</u>. **17.** When they reached the earth, their chief told them to divide the fire <u>among</u> all people, so Horsefly and Hummingbird carried the fire to all <u>parts</u> of the country.

Sentence Practice: Embedding Adjectives, Adverbs, and Prepositional Phrases

You have now learned to identify the basic parts of a sentence, but this skill in itself is not very helpful unless you can use it to compose clear and effective sentences. Obviously, you have some flexibility when you compose sentences, but that flexibility is far from unlimited. The following sentence has a subject, a verb, five modifiers, one conjunction, and two prepositional phrases, but it makes no sense at all.

> Architect the quickly president for the drew up building new and plans the them to showed company.

With the parts arranged in a more effective order, the sentence, of course, makes sense.

> The architect quickly drew up plans for the new building and showed them to the company president.

There is no single correct pattern for the English sentence. The patterns you choose will be determined by the facts and ideas you wish to convey. For any given set of facts and ideas, there will be a relatively limited number of effective sentence patterns and an enormous number of ineffective ones. Knowing the parts of the sentence and how they function will help you choose the most effective patterns to communicate your thoughts.

Assume, for example, that you have four facts to communicate:

1. *Moby Dick* was written by Herman Melville.

2. *Moby Dick* is a famous novel.

3. *Moby Dick* is about a whale.

4. The whale is white.

You could combine all these facts into a single sentence:

> *Moby Dick* was written by Herman Melville, and *Moby Dick* is a famous novel, and *Moby Dick* is about a whale, and the whale is white.

Although this sentence is grammatically correct, it is repetitious and sounds foolish.

If you choose the key fact from each sentence and combine the facts in the order in which they are presented, the result is not much better:

> *Moby Dick* was written by Herman Melville, a famous novel about a whale white.

A much more effective approach is to choose the sentence that expresses the fact or idea you think is most important and to use that as your **base sentence**. Of course, the sentence you choose as the base sentence may vary depending upon the fact or idea you think is most important, but, whichever sentence you choose, it should contain the essential fact or idea that the other sentences somehow modify or explain. Once you have found the base sentence, you can **embed** the other facts or ideas into it as **adjectives, adverbs,** and **prepositional phrases.**

For example, let's use "*Moby Dick* is a famous novel" as the base sentence since it states an essential fact about *Moby Dick*—that it is a famous novel. The idea in sentence number 1 can be embedded into the base sentence as a **prepositional phrase:**

   by Herman Melville
Moby Dick ⋀ is a famous novel.

The idea in sentence 3 can now be embedded into the expanded base sentence as another **prepositional phrase:**

                                                                  about a whale
Moby Dick, by Herman Melville, is a famous novel ⋀.

Sentence 4 contains an **adjective** that modifies the noun *whale,* so it can be embedded into the sentence by placing it before *whale:*

Moby Dick, by Herman Melville, is a famous novel

        white
about a ⋀ whale.

Thus, your final sentence will read:

Moby Dick, by Herman Melville, is a famous novel about a white whale.

The same facts could be embedded in a number of other ways. Two of them are:

Moby Dick, a famous novel by Herman Melville, is about a white whale.

Herman Melville's *Moby Dick* is a famous novel about a white whale.

This process of embedding is called **sentence combining.** The purpose of practicing sentence combining is to give you an opportunity to apply the grammatical concepts you have learned in the chapter. For instance, in the above example the base sentence was expanded into a more interesting sentence by means of prepositional phrases and an adjective. Practicing this process will also help you develop greater flexibility in your sentence structure and will show you how to enrich your sentences through the addition of significant details. After all, the use of specific details is one of the most important ways of making writing interesting and effective.

PRACTICE   a. The rock star was aging.
b. The rock star was standing outside the bar.
c. The rock star was in a tuxedo.
d. The tuxedo was glittering.
e. The rock star was tired.

1. In the space below, write the base sentence, the one with the main idea.

_____

_____

2. Embed the **adjective** from sentence a into the base sentence by placing it before the noun that it modifies.

_____

_____

3. Embed the **prepositional phrase** from sentence c into the sentence by placing it after the word that it modifies.

_____

_____

4. Embed the **adjective** from sentence d into the sentence by placing it before the noun that it modifies.

_____

_____

5. Change the **adjective** in sentence e into an **adverb** (add "ly") and embed it into the sentence by placing it after the verb that it modifies.

_____

_____

Sentence Combining: Exercise A

In each of the following sets of sentences, use the first sentence as the base sentence. Embed into the base sentence the adjectives, adverbs, and prepositional phrases underlined in the sentences below it.

EXAMPLE
a. A man strode into the nightclub.
b. The man was <u>young</u>.
c. He was <u>in a bright orange bathrobe</u>.
d. He strode <u>confidently</u>.
e. The nightclub was <u>fashionable</u>.

A young man in a bright orange bathrobe strode confidently into the fashionable nightclub.

1. a. Snoop Dogg fired his accountant.
 b. The accountant was <u>outraged</u>.
 c. The accountant was <u>incompetent</u>.

_____

_____

2. a. Jennifer Lopez fell asleep at the table.
 b. Jennifer Lopez was <u>exhausted</u>.
 c. The table was <u>on the *American Idol* stage</u>.
 d. The table was <u>green</u>.

_____

_____

3. a. Ronald Reagan appeared in movies.
 b. He appeared <u>before becoming president</u>.
 c. He appeared in <u>many</u> movies.
 d. Many of those movies were <u>western</u> movies.
 e. The movies were made <u>in Hollywood</u>.

_____

_____

Sentence Combining: Exercise A

continued

4. a. Siddiqui climbed the mountain.
   b. The mountain was <u>in the Himalayas</u>.
   c. He climbed the mountain <u>steadily</u>.
   d. He climbed the mountain <u>slowly</u>.
   e. The mountain was <u>famous</u>.

   _____

   _____

5. a. The bartender mixed the drink.
   b. The bartender was <u>from Germany</u>.
   c. He mixed the drink <u>energetically</u>.
   d. The drink was made <u>with many types of liquor</u>.
   e. He mixed the drink <u>for the customer</u>.
   f. The customer was <u>elegantly dressed</u>.

   _____

   _____

Sentence Combining: Exercise B

First, choose a base sentence and circle the letter next to it. Then, using adjectives, adverbs, and prepositional phrases, embed the other facts and ideas into the base sentence.

⊚⊚ **EXAMPLE**
    a. The mountains were tall.
    b. The mountains were snow-covered.
    ⓒ The mountains towered over the hikers.
    d. There were three hikers.
    e. The hikers were from France.
    f. The hikers were lost.
    g. The mountains towered menacingly.

The tall, snow-covered mountains towered menacingly

over the three lost hikers from France.

1. a. The writer was hungry.
   b. The writer looked at the chile relleno.
   c. The chile relleno was delicious.
   d. The chile relleno was on the table.
   e. The table was next to his desk.

   _____

   _____

2. a. The drummer was swaying.
   b. The drummer moved.
   c. She moved gracefully.
   d. She moved to the rhythm of the music.
   e. The music was reggae.

   _____

   _____

3. a. The dolphin was clever.
   b. The tuna was large.
   c. The net was in the ocean.
   d. The dolphin and the tuna evaded the net.
   e. They evaded the net swiftly.

   _____

   _____

Sentence Combining: Exercise B

continued

4. a. The noise was loud.
   b. The noise was piercing.
   c. The noise was from a video game.
   d. The video game distracted the student.
   e. The student was busy.

_____

_____

5. a. The couple was happy.
   b. The couple traveled to South Africa.
   c. The couple was newly married.
   d. The couple had a first-class ticket.
   e. The couple traveled by ship.

_____

_____

6. a. A person has invented a talking tombstone.
   b. The person is imaginative.
   c. It was invented recently.
   d. The talking tombstone is solar powered.

_____

_____

7. a. A statement is tape-recorded.
   b. The case is Plexiglas.
   c. A statement is placed in a case.
   d. It is a case that sits in an area of the tombstone.
   e. The area is hollowed out.

_____

_____

Sentence Combining: Exercise B

continued

8. a. A speaker is small.
   b. A speaker and a panel are installed.
   c. It is a solar panel.
   d. A speaker and panel are on the tombstone.
   e. It is a three-inch panel.

   _____

   _____

9. a. The recording can be activated with the correct key.
   b. You can activate the recording and listen to a statement.
   c. The recording is in the case.
   d. The statement is from the grave's occupant.

   _____

   _____

10. a. The sunlight must be enough.
    b. With sunlight, the recording will run.
    c. The recording will run for as long as two hours.
    d. The recording is in the tombstone.
    e. The tombstone costs $10,000.

    _____

    _____

Paragraph Practice: Narrating an Event

If you have ever sat for hours before a blank sheet of paper or stared for what seemed like forever at a blank computer screen, you know how difficult and frustrating it can be to write a paper. In fact, some people have such trouble simply *starting* their papers that, for them, writing becomes a truly painful experience.

Fortunately, writing does not have to be so difficult. If you learn how to use the steps involved in the process of writing, you can avoid much of the frustration and enjoy more of the satisfaction that comes from writing a successful paper. In this section, you will practice using the three general activities that make up the writing process—**prewriting, writing**, and **rewriting**—to produce a paragraph based on the following assignment.

Assignment

In each section of this chapter, there are paragraphs that tell stories. Whether it is a story about the past (Egyptian women), a story relating facts (how the American penny developed), a cultural story (how Woodpecker brought fire to the earth), or a background story about a movie (*Indiana Jones*), all stories have a starting point and then develop a narrative, a story line that heads toward a kind of conclusion or ending. Telling some stories requires research, but we already have the knowledge to write stories about events that occurred in our own lives.

For this writing assignment, use the writing process explained below to describe an event that has happened to you. Ask yourself, "What events— either from the distant past or from more recent times—have happened to me that I remember well?" Perhaps you remember your first date, your first traffic ticket, or even your first child. Or perhaps you remember the day you won a race in a track meet, performed alone on a stage, or attended your first college class. Often the best event to write about will not be the first one you think of.

Prewriting to Generate Ideas

Prewriting is the part of the writing process that will help you get past "writer's block" and into writing. It consists of anything you do to generate ideas and get started, but three of the most successful prewriting techniques are **freewriting, brainstorming,** and **clustering.**

Freewriting

Freewriting is based on one simple but essential idea: When you sit down to write, you write. You don't stare at your paper or look out the window, wondering what in the world you could write about. Instead, you <u>write down</u> your thoughts and questions even if you have no idea what topic you should focus on. In addition, as you freewrite, you do not stop to correct spelling, grammar, or punctuation errors. After all, the purpose of freewriting is to generate ideas, not to write the final draft of your paper.

Here is how some freewriting might look for the assignment described above.

> To describe an event? What could I write about that? I don't have a lot of "events" that I can think of—but I suppose I must have some. What do I remember? How about recently? Have I gone anywhere or has anything happened to me? I went skiing last month and took a bad fall—but so what? That wouldn't be very interesting. How about something I remember that I didn't like—like what? Death? Too depressing. Besides, I have never been closely involved in death. I was in a car accident once, but that was too long ago, and it doesn't really interest me. How about—what? I'm stuck. How about events I have good memories about—wait—I remember almost drowning when I was practicing for water polo in high school. <u>That</u> was a wild event. I could do it. Any other possibilities? How about good memories—like the time I made that lucky catch in Little League. That would be good. Or the fish I caught with my dad when I was a kid. Lots of good memories there. Any others? Yeah—I joined a softball league recently—that was a real experience, especially because it'd been so long since I'd played baseball. But I can't think of any particular thing I'd write about it.—Of all these, I think I like the drowning one best. I <u>really</u> remember that one and all the feelings that went with it.

You can tell that the above writer was not trying to produce a clean, well-written copy of his paper. Instead, he wrote down his thoughts as they occurred to him, and the result was a very informal rush of ideas that eventually led him to a topic, a near-drowning that occurred when he was in high school. Now that he has his topic, he can continue to freewrite to generate details about the event that he can use in his paper.

Prewriting Application: Freewriting

1. Freewrite for ten minutes about any memories you have of events that were important to you. Don't stop to correct any errors. Just write about as many events as you can remember. If you skip from one event to another, that's fine. If you get stuck, just write "I'm stuck" or something like that over and over—but keep writing for ten minutes.

2. Now reread your initial freewriting. Is there some event in there that interests you more than the others? Choose one event and freewrite only on it. Describe everything you can remember about the event, but don't stop to correct errors—just write.

Brainstorming

Brainstorming is another prewriting technique that you can use to generate ideas. Brainstorming is similar to freewriting in that you write down your thoughts without censoring or editing them, but it differs in that the thoughts usually appear as a list of ideas rather than as separate sentences. Here is an example of how the above freewriting might have looked as brainstorming.

> An event I remember well—what could I use?
>
> recently?
>
>   fall while skiing—no
>
> things I didn't like
>
>   death? too depressing
>
>   car accident I was in? too long ago
>
>   almost drowned at practice—<u>good one</u>
>
> good memories?
>
>   lucky catch in Little League
>
>   fishing with Dad
>
> <u>Use the one about almost drowning</u>.

Prewriting Application: Brainstorming

1. Make a brainstorming list of events from your life that were important to you. Include events from as far back as your early childhood to as recently as yesterday.

2. Choose the event that interests you the most. Make a brainstorming list of everything you can remember about it.

Clustering

Clustering is a third prewriting technique that many people find helpful. It differs from brainstorming and freewriting in that it is written almost like an informal map. To "cluster" your ideas, start out with an idea or question and draw a circle around it. Then connect related ideas to the circle and continue in that way. Here is how you might use clustering to find a memorable event to write about.

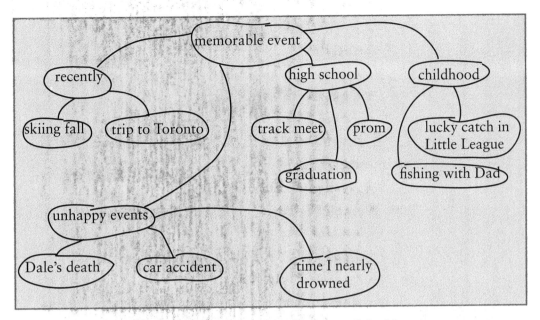

As you can see, clustering provides a mental picture of the ideas you generate. As such, it can help you organize your material <u>as</u> you think of it.

Prewriting Application: Clustering

1. Develop a "memorable events" cluster of your own. Include as many associations as you can to find the one event that interests you the most.

2. Now choose the event that interests you the most and use it as the center of a new cluster. Write in as many memories of the event as you can.

Freewriting, brainstorming, and clustering are only three of many techniques to help you get started writing. When you use them, you should feel free to move from one to the other at any time. And, of course, your instructor may suggest other ways to help you get started. Whatever technique you use, the point is to <u>start writing</u>. Do your thinking on paper (or at a computer), not while you are staring out a window. Here's a good motto that you should try to follow whenever you have a writing assignment due: **Think in ink.**

Choosing and Narrowing the Topic

Choosing the Topic

Perhaps you have already found the event that most interests you. If you have, continue to prewrite to develop as many details as you can. If you are still undecided about a topic, use the following suggestions to think of possibilities.

1. What experiences of yours have been particularly exciting, happy, or pleasant?

2. What experiences are you most proud of?

3. What events bring you disappointing, unpleasant, or fearful memories?

4. What are your most embarrassing memories?

5. What strange or unusual things have happened to you?

6. What dangerous or frightening experiences have you had?

7. What are the "firsts" in your life? Consider your first day in high school, your first day on a team or as part of a group, your first performance, your first date, your first camping trip, your first traffic ticket.

8. What experiences have inspired you, changed the way you think about life, or made you into a different person?

9. What events do you remember from your early childhood?

10. What events do you remember from elementary school or high school, from vacations or trips?

Narrowing the Topic

Many topics that interest you might be too broad—that is, explaining them might require a much longer paper than has been assigned. And sometimes instructors provide only broad topic ideas when they assign a paper, expecting you to narrow the topic to something appropriate for the length of the assignment. In such cases you need to <u>narrow</u> your topic, discussing, perhaps, only part of the event rather than the entire thing. Learning to narrow a topic is an important step in the writing process because broad topics usually lead to general, unconvincing papers.

For example, let's say you have chosen as your topic a high school football game—the championship game in which you scored the winning touchdown. It would be natural to want to cover the entire game because all of it was important to you, but the topic is much too large to be covered in one paragraph. So you must narrow the topic. A successful single paragraph might describe only one play, the one in which you scored the winning touchdown. It would describe everything about the play, from the noise in the stands to the looks on your teammates' faces in the huddle to the smell of the grass to the sound of the quarterback's voice—everything you can think of to provide detail and add excitement to the event.

What Is a Paragraph?

Since you have been asked to write a paragraph about an experience of your own, it is time to explain what a paragraph is. First and foremost, a paragraph is a kind of visual aid. Just imagine how a text would look if there were no paragraphs; one would end up with one long uninterrupted block of sentences, possibly going on for pages. Such a block would look intimidating and discourage us from reading. Paragraphs visually indicate where one idea—or an aspect or portion of an idea—starts and ends. When you start a new paragraph, you signal to a reader that you shift the topic slightly, or that you turn to another aspect or portion of the larger idea that your essay as a whole is pursuing, or that you are moving to another section of your story. Therefore, the general rule is that one paragraph should explore and develop one idea, or one event, or a portion of a more complicated event or idea. Since that is the case, an event or an idea you want to write about in one paragraph cannot be too complicated. An appropriate paragraph topic has to be specific.

Prewriting Application: Narrowing the Topic

Consider the following events as possible topics for a paragraph. Write "OK" next to any that you think would work. If any seem too broad, explain why and discuss how you might narrow them.

_____ **1.** Giving birth to my first child

_____ **2.** My vacation to Atlanta

_____ **3.** An unusual dinner experience

_____ **4.** The last time I saw my father

_____ **5.** A day at Disney World

_____ **6.** The night I was fired

_____ **7.** Going to a sports event

_____ **8.** My first date

_____ **9.** Getting lost in Tijuana

_____ **10.** Moving to Arizona

Prewriting Application: Talking to Others

Once you have chosen and narrowed your topic, form groups of two, three, or four and tell your experiences to each other. Telling others about an event is a good way to decide what details to include and how much to say. And listening to someone else's story will help you learn what will keep an audience interested in your own story.

As you describe your event to others, make it as interesting as you can by describing what happened, how you felt, and what you thought. As you listen to the stories of others and as you describe your own experience, consider these questions:

1. What are the time and place of the event? How old were you? What time of day did it occur? What time of year? What was the weather like?

2. Can you visualize the scene? What is the name of the place where the event occurred? What physical features are in the area—trees? buildings? furniture? cars? other people?

3. How did you feel as the event progressed? What were you thinking each step of the way?

4. Did your thoughts and feelings change as the event occurred?

5. What parts of the event would be clearer if they were explained more?

Writing a Topic Sentence

The topic sentence is the one sentence in your paragraph that states both your **narrowed topic** and the **central point** you intend to make about the topic. To find your central point, reread your prewriting. Look for related details that seem to focus on <u>one particular reaction</u> to the event. That reaction is your central point.

College texts and your own college papers describe events in order to make a point. In a psychology text, for example, an airplane crash might be described in detail to help the reader understand how such an event can affect the relatives of those involved. And a history text might describe what happened at the Battle of Gettysburg to help the reader understand why it was a major turning point in the Civil War. Certainly in your own college papers, you will be expected to describe events to illustrate the points you are trying to make.

Although the topic sentence can appear in a variety of places, in college paragraphs you should usually write it as the first sentence so that your central point is clear from the very start. Here are some examples of topic sentences drawn from the exercises in this chapter. Note that each topic sentence contains a topic and a central point and that each one is the first sentence of its paragraph.

EXAMPLES

                topic   central point

In ancient Egypt, women enjoyed a <u>better status than women in many other</u>

<u>ancient societies.</u>

                             topic   central point

When confronted with new and unfamiliar foods, <u>many people are afraid</u> <u>to try new things.</u>

                                                   topic

According to many North American Indian stories, the **animal character**

                                 central point

Woodpecker was <u>instrumental in bringing fire to the earth.</u>

The **central point** of your topic sentence needs to be <u>limited</u> and <u>precise</u> so that it is not too broad, general, or vague. For example, in the topic sentence *My first date was an interesting experience,* the central idea that the date was *interesting* is much too vague. It could mean the date was the best experience of your life or that it was absolutely horrible. As a general rule, the more precise the topic sentence, the more effective your paragraph will be. Consider the following characteristics of a well-written topic sentence.

1. A topic sentence must include a central point.

EXAMPLE (weak) My paragraph is about my youngest sister's wedding.

In this sentence the topic (my youngest sister's wedding) is clear, but no central point about that wedding is expressed. An improved topic sentence might be:

EXAMPLE (improved) My youngest sister's wedding last year was one of the most hilarious events I have ever experienced.

In this sentence, a central point—that the wedding was hilarious—has been clearly expressed.

2. A topic sentence does not merely state a fact.

EXAMPLE (weak) A few months ago I saw a car accident.

This sentence simply states a fact. There is no central point to be explained after the fact is stated. An improved topic sentence might be:

EXAMPLE (improved) I will never forget how horrified I was a few months ago when I was an unwilling witness to a major car accident.

This sentence now makes a statement about the accident that causes the reader to want more explanation.

3. A topic sentence must include a narrowed topic and central point.

EXAMPLE (weak) My spring break this year was really something.

Both the topic (spring break) and the central point (it was "something") are far too general to describe in detail in one paragraph. Here is a more focused topic sentence:

EXAMPLE (improved) On the last day of spring break this year, my vacation in Palm Springs, California, turned from wonderful to absolutely miserable in just one hour.

This sentence now focuses on a specific event (the last day of spring break in Palm Springs) and on a precise central point (it changed from wonderful to miserable).

Prewriting Application: Working with Topic Sentences

In each sentence below, underline the topic once and the central point twice.

1. When trying to write essays, I have to overcome my anxiety about writing.

2. My best friend revealed a new side of herself when she shouted at the server at the restaurant.

3. Though I generally do not like video games, last month at my friend's house I discovered I will have to make an exception to that rule.

4. When I stepped onto the stage for my latest audition, I did not know I was in for the biggest surprise of my life.

5. I used to feel anxious about meeting new people, but one day I discovered certain techniques that helped me overcome my fears.

Prewriting Application: Evaluating Topic Sentences

Write "No" before each sentence that would not make a good topic sentence and "Yes" before each sentence that would make a good one. Using ideas of your own, rewrite the unacceptable topic sentences into effective ones.

_____ 1. Last August I visited Lake Ponsett, South Dakota.

_____

_____

_____ 2. Giving birth to my first child made me wonder if I would ever want to have children again.

_____

_____

_____ 3. I never chose to have a dog—instead, my little dachshund chose me when I came home from work one day.

_____

_____

_____ **4.** Last night at the salsa club was interesting.

_____

_____

_____ **5.** One of my earliest memories of my father and me spending time together is also one of my most disappointing ones.

_____

_____

_____ **6.** It all happened when I decided to go skiing in Aspen, Colorado.

_____

_____

_____ **7.** This paragraph will be about my skateboard.

_____

_____

_____

_____ **8.** I was amazed at everything that happened to us while driving from Amarillo, Texas, to Atlanta, Georgia.

_____

_____

_____

_____ **9.** Wilder than a rollercoaster ride—that describes my behavior the evening I put too much wasabi on my sushi.

_____

_____

_____ **10.** A chance encounter at the bus stop last year gave me new insights into the meaning of life.

_____

_____

Organizing Details

When describing an event, you will usually present the details in **chronological order.** That is, you will organize them according to how they occurred in time. However, other assignments might require different organizations to present your supporting details effectively. (Other organizational patterns are discussed in future chapters.)

Prewriting Application: Organizing Supporting Details

The following details describe a time a person almost drowned at a water polo practice. Number the details so that they appear in their probable chronological order.

_____ joined water polo

_____ volunteered to try the challenge set

_____ two laps underwater

_____ felt okay during the first lap

_____ woke up in coach's arms

_____ choking underwater

_____ second lap seemed okay at first

_____ determined to make it

_____ everyone around me when I woke up

_____ everything went black

_____ lungs gave out

_____ saw lane markers just before passed out

Writing the Paragraph

Writing a full draft of your paper is the next step in the writing process. The trick to writing your first draft without getting stuck is to remember that what you write now is not your final copy, so you can allow yourself to make mistakes and to write awkward sentences. Don't worry about how "correct" your writing is. Instead, just write your preliminary topic sentence and then describe your experience as thoroughly as you can.

Here is a sample first draft of the paper on drowning. As you read it, notice that the writer has not yet corrected any errors it may contain.

The Challenge Set (First Draft)

An unusual experience happened to me when I was sixteen. It all happened one day at practice for water polo. I was a sophomore on the Kearney High School water polo team. One day I volunteered for the dreaded "Challenge Set." I had just finished the first lap underwater. I still felt good. As I come to the wall, I make the decision to go for another lap, I keep swimming, but my lungs collapse. I took a few more strokes, and then it happened. I blacked out. All I remember was seeing black. I felt completely relaxed. Then I remember hearing voices. Suddenly, starting to cough violently. When I opened my eyes, the first person I saw was my coach. He told me what had happened, I was a little shaken. I couldn't believe that I almost died. This was really a frightening experience that I remember whenever I go for a swim.

The above first draft is far from perfect. It contains writing errors and could use more descriptive details. However, it has accomplished its purpose: *It has given the writer a draft to work with and to improve.*

Writing Application: Producing Your First Draft

Now write the first draft of your paragraph. Remember that your goal is *not* to write an error-free draft. Instead, it is to write a *first* draft that opens with a preliminary topic sentence, a draft that you can then continue to work on and improve.

Rewriting and Improving the Paragraph

Rewriting consists of two stages: **revising** and **proofreading.** In the **revising** stage of the writing process, you improve the "larger" areas of your paper—its content, organization, and sentence structure. Here are some suggestions.

- Improve your preliminary topic sentence.

  You can often improve your topic sentence *after* you have written your first draft because now you really have something to introduce. In fact, if you look at the *concluding* sentences of your first draft, you may find a clearer statement of the central point of your paragraph than the one you have in your preliminary topic sentence. If that is the case, rewrite your topic sentence to include that statement.

- Add more details.

  After you have written the first draft, add any further details that might improve your paper. Look especially for those that will emphasize the central point of your topic sentence.

- Reorganize the details in the first draft.

  There are many ways to organize a paper, but one of the most common ones is to save the most important details for last. Another way to organize details, especially if you are describing an event, is to list the details in chronological order. Whichever way you choose, now is the time to make any changes in the order of your material.

- Combine related sentences and ideas.

  Combine sentences that are obviously related. Where possible, use sentence-combining techniques to embed material from one sentence into another. (Sentence-combining techniques are discussed in Section Four of each chapter.)

Improving Supporting Details

The supporting details in many first drafts tend to be vague, colorless, and mediocre. But with just a little work they can be transformed into strong, dramatic sentences. Consider adding details that emphasize specific sights and sounds. Wherever you can, use the precise names of people, places, and things. Look especially for new details and words that will emphasize the central point of your paragraph. Note how the colorless example below is transformed with precise, descriptive details.

EXAMPLE   (weak)   My father went in one direction while I went in another. I saw a fence covered with all sorts of decorations from local Indians. Inside the fence on the ground was the medicine wheel. I stared at it silently.

EXAMPLE   (improved)   My father veered off to the west as I continued straight ahead, toward what I perceived to be the main attraction. It was a protective, circular chain link fence sixty feet in diameter, decorated with ribbons, scraps of paper, little totem bags made by the local Indian women and girls, and eagle feathers and strings of beads. All of these decorations were meant as offerings and prayers. Inside the fence was the medicine wheel, a fifty-foot spoked wheel etched into the dust. I stopped and felt the wind and the still sacredness of the view.

Rewriting Application: Improving Supporting Details

Read the following brief paragraphs and identify places where the support could be more descriptive and precise. Then rewrite the paragraphs, adding stronger, more dramatic details.

A. My trip to the grocery store turned into a complete nightmare. When I walked down one of the aisles, I saw a person shoplifting, so I told the manager. She stopped the shoplifter, and they argued. Then the manager said I had to stay to talk to the police. I had some important things to do, so I said I had to leave. As I walked to my car, the manager became really mad at me too.

B. One of the highlights of my short career playing Little League baseball happened when my best friend was at bat. He and I played on opposing teams. I was in the outfield when he hit the ball toward me. It was going to go over my head, so I backed up. When I reached the fence, I stuck up my glove and caught the ball. I looked at the stands and saw people standing and cheering for me. It was a great experience.

Proofreading

Proofreading is the final step in the writing process. It consists of correcting spelling, grammar, and punctuation errors. **Do not skip this step.** A paper focused on an excellent topic and developed with striking details will almost always still receive a poor grade if it is full of distracting writing errors. Here are some suggestions to help you proofread successfully.

- If you use a computer, run the spelling-checker program. (But don't rely only on that program. Read each word carefully yourself.)

- Use a dictionary to check the spelling of any words you are unsure of.

- Watch for incomplete sentences and run-on sentences. (These errors will be discussed in Chapter Two.)

- Look closely at your verbs and pronouns. If you are describing an event from the past, use past-tense verbs. (Verb and pronoun errors will be discussed in Chapter Four.)

- Ask someone you trust to read your paper. If your school has tutors available, use them. They can help you find many writing errors that you might have overlooked. **However, please note:** If a friend reads your paper, do not allow him or her to rewrite sentences for you. Most instructors consider that kind of help to be plagiarism.

- When you are satisfied with your paper, print a final copy, and then *read that copy one more time.* You will be surprised how often more errors seem to appear out of nowhere. If you find more errors, fix them and print another copy.

Rewriting Application: Responding to Writing

Reread the first draft of "The Challenge Set" on page 71. Then respond to the following questions:

1. What is the writer's central feeling about his experience? Where is it stated? How would you reword the opening sentence to express that central feeling?

2. Where should the writer add more details? What kind of details would make his paragraph more colorful and descriptive?

3. Should any of the details be reorganized or presented in a different order?

4. What sentences would you combine because they contain related ideas?

5. What changes should the writer make in spelling, grammar, or punctuation?

Here is how the student who nearly drowned revised his first draft. Compare it to his first draft.

	The Challenge Set
Revised opening sentence includes reaction to the event.	**When I was sixteen, I had a frightening experience that I still remember whenever I go for a swim.** This took place when I was a sophomore on the Kearney High School water polo team. One day at practice, I volunteered to try the dreaded "Challenge Set." **It consisted of three to four players attempting to swim fifty yards, two laps of the pool, on a single breath.**
Added details	**I dove into the cool, clear water full of confidence, but I had no idea what was about to happen.** When I came to the wall at the end of the first lap, I was well ahead of my teammate, Bryan, who was in the lane to my right. I felt great, as if I could hold my breath forever, so I decided to go for the second lap. I made the flip turn and pushed off **the blue tiles.** I still felt okay, but without my knowing it, my lungs had started to collapse.
Added details	**I remember beginning to feel pressure in my chest** when I saw the blue hash marks, **the halfway markers.** I had just a little way to go, but my head was whirling, and my chest felt like it was about to explode. **Suddenly everything slowed down.** I knew I should stop and take a breath, but I refused to do it. I took a few more strokes, and then it happened. I started to black out.
Combined sentences	**All I remember is seeing black and feeling completely relaxed.** The next thing I knew, it seemed like someone was shaking me. As I began to hear voices, I started to cough violently. **Every time I tried to take a breath, a searing pain shot through me. I was terrified.** When I opened my eyes, the first person I saw was Coach Leonard, **a state beach lifeguard. I was lying in his arms, not knowing where I was or what had happened to me.** When
Added details	he told me that I had passed out in the pool and that Bryan had pulled me
Added details	out, **I was really shaken. I couldn't believe I had almost drowned. I got out of the pool, got dressed, and sat in the stands waiting for practice to end.** I don't think I'll ever forget that day.

Rewriting Application: Revising and Proofreading Your Own Draft

Now revise and proofread your first draft.

1. Improve your topic sentence.

2. Add more details, especially those that emphasize the central point.

3. Reorganize the details.

4. Combine related sentences and ideas.

5. Once you have revised, *proofread* for spelling, grammar, and punctuation errors.

As you can tell, thorough revising and editing will involve several new drafts, not just one. Once you have a draft with which you are satisfied, prepare a clean final draft, following the format your instructor has requested.

Chapter 1 Practice Test

A. Identify the underlined words by writing "S" over subjects, "HV" over helping verbs, and "MV" over main verbs. If the underlined word is none of these, leave it blank.

1. The government agency <u>said</u> that the nuclear power <u>plant</u> was safe.

2. It is hard to <u>see</u> anything new if <u>I</u> think that I have seen it all.

3. He <u>would</u> have studied, but the baby was <u>crying</u> all night.

4. There are <u>three</u> <u>options</u>: strawberry, raspberry, and chocolate.

5. In Hinduism, the goal <u>is</u> to become one with the <u>universe</u>.

B. Underline all subjects once and all complete verbs twice in the following sentences.

6. Serena and Venus Williams have shown that they are great tennis players.

7. There are many roads to Rome.

8. Most of the tourists enjoyed the city of Venice.

9. College football might be the most important sport to many people in Nebraska.

10. Are tablets going to replace laptop computers?

11. Do baseball players earn more money than football players, or are basketball players paid even more?

12. The maximum speed for a falling raindrop is eighteen miles per hour.

13. Many people think that Sidney is the capital of Australia, but the capital is actually Canberra.

14. Measles does not actually come from Germany.

15. Although some Greeks and Turks will deny it, coffee really originated in Ethiopia.

continued

C. Write sentences of your own that follow the suggested patterns.

16. A statement with one subject, one helping verb, and one main verb (S-HV-MV).

_____

_____

17. A question with one helping verb, two subjects joined by "and," and one main verb (HV-S "and" S-MV):

_____

_____

18. A statement with one subject and two main verbs joined by "and" (S-MV "and" MV).

_____

_____

19. A statement starting with "Before" and followed by one subject, one helping verb, and one main verb, and then another subject and main verb ("Before" S-HV-MV, S-MV):

_____

_____

20. A statement with a subject, two helping verbs, and a main verb followed by "when" and another subject and main verb (S-HV-HV-MV "when" S-MV):

_____

_____

D. In the following sentences, identify all adjectives by writing "Adj" above them, and identify all adverbs by writing "Adv" above them.

21. The vampire was very sad because many teenagers lost interest in him.

22. The industrious student decided to spend her hard-earned money on textbooks.

23. The Iroquois formed a powerful confederacy that decisively influenced the

Constitution of the United States.

continued

24. Would you rather go to Disneyland, or do you still prefer to go to Universal Studios?

25. Movie directors always seem to find ways to make longer and more destructive chase scenes.

E. In the following sentences, correct any errors in the use of adjectives and adverbs (or in the use of *then* and *than*) by crossing out any incorrect words and writing the correct words above them.

26. Chile has a longer coastline then Peru, but Peru has more higher mountains.

27. Of the two dishes, sweet potato pie is the best one.

28. The pizza tasted so well that I ordered some more real fast.

29. Though the Ferrari did not perform as good as the Porsche, I still think it is the most attractive car of the two.

30. Among Albert Einstein, Lao Tzu, and King Solomon, who was the more intelligent, who lived earliest, and who was the wiser one?

F. In the following sentences, place all prepositional phrases in parentheses.

31. When he arrived at the doors of Nirvana with his Rolex, the universe decided he was not ready to enter.

32. The salsa tune was accompanied by congas, and several brass instruments contributed to the rhythmic arrangement of the music.

33. When the Israelites fled from Egypt, the Red Sea is said to have divided in front of them so that they could walk through it.

34. Benjamin Franklin looked at the sky and decided this would be a good time to test his new invention.

35. In the Middle Ages, Baghdad was known as the largest city in the world, and it was famous for its scholars and for its cultural treasures.

continued

G. In the following sentences, add coordinating conjunctions that show the relationship indicated in parentheses.

36. Celia Cruz was singing, _____ Tito Puente accompanied her on the timbales. (addition)

37. James did not like the looks of the hotdog, _____ he asked the ballpark vendor to give him another one. (result)

38. Ghengis Khan had conquered most of northern Asia, _____ eventually he and his army got tired. (contrast)

39. Michael could learn how to play rock 'n roll on his guitar, _____ he could learn how to play flamenco. (alternative)

40. Hester did not want to wear the scarlet letter, _____ she had not done anything wrong. (cause)

H. Identify the underlined words in these sentences by writing one of the following abbreviations above each word: noun (N), pronoun (Pro), verb (V), adjective (Adj), adverb (Adv), conjunction (Conj), or preposition (Prep).

41. Climate change <u>has</u> caused some Pacific Island countries' governments to consider moving the <u>entire</u> population to other places.

42. Miami, Florida, has a large <u>population</u> <u>of</u> Cubans.

43. Dolphins are considered to be among the <u>most</u> intelligent animals on the planet, <u>and</u> they are not fish but mammals.

44. Even though he had a GPS <u>device</u>, he was <u>still</u> unable to find the bakery.

45. Phil and Tiger are competing to be remembered as the best golfer <u>who</u> ever played, <u>but</u> some think neither one will be.

46. Emma had updated her Facebook page <u>many</u> times, and Camille noticed all the <u>changes</u>.

continued

47. Coal mining used to be an <u>important</u> industry that employed many people, but a lot of

    coal miners have been replaced <u>by</u> machines

48. The children did <u>not</u> seem to be learning, <u>so</u> the administration came up with another

    standardized test.

49. Do <u>you</u> think *Dumb and Dumber* is a funny movie, or do you <u>prefer</u> *Beverly Hills Cop?*

50. Hannibal <u>checked</u> <u>on</u> all the elephants before he crossed the Alps.

Understanding Sentence Patterns

In Chapter One you learned the terms that describe how words function in a sentence. These terms will help you understand how the various word groups operate in a sentence. Understanding these word groups will help you see not only how sentences are put together but also how to revise your writing effectively and systematically. Without some knowledge of these word groups, you really can't even define what a sentence is.

Consider, for example, two common definitions of a sentence:

1. A sentence is a group of words that expresses a complete thought.

2. A sentence is a group of words that contains a subject and a verb.

These definitions may seem adequate, but, if you consider them carefully, you will see that neither of them is really accurate. For example, some sentences do not seem to express "a complete thought." Consider the sentence "*It fell.*" Do these two words really convey a complete thought? In one sense they do: A specific action is communicated, and a subject, though an indefinite one, is identified. However, the sentence raises more questions than it answers. What fell? Why did it fall? Where did it fall to? The sentence could refer to an apple, a star, the sky, or the Roman Empire. If someone walked up to you in the street and said, "*It fell,*" you certainly would not feel that a complete thought had been communicated to you, and yet the two words do form a sentence.

The second definition is no more satisfactory. The words "*Because his father was sleeping*" do <u>not</u> make up a sentence even though they contain both a subject (*father*) and a verb (*was sleeping*). Although it is true that all sentences must contain a subject and a verb, it does not necessarily follow that every group of words with a subject and a verb is a sentence.

The only definition of a sentence that is <u>always</u> correct is the following one: A sentence is a group of words that contains at least one main clause.

---

sentence

A sentence is a group of words that contains at least one main clause.

You will understand this definition easily if you know what a **main clause** is, but it will be incomprehensible if you do not. Thus, it is critical that you be able to identify this word group, for, if you cannot identify a main clause, you cannot be certain that you are using complete sentences in your writing.

Clauses

Main Clauses and Subordinate Clauses

A clause is a group of words that contains at least one subject and at least one verb.

> **clause**
>
> A clause is a group of words that contains at least one subject and at least one verb.

The two types of clauses are **main clause** and **subordinate clause.**

1. A **main clause** is a group of words that contains at least one subject and one verb and that <u>expresses a complete idea</u>.

2. A **subordinate clause** is a group of words that contains at least one subject and one verb but that <u>does not express a complete idea</u>. All subordinate clauses begin with **subordinators.**

◎◎ **EXAMPLE**

            sub. clause   main clause

[Although he seldom plays,] [Raymond is an excellent golfer.]

This example contains two clauses, each with a subject and a verb. As you can see, the clause *Raymond is an excellent golfer* could stand by itself as a sentence. But the clause *Although he seldom plays* cannot stand by itself (even though it has a subject and a verb) because it needs the main clause to complete its thought and because it begins with the subordinator *although*.

Subordinators

Subordinators indicate the relationship between the subordinate clause and the main clause. Learning to recognize the two types of subordinators—subordinating conjunctions and relative pronouns—will help you identify subordinate clauses.

Subordinating Conjunctions		*Relative Pronouns*	
<u>after</u>	so that	that	who(ever)
although	than	which	whom(ever)
<u>as</u>	though		whose
as if	unless		
as long as	<u>until</u>		
because	when		
<u>before</u>	whenever		
even though	where		
if	wherever		
<u>since</u>	while		

NOTE: Some of the words in the above list of subordinators are underlined (*after, as, before, since, until*). These words are used as prepositions when they do not introduce a subordinate clause.

◎◎ **EXAMPLES**   prepositional phrase: *after dinner*

subordinate clause: *after I eat dinner*

The following are examples of sentences containing subordinate clauses. (Note that each subordinate clause begins with a subordinator.)

◎◎ **EXAMPLES**

                          sub. clause   main clause
[**Before** his horse had crossed the finish line,] [the jockey suddenly stood up in his saddle.]

          main clause   sub. clause
[Fried Spam is a dish] [**that** few people love.]

             main clause   sub. clause
[Antonio won the spelling bee] [**because** he spelled *penicillin* correctly.]

◎◎ **PRACTICE**   Identify the following word groups as main clauses (MC) or subordinate clauses (SC) or neither (N).

1. Although Prometheus came to like the vultures.   *SC*

2. That the farmer fed his horses.   _____

3. We took a cold shower.   _____

4. Which we found under the Queen of Hearts's crown.   _____

5. We had ham and black-eyed peas.   _____

6. Because she turned into a beautiful princess. _____

7. While Custer was not looking. _____

8. In spite of their lack of ammunition. _____

9. Whom the fans idolized. _____

10. If Karl Marx had written it. _____

PRACTICE   Identify the following word groups as subordinate clauses (SC) or prepositional phrases (PP).

1. Since Michelle ate the crab legs. _____SC_____

2. Since the end of the Olympics. _____

3. Since no one has answered the bell. _____

4. After the delicately buttered popcorn. _____

5. After UPS delivers the package. _____

6. Until the fall of Constantinople. _____

7. Until you finish *The Hunger Games*. _____

8. Before we decided on our latest strategy. _____

9. Before winter and the first deep snow. _____

10. Before the arrival of Macintosh computers. _____

PRACTICE   Underline the subordinate clauses in the following sentences and circle the subordinators. Not all sentences contain subordinate clauses.

1. A misanthrope is a person (who) does not like people.

2. Lewis Carroll created the word *chortle*, which is a combination of two other words.

3. After the battle in the lake, Beowulf returned to the hall.

4. Puck gave the potion to Titania, who was sleeping.

5. Even though I have seen *Hugo* seven times, you should still go with me.

6. A reformed slave trader wrote "Amazing Grace," which is played at police officers' funerals.

7. Michelle decided not to visit Saudi Arabia because Saudi culture is so hard on women.

8. My math teacher, who otherwise seemed sane, wore an *Angry Birds* hat everywhere.

9. I am going to complain if I have to see that Budweiser commercial one more time.

10. The Battle of Bull Run was the place where the first real engagement of the Civil War occurred.

Adverb and Adjective Subordinate Clauses

Subordinate clauses may function as adverbs, adjectives, or nouns in their sentences. Therefore, they are called **adverb clauses, adjective clauses,** or **noun clauses.** We will be discussing adverb and adjective clauses, but not noun clauses. Although we frequently use noun clauses in our writing, they seldom present problems in punctuation or clarity.

Adverb Clauses

Like single-word adverbs, adverb subordinate clauses can modify verbs. For example, in the sentence *Clare ate a big breakfast because she had a busy day ahead of her,* the adverb clause *because she had a busy day ahead of her* modifies the verb *ate*. It explains <u>why</u> Clare ate a big breakfast.

Another characteristic of adverb clauses is that they begin with a **subordinating conjunction,** not a relative pronoun. In addition, in most cases an adverb clause can be moved around in its sentence, and the sentence will still make sense.

☍☍ EXAMPLES   [**When** she ate the mushroom,] Alice grew taller.

Alice grew taller [**when** she ate the mushroom.]

Alice, [**when** she ate the mushroom,] grew taller.

NOTE: When the adverb clause begins the sentence, it is followed by a comma, as in the first example. When the adverb clause ends a sentence, no comma is needed. When the adverb clause interrupts the main clause, it is enclosed by commas.

PRACTICE Underline the adverb clauses in the following sentences. Circle the subordinating conjunctions.

1. (If) you leave now, you will miss the eruption of Vesuvius.

2. Whenever Deborah wants a snack, she eats an apple.

3. Because she was wandering in an isolated part of the mountains, Ruth dressed warmly.

4. Although he suffered greatly, Dr. Urbino delayed his marriage to his beloved Fiorentino.

5. James Barrie was inspired to write *Peter Pan* after he told stories of Peter to the children of a friend.

PRACTICE Add adverb clauses of your own to the following main clauses in the spaces indicated. Use commas where they are needed.

1. He laid his daughter Regan down for a nap *because she had been acting tired all morning.*

2. _____ , Robert E. Lee was appointed president of a college.

3. Colin always waits until spring _____

   _____ .

4. Pooh was happy to see the swarm of bees _____

   _____

5. _____ , the emperor walked naked into the village.

Adjective Clauses

Adjective subordinate clauses modify nouns or pronouns just as single-word adjectives do. Adjective clauses follow the nouns or pronouns they modify, and they usually begin with a **relative pronoun**—*who, whom, whose, which, that* (and sometimes *when* or *where*). As you can see in the examples below, relative pronouns sometimes serve as subjects of their clauses. We will discuss the rules for punctuating adjective clauses in Chapter Three.

EXAMPLES   The horse [that Mr. Lee liked best] was named Traveller. (The adjective clause modifies *horse*.)

On the top shelf was the trophy [**that** Irma had won for her model of the Battle of Shiloh]. (The adjective clause modifies *trophy*.)

Hampton, [**which** is Michelle's hooded rat,] resides at the foot of her bed. (The adjective clause modifies *Hampton,* and the relative pronoun *which* is the subject of the clause.)

NOTE: As you can see in the example above, the adjective clause often appears between the subject and the verb of the main clause. In addition, as you can see in the following example, sometimes the relative pronoun is left out.

EXAMPLE   The man [I met yesterday] works for the CIA. (Here the adjective clause modifies the noun *man*, but the relative pronoun *whom* is left out.)

A note about relative pronouns:

1. Use *who* or *whom* to refer to people only.

2. Use *which* to refer to nonhuman things only, such as animals or objects.

3. Use *that* to refer to either people or nonhuman things.

PRACTICE   Underline the adjective clauses in the following paragraph and circle the relative pronouns.

1. Beethoven's Fifth is the new bar (that) opened on Verde Avenue. **2.** A cello player whom the owner knew led the house band. **3.** The next player hired was a pianist who was the wife of the cellist. **4.** Rum Adagio, which is my favorite drink, is always served in a bright red glass. **5.** A Persian cat that everyone calls Ludwig begs for treats on the bar.

PRACTICE Add adjective clauses of your own to the following main clauses.

1. Ludwig has her own special dish by the back door.

Ludwig, who is picky, has her own special dish by the back door.

_____

2. *Game of Thrones* features a beautiful blonde woman.

_____

_____

3. Many people reported sighting a blue whale off the coast of Pismo Beach.

_____

_____

4. Bill wanted to go to Tennessee to talk to a native of the Cherokee nation.

_____

_____

5. Elephants do not have special places for graveyards.

_____

_____

PRACTICE In the following sentences, underline the subordinate clauses and identify them as adverb clauses (Adv) or adjective clauses (Adj).

1. After the first robin appears, the worms run for their lives.   *Adv*

2. Lady Gaga gets attention wherever she goes.   _____

3. Manuel was looking for someone who would go fishing

   with him.   _____

4. Although Ireland had become prosperous, Fergal would

not return. _____

5. The carousel that is near Balboa Park is Katie's favorite place. _____

PRACTICE Add subordinate clauses of your own to the following main clauses and indicate whether you have added an adverb clause (Adv) or an adjective clause (Adj).

1. Rupert decided to sell his stamp collection.

Rupert, who was desperate for extra money, decided

to sell his stamp collection. (Adj)

2. *Rescue Me* was a series about a group of firefighters.

_____

_____

3. The nuns cared for homeless people.

_____

_____

4. Prometheus warmed his hands by the fire.

_____

_____

5. Microsoft has developed some controversial software.

_____

_____

Section One Review

1. A **clause** is a group of words <u>that contains at least one subject and at least one verb</u>.

2. A **main clause** is a group of words that contains at least one subject and one verb and that <u>expresses a complete idea</u>.

3. A **subordinate clause** is a group of words that contains at least one subject and one verb but that <u>does not express a complete idea</u>.

4. **Subordinate clauses** begin with <u>subordinators</u>.

5. **Adverb subordinate clauses** usually modify verbs and begin with <u>subordinating conjunctions</u>.

6. **Adjective subordinate clauses** modify nouns or pronouns and begin with <u>relative pronouns</u>.

Exercise 1A

Listen to or watch the news, or read a magazine, newspaper, or book. Identify which news program, magazine, newspaper, or book you used. Write down five sentences that contain adjective subordinate clauses and five that contain adverb subordinate clauses. Underline and identify each subordinate clause.

1. _____

   _____

2. _____

   _____

3. _____

   _____

4. _____

   _____

5. _____

   _____

6. _____

   _____

7. _____

   _____

8. _____

   _____

9. _____

   _____

10. _____

   _____

Exercise 1B

Underline all subordinate clauses and circle the subordinators. In the spaces provided, indicate whether the subordinate clause is an adverb clause (Adv) or an adjective clause (Adj). If a sentence contains no subordinate clause, do nothing to it.

1. The chairman suggested a solution (that) he thought would help the homeless

   people in his town.   *Adj*

2. As Mr. Hyde made his appearance, Dr. Jekyll disappeared.   _____

3. After the poetry reading, we stopped by some snowy woods.   _____

4. Monet almost always painted the water lilies that were outside his house.   _____

5. While the professor was talking, the students were texting.   _____

6. The house burned completely, although Oscar was able to rescue his photographs. _____

7. The picture that Calvin had tattooed on his back was a goofy dog.   _____

8. When Oedipus realized the truth, he was somewhat upset.   _____

9. Because he was so enthusiastic, Tigger was eager to begin the adventure.   _____

10. After finishing *David*, Michelangelo was worried about leaving the sculpture

    outside in the storm.   _____

11. *House*, which featured a drug-addicted, cynical doctor, was one of the most

    popular television shows in 2008.   _____

12. World War I had more men that died of disease than from wounds.   _____

13. When the Lilliputians untied him, Gulliver slowly stood up.   _____

14. You will see the Nike in the Louvre if you look closely.   _____

15. Everyone still loved Steve even though he had moved into administration.   _____

Exercise 1C

A. Join the pairs of sentences below by making one of them either an adverb or an adjective subordinate clause. You may need to delete or change some words.

1. The zookeeper comforted the frightened king cobra.
   The cobra had been attacked by a mongoose.

   The zookeeper comforted the frightened king cobra that had

   been attacked by a mongoose.

2. Mick Jagger draws huge crowds.
   He is over sixty-five years old.

   _____

   _____

3. The two of them looked for the feathers.
   The feathers had fallen into the maze.

   _____

4. The athlete was disgraced.
   He stayed in isolation in his home.

   _____

   _____

5. Josefina celebrated her quinceañera in a restaurant.
   It was snowing.

   _____

B. Write subordinate clauses (adjective or adverb) in the blanks as indicated in parentheses at the beginning of the sentence. Make sure your clauses have subjects and verbs.

6. (Adv) *Because he was absolutely famished,* Homer added some pigs' feet to
   his casserole.

7. (Adj or Adv) President Obama and his wife toured the Louvre _____

   _____

8. (Adj) Adrian Monk, _____, washes his hands at least ten times
   each day.

Exercise 1C

continued

9. (Adv) _____ , Ahmed slept like a baby.

10. (Adv or Adj) Skateboarding can lower your IQ _____

_____

C. To the main clauses below, add the types of subordinate clauses indicated in parentheses. Add your clause at any place in the sentence that you feel is appropriate. For instance, you may add an adjective clause to any noun in a sentence.

11. (Adv) Driving your car along the Northwest Coast is a beautiful trip.

If you take the time to enjoy the view, driving your car along

the Northwest Coast is a beautiful trip.

12. (Adj) The marine drove the vehicle along the narrow dirt road.

_____

_____

13. (Adj) Caesar wanted to cross the Rubicon River.

_____

_____

14. (Adv or Adj) Jackson Pollock was once called "Jack the Dripper."

_____

_____

15. (Adv) The sun rises in the east and sets in the west.

_____

_____

Exercise 1D

Underline all subordinate clauses and identify the type of clause (adjective or adverb) in the spaces provided.

1. One of my favorite places is San Francisco's Pier 39, <u>which I will always remember for its wonderful blend of unique sights, sounds, and smells.</u> *Adj* **2.** As I walked down the pier one weekend last summer, I noticed a cook dressed all in white tossing pizza dough to lure hungry customers. _____ **3.** Near him I saw cooks who were roasting and baking all kinds of seafood. _____ **4.** Among the foods that caught my attention were lobster, shark, and clam chowder on sourdough bread. _____ **5.** I soon encountered some people being entertained by hundreds of sea lions making a tremendous racket as they played on the rocks and sunbathed by the pier. _____ **6.** When I turned away from the sea lions, my nose followed an aroma coming from a waffle ice cream stand. _____ **7.** Because I could not resist, I ordered vanilla ice cream with M&M's mixed in. _____ **8.** The hot waffle cone warmed my hand while the cold ice cream refreshed my throat. _____ **9.** Next, I came across a delightful shop, where I found all sorts of posters for children's books like *James and the Giant Peach.* _____ **10.** After I left the poster place, I spotted a chocolate shop and almost swooned in anticipation. _____ **11.** Although I was tempted, I declined the chocolate models of Alcatraz and the Golden Gate Bridge. _____ **12.** Across from the chocolate shop, I saw a restaurant that was built to look like Alcatraz Prison. _____ **13.** People could have their pictures taken in a prison cell while they were waiting to eat. _____ **14.** Close by I saw the tour boat that was taking tourists to Alcatraz Island. _____ **15.** As night fell across San Francisco Bay, I could admire the beauty of the Golden Gate Bridge from the tip of Pier 39. _____ **16.** Before I left, I felt the salty mist of the bay on my skin, a final remembrance of Pier 39. _____

Simple, Compound, Complex, and Compound-Complex Sentences

Sentences are categorized according to the number and types of clauses they contain. The names of the four types of sentences are **simple, compound, complex,** and **compound-complex.** You need to be familiar with these sentence patterns for a number of reasons:

1. **Variety.** Varying your sentence patterns creates interest and avoids monotony. Repeating a sentence pattern endlessly will bore even your most interested reader.

2. **Emphasis.** You can use these sentence patterns to emphasize the ideas that you think are more important than others.

3. **Grammar.** A knowledge of the basic sentence patterns of English will help you avoid the major sentence structure errors discussed in Section Three.

Being able to recognize and use these sentence patterns will help you control your writing and thus express your ideas more effectively.

The Simple Sentence

The introduction to this chapter points out that a sentence must contain at least one main clause. A sentence that contains only one main clause and no other clauses is called a **simple sentence.** However, a simple sentence is not necessarily an uncomplicated or short sentence because, in addition to its one main clause, it may contain a variety of phrases and modifiers.

The basic pattern for the simple sentence is subject–verb (SV). This pattern may vary in several ways:

EXAMPLES

                  S   V
subject–verb (SV): The plane flew over the stadium.

                       V   S
verb–subject (VS): Over the stadium flew the plane.

                      S   S   V
subject–subject–verb (SSV): The plane and the helicopter flew over the stadium.

                 S   V   V
subject–verb–verb (SVV): The plane flew over the stadium and turned north.

S   S   V
subject–subject–verb–verb (SSVV): The plane and the helicopter flew

V
over the stadium and turned north.

S   V
A simple sentence can be brief: It rained.

S
Or it can be rather long: Enraged by the taunting of the boys, the huge gorilla

V   V
leaped from his enclosure and chased them up a hill and down a pathway to
the exit gates.

The important thing to remember about the simple sentence is that it has
only one main clause and no other clauses.

◎ PRACTICE   Write your own simple sentences according to the instructions.

1. A simple sentence with the pattern subject–subject–verb:

   Two supermarkets and a department store collapsed in the

   recent earthquake.

2. A simple sentence that contains a prepositional phrase.

   _____

   _____

3. A simple sentence that begins with *there* and has the pattern verb–subject.

   _____

   _____

4. A simple sentence that expresses a command:

   _____

   _____

5. A simple sentence that has the pattern subject–subject–verb–verb:

_____

_____

The Compound Sentence

Simply put, a **compound sentence** contains two or more main clauses but no subordinate clauses. The basic pattern of the clauses may be expressed as subject–verb/subject–verb (SV/SV). The main clauses are always joined in one of three ways:

1. Two main clauses may be joined by a comma and one of the seven coordinating conjunctions (*and, or, nor, but, for, so, yet*).

EXAMPLE

     S   V   S   V

Maria registered for all of her classes by mail, **but** Brad was not able to do so.

Remember, the two main clauses must be joined by **both a comma and a coordinating conjunction,** and the comma always comes before the coordinating conjunction.

2. Two main clauses may be joined by a semicolon (;).

EXAMPLE

     S   V   S   V

Maria registered for all of her classes by mail; Brad was not able to do so.

3. Two main clauses may be joined by a semicolon and a transitional word or phrase. Such transitional words or phrases are followed by a comma.

EXAMPLE

     S   V   S

Maria registered for all of her classes by mail; **however,** Brad

     V

was not able to do so.

Below is a list of the most commonly used transitional words and phrases. Do not confuse these words or phrases with coordinating conjunctions or subordinating conjunctions.

accordingly	furthermore	nevertheless	that is
also	hence	next	therefore
besides	however	nonetheless	thus
consequently	instead	on the other hand	undoubtedly
finally	meanwhile	otherwise	
for example	moreover	similarly	
for instance	namely	still	

@@ PRACTICE   Write compound sentences of your own according to the instructions.

1. A compound sentence that uses a comma and *but* to join two main clauses:

    I was very hungry after the game, but I decided not

    to eat anything.

2. A compound sentence that joins two main clauses with a semicolon:

    _____

    _____

3. A compound sentence that joins two main clauses with a semicolon and an appropriate transitional word or phrase followed by a comma:

    _____

    _____

4. A compound sentence that joins two main clauses with a comma and *yet*.

    _____

    _____

5. A compound sentence that joins two main clauses with a semicolon followed by the transitional word *however* or *therefore*:

    _____

    _____

PRACTICE   In the following paragraph, write "S" above each subject and "V" above each verb. Then, in the spaces provided, identify each sentence as either **simple** or **compound**.

        S   *V*
 1. Some of the earliest forms of writing appeared around 3500 BCE.

 *simple* **2.** The Sumerians needed to keep track of food, grain, and

 other materials used in trade, so they made pictures of the items on clay

 tablets. _____ **3.** These pictures were the first form of writing. _____

 4. The clay tablets were baked in a kiln; as a result, thousands of them have

 lasted throughout the centuries. _____ **5.** The pictures were created with a

 wedge-shaped instrument; this type of writing is called *cuneiform*. _____

 6. Gradually, these pictures came to represent the syllables of the Sumerian

 language. _____ **7.** Rather than clay, ancient Egyptians recorded their

 writing on leather or on a more fragile material. _____ **8.** This fragile

 material was papyrus, and it later came to be called paper. _____

 9. About eighteen hundred years ago, a Chinese inventor made paper from

 bark and rags. _____ **10.** Chinese books were soon written on paper,

 but the knowledge of paper-making did not reach Europe for a thousand

 years. _____

The Complex Sentence

The **complex sentence** has the same subject–verb pattern (SV/SV) as the compound sentence. However, the complex sentence features only one main clause and always contains at least one subordinate clause and sometimes more than one. The subordinate clauses in a complex sentence may occur at any place in the sentence.

EXAMPLES

                                    S   V   S   V
Before a main clause: <u>After he retired from the Army,</u> Eisenhower ran for president.

                        S V   S   V   V
After a main clause: Rugby is a sport <u>that I have played only once</u>.

S   S   V

Interrupting a main clause: Emilio's grandfather, <u>who fought</u> in World

      V

<u>War II,</u> told him about his experiences during the war.

                                     S   V

Before and after a main clause: <u>When the pianist sat down at the piano,</u>

S   V   S   V   V

she played a melody <u>that she had written recently.</u>

PRACTICE

Write complex sentences of your own according to the instructions.

1. A complex sentence that includes an adjective clause using the relative pronoun *who*:

   Zelda searched for three days to find the

   person who had lost the German shepherd.

2. A complex sentence that ends with an adverb clause:

   _____

   _____

3. A complex sentence that contains an adjective clause using the relative pronoun *which*:

   _____

   _____

4. A complex sentence that begins with an adverb clause:

   _____

   _____

5. A complex sentence that contains an adjective clause that uses the word *where*:

   _____

   _____

The Compound-Complex Sentence

The **compound-complex sentence** is a combination of the compound and the complex sentence patterns. It is made up of two or more main clauses and one or more subordinate clauses. Therefore, it must contain a minimum of three sets of subjects and verbs (<u>at least</u> two main clauses and <u>at least</u> one subordinate clause).

EXAMPLES

                         main clause   sub. clause

[On the day-long bicycle trip, Ophelia ate the food] [that she had packed,]

           main clause

[but Henry had forgotten to bring anything to eat.]

         sub. clause   main clause

[Although he was exhausted,] [Ernesto cooked dinner for his mother,]

             main clause

[and after dinner he cleaned the kitchen.]

        main clause   sub. clause

[The travelers were excited] [when they arrived in Paris;]

            main clause

[they wanted to go sightseeing immediately.]

PRACTICE   Write compound-complex sentences of your own according to the instructions.

1. A compound-complex sentence that contains two main clauses joined by *and* and one adjective clause beginning with *who*:

   Murphy, who works at the Mazda dealership, sold ten Miatas

   last month, and this month he plans to sell even more.

2. A compound-complex sentence that contains two main clauses and an adverb clause. Use *or* to join the two main clauses.

   _____

   _____

3. A compound-complex sentence that contains two main clauses and an adjective clause. Use a semicolon and a transitional word or phrase to join the two main clauses.

   _____

   _____

4. A compound-complex sentence that contains two main clauses and two adverb clauses:

_____

_____

5. A compound-complex sentence with a pattern of your own choice:

_____

_____

⊚⊚ PRACTICE

In the following **paragraph**, write "S" above each subject and "V" above each verb. Then, in the spaces provided, identify each sentence as either **simple, compound, complex,** or **compound-complex**

         S   V

1. *Cinderella* is a European fairy tale with over five hundred versions. _*simple*_

2. The oldest versions are from the ninth century; those early stories do not give Cinderella glass slippers. _____ **3.** The glass slippers appeared when a French version of the story was translated incorrectly. _____ **4.** In older versions, Cinderella's shoes were made of a rare metal or some other valuable covering. _____ **5.** The French story used white squirrel fur for the slippers, but the French word that meant *fur* was similar to the word that meant *glass*. _____ **6.** Charles Perrault, who translated the story in 1697, was the first person to describe the slippers as glass. _____ **7.** Almost all later versions of the story depict Cinderella as wearing glass slippers. _____ **8.** In most of the stories, Cinderella is helped by her fairy godmother; however, some versions use other characters. _____ **9.** Although Cinderella's mother is dead, she magically appears in one story, and she takes the place of the fairy godmother. _____ **10.** Sometimes cows or goats assist Cinderella, but in the Disney version mice come to her aid. _____

Section Two Review

1. A **simple sentence** contains only one main clause and no other clauses.

2. A **compound sentence** contains two or more main clauses that are joined by a comma and a coordinating conjunction **or** a semicolon **or** a semicolon and a transitional word or phrase.

3. A **complex sentence** contains only one main clause and one or more subordinate clauses.

4. A **compound-complex sentence** contains two or more main clauses and one or more subordinate clauses.

Exercise 2A

Examine one of your textbooks, a newspaper, a magazine, or a book from your home and find two simple sentences, three compound sentences, three complex sentences, and two compound-complex sentences. Label the types of sentences you have found as simple, compound, complex, or compound-complex.

1. _____

    _____

2. _____

    _____

3. _____

    _____

4. _____

    _____

5. _____

    _____

6. _____

    _____

7. _____

    _____

8. _____

    _____

9. _____

    _____

10. _____

    _____

Exercise 2B

In the spaces provided, identify the sentences in the following paragraph as simple, compound, complex, or compound-complex.

1. Alex was the name of a famous African gray parrot. _simple_ **2.** Irene Pepperberg, who is a comparative psychologist, bought Alex from a pet shop in 1977. _____ **3.** For twenty-two years, Dr. Pepperberg taught Alex to do tasks that only a few nonhuman species can do.

_____ **4.** Alex seemed to use words creatively. _____ **5.** Alex's speech was not just imitation; instead, it suggested reasoning and choice. _____ **6.** Dr. Pepperberg used a novel approach to teach Alex. _____ **7.** Another trainer competed with Alex for a reward, and Alex would learn by watching the other trainer. _____ **8.** When Alex was shown a blue paper triangle, he could identify the color, the shape, and the material. _____ **9.** He had not simply memorized the colors that go with objects; he also identified the correct colors of new objects. _____ **10.** Alex could identify fifty different objects, recognize quantities up to six, distinguish seven colors and five shapes, understand "bigger," "smaller," "same," and "different," and was learning the concepts of "over" and "under." _____ **11.** If Dr. Pepperberg asked Alex to identify the object that was orange and three-cornered, he would choose the right one. _____ **12.** Sometimes Alex would grow tired of the questions, so he would ask to go back to his cage. _____ **13.** Although many researchers dispute Dr. Pepperberg's claims, others believe Alex demonstrated the intelligence of a five-year-old human. _____

14. According to some scientists, Alex expressed conscious thoughts and feelings. _____

15. African gray parrots often live for fifty years, but Alex died unexpectedly during the night in 2009 when he was less than thirty years old. _____

Exercise 2C

A. Combine each set of sentences to create the sentence type asked for. You may need to delete or change some words.

1. A simple sentence with the pattern verb–subject:
   a. The ship was in the harbor.
   b. The ship was a nineteenth-century three-masted schooner.

In the harbor was a nineteenth-century three-masted schooner.

2. A compound sentence:
   a. Little Miss Muffet was uneasy beside the spider.
   b. She moved away from the log.

3. A complex sentence:
   a. Bob Dylan was in love.
   b. He wrote the song called "Love Minus Zero/No Limit."

4. A simple sentence:
   a. The rain flooded our yard.
   b. It also washed away our newly planted garden.

5. A complex sentence:
   a. Ovetta's friends could see all of her private posts.
   b. She had left her computer on.

continued

6. A simple sentence:
   a. The rain did not bother the man fishing in the Deschutes River.
   b. The wind did not bother him either.

   _____

   _____

7. A compound sentence:
   a. The tsunami ruined their home.
   b. They returned and built an even more beautiful one.

   _____

   _____

8. A compound-complex sentence:
   a. Legoland is a popular attraction.
   b. My daughter and I enjoy visiting it every summer.
   c. I don't think we'll be able to go there this year.

   _____

   _____

   _____

9. A compound-complex sentence:
   a. "Richard Cory" is a song composed by Paul Simon.
   b. It is included in Simon and Garfunkel's album *Sounds of Silence*.
   c. It is originally a poem composed by Edwin Arlington Robinson.

   _____

   _____

B. Following the instructions, construct sentences of your own.

10. A compound-complex sentence that uses a semicolon:

    _____

    _____

Exercise 2C

continued

11. A complex sentence that includes an adjective clause:

_____

_____

12. A compound sentence that uses a semicolon and a transitional word:

_____

_____

13. A simple sentence:

_____

_____

14. A complex sentence that includes an adverb clause at the beginning of the sentence:

_____

_____

15. A compound-complex sentence that does not use a semicolon:

_____

_____

Exercise 2D

Identify the sentences in the following paragraph as simple, compound, complex, or compound-complex.

1. I was twenty, so you can imagine my surprise as I stepped aboard my first U.S. Navy ship, the USS *Meeker County*. *compound-complex* **2.** Everything in my environment had been renamed. _____ **3.** The floors were no longer floors; they were "decks." _____ **4.** Above me were no longer ceilings, but "overheads." _____ **5.** When I wanted a drink of water, I got it from a "scuttlebutt." _____ **6.** As I was rudely awakened at 6:00 each morning, I was in my "rack" rather than my bed. _____ **7.** While I dressed, the thing I placed on my head was my "cover," and I wore a "blouse" rather than a shirt. _____ **8.** Moreover, I went to "chow," not breakfast, lunch, or dinner. _____ **9.** I didn't carry a gun or pistol, but a "piece" or "sidearm." _____ **10.** "Reveille" was in the morning, and "taps" was in the evening. _____ **11.** I did not place my cigarettes in ash trays; I placed them in "butt kits." _____ **12.** When I wanted to reach another deck, I used "ladders" rather than stairs. _____ **13.** I did not leave the ship and go into town; I went on "liberty." _____ **14.** My meals were not taken in a dining room. _____ **15.** I ate in the "mess," and all around me were not walls, but "bulkheads." _____ **16.** At first, I grew dizzy as I tried to remember all of these new names, but they quickly became commonplace aboard my "ship" (never a "boat"). _____

Fragments, Fused Sentences, and Comma Splices

Now that you are combining main and subordinate clauses to write different types of sentences, we need to talk about a few of the writing problems you might encounter. Fortunately, the most serious of these problems—the **fragment**, the **fused sentence**, and the **comma splice**—are also the easiest to identify and correct.

Fragments

The easiest way to identify a **sentence fragment** is to remember that <u>every sentence must contain a main clause</u>. If you do not have a main clause, you do <u>not</u> have a sentence. You can define a fragment, then, like this: A sentence fragment occurs when a group of words that lacks a main clause is punctuated as a sentence.

---

sentence fragment

A sentence fragment occurs when a group of words that lacks a main clause is punctuated as a sentence.

Using this definition, you can identify almost any sentence fragment. However, you will find it easier to locate fragments in your own writing if you know that fragments can be divided into three basic types.

Three Types of Sentence Fragments

1. <u>Some fragments contain no clause at all.</u> This type of fragment is simple to spot. It usually does not even sound like a sentence because it lacks a subject or verb or both.

EXAMPLE The snow in the street.

2. <u>Some fragments contain a verbal but still no clause.</u> This fragment is a bit less obvious because a verbal can be mistaken for a verb. But remember, neither a participle nor an infinitive is a verb. (See Chapter One if you need to review this point.)

EXAMPLES The snow **falling** on the street. (participle)

To slip on the snow in the street. (infinitive)

3. Some fragments contain a **subordinate clause** but no **main clause.** This type of fragment is perhaps the most common because it does contain a subject and a verb. But remember, <u>a group of words without a main clause is not a sentence.</u>

EXAMPLES   After the snow had fallen on the street.

Because I had slipped on the snow in the street.

Repairing Sentence Fragments

Once you have identified a fragment, you can correct it in one of two ways.

1. Add words to give it a main clause.

EXAMPLES   (fragment)   The snow in the street.

(sentence)   **I gazed** at the snow in the street.

(sentence)   The snow **was** in the street.

(fragment)   The snow falling in the street.

(sentence)   The snow falling in the street **covered my car.**

(sentence)   The snow **was** falling in the street.

(fragment)   After the snow had fallen in the street.

(sentence)   **I looked for a shovel** after the snow had fallen in the street.

2. Join the fragment to a main clause written before or after it.

EXAMPLES   (incorrect)   I love to see the ice on the lake. And the snow in the street.

(correct)   I love to see the ice on the lake and the snow in the street.

(incorrect)   My back was so sore that I could not stand straight. Because I had slipped on the snow in the street.

(correct)   My back was so sore that I could not stand straight because I had slipped on the snow in the street.

One final point might help you identify and correct sentence fragments. Remember that we all speak in fragments every day. (If a friend asks you how you are, you might respond with the fragment "Fine.") Because we speak in fragments, you may find that your writing seems acceptable even though it contains fragments. When you work on the exercises in this unit, do not rely on your "ear" alone. Look at the sentences. **If they do not contain main clauses, they are fragments, no matter how correct they may sound.**

⊚⊚ **PRACTICE**   Underline any fragment you find. Then correct it either by adding new words to give it a main clause or by joining it to a main clause next to it.

1. The aircraft carrier *Midway* floats in San Diego Bay. <u>A tourist attraction.</u>

The aircraft carrier Midway floats in San Diego Bay as a

tourist attraction.

2. The cat that was trapped in the tree.

_____

_____

3. Because the Red Hot Chili Peppers were appearing in the Hollywood Bowl. The tickets were sold out.

_____

_____

4. Amy's mother refused to let her go to the party. To punish her for staying out so late.

_____

_____

5. When Amy's 6'10" boyfriend arrived. Her mother dialed 911.

_____

_____

6. Hugo liked working on the clocks. That were in the Paris train station.

_____

_____

7. As the election neared. The candidates started mentioning religion.

Which irritated Brandy.

_____

_____

8. Elton John appeared at my church. Wearing his usual outlandish costume.

_____

_____

9. To see the cranes that were nesting on my roof.

_____

_____

10. You must finish the final exam. If you want to go to Rome.

_____

_____

Fused Sentences and Comma Splices

The **fused sentence** and **comma splice** are serious writing errors that you can correct with little effort. Either error can occur when you write a compound or compound-complex sentence. The fused sentence occurs when two or more main clauses are joined without a coordinating conjunction and without punctuation.

---

fused sentence

The fused sentence occurs when two or more main clauses are joined without a coordinating conjunction and without punctuation.

EXAMPLE   (fused)   Raoul drove by his uncle's house he waved at his cousins.

As you can see, the two main clauses in the above example (*Raoul drove by his uncle's house* and *he waved at his cousins*) have been joined without a coordinating conjunction and without punctuation of any kind.

The comma splice is a similar error: The comma splice occurs when two or more main clauses are joined with a comma but without a coordinating conjunction.

---

comma splice

The comma splice occurs when two or more main clauses are joined with a comma but without a coordinating conjunction.

EXAMPLE   (comma splice)   The hot sun beat down on the construction workers, they looked forward to the end of the day.

In this example, the two main clauses (*The hot sun beat down on the construction workers* and *they looked forward to the end of the day*) are joined by a comma, but a comma alone is not enough to join main clauses.

NOTE: One of the most frequent comma splices occurs when a writer joins two main clauses with a comma and a transitional word rather than with a semicolon and a transitional word.

EXAMPLE   (comma splice)   I wanted a dog for Christmas, however, my parents gave me a cat.

Repairing Fused Sentences and Comma Splices

Because both fused sentences and comma splices occur when two main clauses are joined, you can correct either error using one of five methods. Consider these two errors:

EXAMPLES   (fused)   Jack left for work early he arrived late.

(comma splice)   Jack left for work early, he arrived late.

Both of these errors can be corrected in one of five ways:

1. <u>Use a comma and a coordinating conjunction.</u>
   Jack left for work early, **but** he arrived late.

2. <u>Use a semicolon.</u>
   Jack left for work early; he arrived late.

3. <u>Use a semicolon and a transitional word or phrase.</u>
   Jack left for work early; **however,** he arrived late.

   NOTE: Do <u>not</u> use a semicolon before a transitional word that does <u>not</u> begin a main clause. For example, in the following sentence, *however* does not need a semicolon.

EXAMPLE   I have not seen my father, **however,** for ten years.

4. <u>Change one of the clauses to a subordinate clause by beginning it with a subordinator.</u>
   Although Jack left for work early, he arrived late.

5. <u>Punctuate the clauses as two separate sentences.</u>
   Jack left for work early. He arrived late.

NOTE: Sometimes the two main clauses in a fused sentence or comma splice are interrupted by a subordinate clause. When this sentence pattern occurs, the two main clauses must still be connected in one of the five ways.

EXAMPLES   (fused)   Alma bought a new Mercedes even though she could not afford one she fell behind in her monthly payments.

(comma splice)   Alma bought a new Mercedes even though she could not afford one, she fell behind in her monthly payments.

⊙⊙ PRACTICE

Identify the following sentences as fused (F), comma splice (CS), or correct (C). Then correct the incorrect sentences. Use a different method of correction each time.

_CS_ 1. Butler had wanted to join his brother in New York, his business was going too well for him to leave.

Butler had wanted to join his brother in New York,

but his business was going too well for him to leave.

_____ 2. The line for buying one of the new Cannibal surfboards was extremely long we were sure they would sell out.

_____ 3. The political candidate tried to skip up the stairs, he tripped and broke his wrist.

_____ 4. Barbara thinks *Grey's Anatomy* has been on too long, on the other hand, Horst hopes it runs forever.

_____ 5. The city installed a new skateboard park it was twelve yards from my house.

_____ **6.** When the tornado suddenly touched down, we had no time to escape.

_____

_____

_____ **7.** Eeyore saw the swarm of honey bees he did not want to follow it with the others.

_____

_____

_____

_____ **8.** Everything at the wedding was perfect, therefore, the organizer received a huge tip.

_____

_____

_____ **9.** Charlie's speech at the royal wedding, however, was a complete disaster.

_____

_____

_____ **10.** Mr. Nosferatu came over for dinner last night, he kept staring at my fiancée's neck.

_____

_____

Section Three Review

1. A **sentence fragment** occurs when a group of words that lacks a main clause is punctuated as a sentence.

2. There are three types of sentence fragments.

   a. Some contain no clause at all.

   b. Some contain a verbal but still no clause.

   c. Some contain a subordinate clause but no main clause.

3. You can correct a sentence fragment in one of two ways.

   a. Add words to give it a main clause.

   b. Join it to an already existing main clause.

4. The **fused sentence** occurs when two or more main clauses are joined without a coordinating conjunction and without punctuation.

5. The **comma splice** occurs when two or more main clauses are joined with a comma but without a coordinating conjunction.

6. You can correct fused sentences and comma splices in one of five ways.

   a. Use a comma and a coordinating conjunction.

   b. Use a semicolon.

   c. Use a semicolon and a transitional word or phrase.

   d. Change one of the clauses to a subordinate clause by adding a subordinator at the beginning of it.

   e. Punctuate the clauses as two separate sentences.

Exercise 3A

Identify each of the following as correct (C), fused (F), comma splice (CS), or sentence fragment (Frag). Then correct each error using any of the methods discussed in this unit.

Frag 1. Because it was so cold and slimy and ugly that Carl was becoming nauseated just looking at it.

It was so cold and slimy and ugly that Carl was becoming

nauseated just looking at it.

_____ 2. My cat, Rainy, likes to sit on my desk, however, she hops off at the sound of my footsteps.

_____ 3. Please buy some orange marmalade at the grocery store.

_____ 4. Vincent was driving back to Arles suddenly he realized he had forgotten to buy canvas.

_____ 5. The prime minister of Holland, wondering how to strengthen the system of dikes in his country.

_____ 6. Meriwether Lewis began his journey home in 1806, William Clark accompanied him.

Exercise 3A

continued

_____ **7.** The worms on the mulberry trees are the source of silk, so they are treated with care.

_____

_____

_____ **8.** Chelsea enjoyed her job as a flight attendant however she was not paid very well.

_____

_____

_____ **9.** Julio knew that the name of the mythological river started with *L* he couldn't remember its exact name.

_____

_____

_____ **10.** The weather was so cold that Garrison's tongue stuck to the pump handle.

_____

_____

_____ **11.** The senator from New York could not believe that he had lost the nomination, his wife was even more surprised.

_____

_____

_____ **12.** Forgetting to back up the work on his autobiography.

_____

_____

Exercise 3A

continued

_____13. The student from Hawaii knew the history of his state, nevertheless, he did not know where the Sandwich Islands were.

_____

_____

_____14. Before Cyrano agreed to an operation on his nose.

_____

_____

_____15. The wolves were confined to a small enclosure on the other hand they looked happy, healthy, and well fed.

_____

_____

Exercise 3B

A. Correct the following sentence fragments by adding words to them to make them complete sentences.

1. Shannon, who had been standing in the rain for two hours.

   Shannon, who had been standing in the rain for two hours,

   finally decided to give up and go home.

2. Carl, forgetting the code to his security system.

   _____

   _____

3. If the asteroid would destroy the earth.

   _____

   _____

4. The cluster of penguins that patiently waited by the restrooms.

   _____

   _____

5. To the first person who walks through the door.

   _____

   _____

B. Join the following main clauses by using a comma and a coordinating conjunction, a semicolon, a semicolon and a transitional word or phrase, or by making one of the clauses a subordinate clause. Use each of these four methods at least once.

6. Regan asked Cordelia for her third of the kingdom. Eventually, Cordelia gave it to her and left for France.

   Regan asked Cordelia for her third of the kingdom;

   eventually, Cordelia gave it to her and left for France.

continued

7. Hester told their secret to everyone. Dimmesdale would not tell anyone.

_____

_____

8. Herb went to Prairie View University for four years. He failed to see one prairie dog in all that time.

_____

_____

9. Leonardo looked at the new Picasso. The Picasso had just been purchased by the museum.

_____

_____

10. Theodore Roosevelt had many health problems in his youth. By exercise and diet he grew into a healthy, robust young man who constantly hunted and who eventually became president of the United States.

_____

_____

C. Expand each of the following sentences by adding a **clause** to it. Vary the placement of the clauses. (Don't place every clause at the end of its sentence.) When you add the clauses, use each of the following methods at least once: (a) use a comma and a coordinating conjunction; (b) use a semicolon; (c) use a semicolon and a transitional word or phrase; (d) make one clause a subordinate clause.

11. Sitting in their patrol car, the police officers tried to comfort the lost child.

Sitting in their patrol car, the police officers tried to

comfort the lost child; however, the child would not stop crying.

12. Savion Glover is a contemporary tap dancer.

_____

_____

continued

13. The polluted creek recovered at a surprising rate.

_____

_____

14. Sydney tried to flirt with Ambrosia.

_____

_____

15. The riot squad could barely control the people waiting to see the latest vampire film.

_____

_____

Exercise 3C

In the following paragraph, correct any fragments, fused sentences, or comma splices.

1. *La Tzararacua* is an awe-inspiring cascade. **2.** ~~L~~ocated near my hometown in Mexico. *(correction: ⟨r⟩ located)*

3. The last time I visited it, I walked for two hours through the wet, slippery forest. **4.** As I approached the cascade, I could hear the falling water, red and yellow birds were screeching and singing all around us. **5.** I enjoyed the fresh air and the gentle breeze on my skin. **6.** As well as the fresh, relaxing smell of the many tropical bushes and trees. **7.** I walked forward and sat down on a huge boulder right by the river it was so smooth and warm that I could not resist lying down on it. **8.** Later I walked to the main waterfall, it is over one hundred meters high. **9.** And is surrounded by thousands of little cascades. **10.** I could hear water running underneath the rocks that I was walking on. **11.** The water of *La Tzararacua* seems to spring from the rocks, the waterfall is amazingly clear. **12.** Behind the huge waterfall, green moss covering huge boulders. **13.** The water originates in the middle of the forest it is fresh, pure, and satisfying. **14.** I did not worry about contamination. **15.** As I cupped it in my hands and took a deep drink.

Sentence Practice:
Combining Main and Subordinate Clauses

In this chapter you have learned the basic sentence patterns of English, and you have seen that you can combine the major word groups of a sentence—the clauses—in various ways. Of course, how you present your ideas in your sentences can affect the way a reader perceives your ideas. Take, for instance, the following sentences.

1. Subcompact cars are economical.

2. Subcompact cars are easy to handle.

3. Subcompact cars are simple to park.

4. Full-size sedans are roomier.

5. Full-size sedans are safer.

6. Full-size sedans are quieter.

You can present these ideas in six simple sentences like those above, but doing so makes the writing choppy and simplistic. On the other hand, you can use the sentence patterns discussed in this chapter to combine these six ideas in several ways.

1. You can present these ideas as two simple sentences.

EXAMPLE   Subcompact cars are economical, easy to handle, and simple to park.
Full-size sedans are roomier, safer, and quieter.

2. Or you can group the ideas into one compound sentence by using a comma and a coordinating conjunction.

EXAMPLE   Subcompact cars are economical, easy to handle, and simple to park, but full-size sedans are roomier, safer, and quieter.

Note that the coordinating conjunction *but* allows you to emphasize the contrast between the ideas in the two main clauses.

3. You can also group these ideas into a compound sentence by using a semicolon as a connector.

EXAMPLE   Subcompact cars are economical, easy to handle, and simple to park; full-size sedans are roomier, safer, and quieter.

In this sentence the contrast in the ideas is implied rather than directly stated.

4. Of course, you can add a transitional word after the semicolon.

EXAMPLE

Subcompact cars are economical, easy to handle, and simple to park; however, full-size sedans are roomier, safer, and quieter.

Note that *however* now signals the contrast between the ideas in the two clauses.

5. Finally, you can group the ideas into a main clause and a subordinate clause by adding a subordinator. Now you have a complex sentence.

EXAMPLE

Although subcompact cars are economical, easy to handle, and simple to park, full-size sedans are roomier, safer, and quieter.

Like the other sentences, this sentence shows the reader the contrast between the ideas in the two clauses. However, it also shows the ideas the writer thinks are most important—the ones in the main clause.

Sentence Combining Exercises

Using the knowledge of sentence patterns that you have gained from this chapter, combine the following lists of sentences into longer sentences according to the directions. Be sure to punctuate carefully to avoid comma splices or fused sentences. Remember to look for a base sentence or a main idea to build upon. The most important idea should be in a main clause.

EXAMPLE   First, combine these ideas into a compound sentence, using one of the three methods presented in Section Two of this chapter. Then form a complex sentence, using a subordinator to make one clause subordinate.

    a. New York City often seems dirty.
    b. New York City often seems overcrowded.
    c. New York City often seems full of crime.
    d. New York City has excitement.
    e. New York City has charming ethnic communities.
    f. New York City has a great variety of cultural attractions.

    A. Compound sentence:

_____

_____

_____

_____

    B. Complex sentence:

_____

_____

_____

_____

Sentence Combining Exercises

continued

1. Combine the following sentences into one complex sentence. Form sentence c into an adverb clause that begins with the subordinating conjunction *although*.

    a. John F. Kennedy was our thirty-fifth president.
    b. He remains one of our most memorable and beloved presidents.
    c. He served only a relatively short term of about one thousand days.

    _____

    _____

    _____

    _____

2. Combine these sentences into one complex sentence. Begin sentence a with the subordinating conjunction *before*. Join the ideas in sentences b and c with *and*.

    a. President Kennedy became president on January 20, 1960.
    b. He had served as a naval officer in World War II.
    c. He had served as a U.S. senator from Massachusetts.

    _____

    _____

    _____

    _____

continued

3. Combine these sentences into one complex sentence with two adverb subordinate clauses. Begin sentence a with the subordinating conjunction *after*. Begin sentence c with the subordinating conjunction *because*.

   a. His small torpedo boat was rammed by a Japanese destroyer, severely injuring him.
   b. The Navy awarded him several medals for bravery.
   c. He had led his men to safety and rescue.

   _____

   _____

   _____

   _____

4. Combine these sentences into one compound-complex sentence by starting sentence a with the subordinating conjunction *when*. Then join sentences b and c with *and*.

   a. He had returned safely from the war.
   b. He successfully ran for U.S. representative from Massachusetts.
   c. Then he became a U.S. senator before running for president.

   _____

   _____

   _____

   _____

Sentence Combining Exercises

continued

5. Combine these sentences into one compound-complex sentence. Join sentences a and b with the conjunction *but*. Then change sentences c and d to subordinate clauses using the subordinating conjunction *because*.

   a. He was elected the first time he ran for president.
   b. It was by a very narrow margin.
   c. He was so young.
   d. The man running against him had much more experience.

   _____

   _____

   _____

   _____

6. Combine these sentences into one sentence. Use the most effective pattern you can find. At the end of your new sentence, indicate which type of sentence you have written.

   a. The American people were enchanted by their new president and his intelligent, beautiful wife.
   b. In fact, they often referred to their time in office as "Camelot."
   c. Jacqueline charmed them by her generosity and her fashions.
   d. The president was quite handsome and gave memorable speeches.

   _____

   _____

   _____

   _____

Sentence Combining Exercises

continued

7. Combine these sentences into one sentence. Use the most effective pattern you can find. At the end of your new sentence, indicate which type of sentence you have written.

   a. Most people at home and abroad thought President Kennedy a dynamic, effective leader.
   b. Unfortunately, dangers lurked in the future.
   c. These dangers would severely try the new president.

   _____

   _____

   _____

   _____

8. Combine these sentences into two sentences. At the end of each sentence, indicate which type of sentence you have written.

   a. At one time, the Soviet Communists challenged the country in a frightening way.
   b. They placed nuclear missiles in Cuba, just a few miles from our shore.
   c. President Kennedy and his advisors bravely demanded that they remove the missiles.
   d. The Russians backed down.

   _____

   _____

   _____

   _____

Sentence Combining Exercises

continued

9. Combine these sentences into two sentences. At the end of each sentence, indicate which type of sentence you have written.

    a. The real story of Camelot does not end happily.
    b. This story does not end happily either.
    c. On November 22, 1963, Lee Harvey Oswald shot and killed President Kennedy.
    d. Lee Harvey Oswald was lone shooter.
    e. He was hiding on the sixth floor of the Texas School Book Depository building.
    f. President Kennedy and his wife were being driven through Dallas, Texas, in a presidential motorcade.

    _____

    _____

    _____

    _____

    _____

    _____

10. Combine these sentences into two sentences. At the end of each sentence, indicate which type of sentence you have written.

    a. America went into deep grief.
    b. The shocking events were shown on television.
    c. The president was laid to rest in Arlington National Cemetery before crowds of thousands.
    d. Many Americans still wonder how the following years might have been different.
    e. They might have been different if John F. Kennedy had not been assassinated.

    _____

    _____

    _____

    _____

Paragraph Practice: Describing a Place

Assignment

In Chapter Two you have read paragraphs that describe a variety of places. Exercise 1D (page 95) describes San Francisco's Pier 39, Exercise 2D (page 110) describes being on a naval ship, and Exercise 3C (page 126) describes the falls called *La Tzararacua*. Your assignment in this writing section is to describe a place that you remember for one particular reason. As you do so, you will practice limiting your paragraph to one idea that is expressed in a topic sentence and developing your paragraph with details that are both specific and concrete.

Prewriting to Generate Ideas

To find a topic, use freewriting, brainstorming, or clustering (or all three) to generate ideas about places that you remember well. Try to develop a list of as many places as you can. Sometimes the most interesting place to describe will be buried deep in your memory, so give prewriting a chance to uncover that memory before you decide on a topic.

Choosing and Narrowing the Topic

As you prewrite, avoid topics that are too broad to cover in one paragraph. For example, a city or an amusement park would be too large of a topic to cover in detail in a brief piece of writing. However, one particular part of a small town or one particular section of an amusement park might work very well.

Prewriting Application: Finding Your Topic

Consider the following questions as you prewrite:

1. What places have you visited in the past several years? Think about vacations you have taken or places you have traveled to.

2. Where have you been in the past two weeks? Make a list of everywhere you have gone.

3. What places from your childhood give you the most pleasant memories?

4. Where do you go to relax, to meditate, or to find peace of mind?

5. Have you ever been somewhere when you felt frightened or concerned for your safety?

6. What are the most beautiful places you have ever seen?

7. What are the most unpleasant ones? What are the strangest ones?

8. Have any places ever made you feel confused or lost?

9. Do you know any places that are particularly chaotic and noisy?

10. Where have you been today? Can you describe an ordinary, everyday place so that a reader sees it in a new way?

Once you have chosen the one place that is most interesting to you, keep prewriting about it. Try to remember as many details as you can about the place. Don't worry about writing well at this point—just brainstorm (make lists) or freewrite to get down as many of the details as you can remember.

Writing a Topic Sentence

After you have written for a while, read over what you have. Look for related details that focus on *one particular impression* of the place. These details and others that give that same impression are the ones you should emphasize in your paragraph. Once you have identified that particular impression, you are ready to write a preliminary **topic sentence.**

Remember, a topic sentence contains both a **topic** and a **central point.** In this writing assignment, your topic will be the place you are describing, and your central point will be the particular impression about the place that your details emphasize and illustrate.

Prewriting Application: Working with Topic Sentences

In each sentence below, underline the topic once and the central point twice.

1. Mammoth Cave, in southwestern Kentucky, is full of eerie, unearthly sights.

2. One of the most confusing places I have ever visited was the Los Angeles International Airport.

3. Snow Summit, in Big Bear, California, is a popular ski resort because it has such a variety of ski runs to choose from.

4. My grandmother's kitchen was one of the few places where I always felt safe and welcome.

5. The artificial decorations and dreary atmosphere were not at all what I had expected when I decided to visit the Excalibur casino in Las Vegas.

Prewriting Application: Evaluating Topic Sentences

Write "No" before each sentence that would not make a good topic sentence and "Yes" before each sentence that would make a good one. Using ideas of your own, rewrite the unacceptable topic sentences into topic sentences that might work.

_____ 1. I like to visit Death Valley in the late fall.

_____

_____

_____ 2. Balboa Island, near Newport Beach, California, is clearly a place designed for the rich and famous.

_____

_____

_____ 3. When my daughter Michelle and I attended Shakespeare's play *Richard III*, we enjoyed the outdoor stage, the setting, and the superb acting.

_____

_____

_____ 4. One of my favorite places to visit is the beach.

_____

_____

_____ **5.** The waiting area in Dr. Larson's dentist office is one of the most welcoming, relaxing places that I have ever seen.

_____

_____

_____ **6.** Last December 30, we had the opportunity to visit Stone Mountain in Atlanta, Georgia.

_____

_____

_____ **7.** My paragraph will describe the Hearst Castle in San Simeon, California.

_____

_____

_____ **8.** The undeveloped canyon behind my house is one place where I can feel free and unrestricted.

_____

_____

_____ **9.** The most unusual restroom that I have ever seen was the one at the Bahia de Los Angeles Research Station in Baja California, Mexico.

_____

_____

_____ **10.** Roberta attended the opening of the Olympics in London.

_____

_____

Prewriting Application: Talking to Others

Before you write your first draft, form groups of two, three, or four people and describe the place that you have decided to write about. Tell the members of your group what central point you are trying to emphasize, and then describe as many details as you can to make that point. As you tell others about the place you have chosen, describe all of the sights, sounds, and smells that contributed to your overall impression of the place. As you listen to the places described by others and as you describe your own place, consider these questions:

1. Where exactly is this place? Has its location been clearly identified? What time of year is it? What time of day? What is the weather like?

2. Can you visualize the place? What physical features are in the area—trees? buildings? furniture? cars? other people? What colors should be included?

3. How did you feel about this place? Is the central point or impression of the place clear?

4. Were there sounds, smells, or physical sensations that should be included in the description of the place?

5. What parts of the scene should be described in more detail?

Organizing Descriptive Details

Writers of descriptive papers use **spatial order** to organize supporting details. Unlike **chronological order,** which describes events as they occur in time, **spatial order** presents details according to their physical placement or characteristics. For example, you might describe the larger, more obvious details of a scene first and then move to the smaller, less obvious details. Or you might mention the details closer to you first and then move to those farther away. Other spatial organizations might involve describing details from left to right or top to bottom or describing the most dominant sense impression first, such as a strong smell, and then moving to other sense impressions.

Descriptions of places often combine spatial and chronological order, especially if you are moving as you describe the place. In such a situation, you might describe what you encounter first in time, then what you encounter second, and so on. If you take such an approach, remember that the purpose of this assignment is to describe the place itself, not to describe what you are doing there.

Prewriting Application: Organizing Supporting Details

Read Exercises 1D (page 95); 2D (page 110); and 3C (page 126). Examine the details in each paragraph and explain why they are organized as they are.

Writing the Paragraph

Once you have a preliminary topic sentence and a list of related details, it is time to write the first draft of your paragraph. Open your paragraph with your topic sentence and then write out the details that illustrate the central point of your topic sentence. Do <u>not</u> worry about writing a "perfect" first draft. You will have the chance to improve the draft when you revise it.

Rewriting and Improving the Paragraph

1. When you have completed the first draft, read it over to see if your preliminary topic sentence accurately states the central point of your paper. If you can improve the topic sentence, do so now.

2. As you read over your draft, see if you can add still more descriptive details that relate to your central point. Add those that come to mind.

3. Check the words and phrases you have used in your first draft. You will find that many of them can be more descriptive if you make them more **specific** and **concrete**.

Adding Specific and Concrete Details

A **specific** detail is limited in the number of things to which it can refer. For example, the word *poodle* is more specific than the word *dog*, and the word *elm* is more specific than *tree*. A **concrete** detail appeals to one of the five senses. It helps a reader **see, hear, smell, taste,** or **feel** what you describe. For instance, rather than writing that your grandmother's kitchen smelled "wonderful," you might write that it was always "filled with the aromas of freshly baked bread and my grandfather's cigar smoke."

Unfortunately, most writers—even most professional writers—do not write specific and concrete details naturally. You need to *add* these details to your draft. You do so by reading back through what you have written and changing words from general to specific and from abstract to concrete. As you read, consider these areas.

- Specificity: Which words could be made more specific? Use precise names of people, places, things, emotions, and actions wherever you can.

- Sight: What sights can be included? Consider colors, shapes, and sizes.

- Sound: What sounds should be added? Were there loud noises; subtle background sounds; peaceful, relaxing sounds; piercing, metallic, or unpleasant sounds?

- Smell: Were any smells present? Were you in a kitchen, near the ocean, passing by a newly oiled street? Were you at a produce stand or in a gymnasium? Many places have distinctive smells that you should include.

- Taste: Taste might be involved even if you did not eat or drink anything. A strong smell often evokes a taste sensation too. A dusty field as well as a dry desert might also elicit a taste reaction.

- Touch: Consider the less obvious touch sensations as well as obvious ones involving pain or pleasure. Were you standing in sand or on hot pavement? Did you touch anything with your hands? Was there a breeze? Was it raining? Did your collar blow up against your face? All of these might involve touch sensations.

Not all senses need to be included, especially if they don't emphasize your central point, but most first drafts have too few specific and concrete details rather than too many.

Rewriting Application: Adding Specific and Concrete Details

In each of the following sentences, identify which words could be made more specific or concrete. Then rewrite the sentence to replace and improve the general, abstract words.

EXAMPLE The house was run-down.

The three-bedroom tract house on the corner of Elm and Vine

had deteriorated into a ruin of broken windows, peeling

paint, and splintered, termite-infested walls.

1. The woman walked through the entrance.

_____

_____

_____

_____

2. The food tasted terrible.

_____

_____

_____

_____

3. The man looked angry.

_____

_____

_____

_____

4. Her bedroom walls were colorful.

_____

_____

_____

_____

5. The trees along the driveway smelled wonderful.

_____

_____

_____

_____

Rewriting Application: Responding to Writing

Read the following description of Breaks Interstate Park. Then respond to the questions following it.

Breaks Interstate Park

There is no more beautiful place in the spring than the Breaks Interstate Park. Last year I spent part of the spring with my father and my grandmother in the Smoky Mountains of Virginia. Because the Smoky Mountains are a very remote area, there was not much to do during my vacation until some of my cousins wanted to go to a place called "The Breaks." We drove into the mountains for about an hour. When we got to the entrance, the first thing I noticed was the incredible number of flowers. There were flowers on the ground, flowers in the trees and on the rocks, and there were some on the log cabins and picnic tables. We pulled off the road to one of the campsites and got out of the car. The smell of spring was everywhere. We could smell honeysuckle, strawberry, and the heady scent of wildflowers. All we could hear were bees working the blossoms and birds bathing in the springs trickling out of the mountainside. My cousin Charon came up to me and told me to follow her. We went across the road and down a winding dirt path, past a sign that said "Twin Towers Overlook." I then beheld one of the most striking and magnificent views I have ever seen in my life. I was on an overlook, looking down at a gorge where the river flowing through it makes a horseshoe-shaped bend and the mountains on the other side look like twin towers. I ran back to the car to get my camera. While on my way back, I slipped on a moss-covered rock and skinned my knee. When I got back to the overlook, I sat down on some strawberry vines, ate wild strawberries, and took pictures. I finally ran out of film and deliciously sweet strawberries, not to mention daylight. We packed it up and went back home; however, I will never forget about the Breaks Interstate Park in the springtime.

---

1. Identify the topic sentence. State its topic and central idea. Is it an effective topic sentence? Why or why not?

2. Identify specific and concrete details. What words do you find particularly effective?

3. Which of the five senses does the writer employ in her description? Identify each of them in the paragraph.

4. What details would you make still more specific or concrete? Would you omit any details because they do not support the central point of the paragraph?

5. What sentences would you combine because they contain related ideas?

Adding Subordinate Clauses

In this chapter you have studied main and subordinate clauses and the four sentence types: simple, compound, complex, and compound-complex. As you rewrite papers, look for opportunities to change main clauses to subordinate clauses.

Rewriting Application: Adding Subordinate Clauses

A. Combine the following sentences by changing some of them to subordinate clauses.

1. a. We pulled off the road to one of the campsites and got out of the car.
   b. The smell of spring was everywhere.

2. a. My cousin Charon came up to me and told me to follow her.
   b. We went across the road and down a winding dirt path, past a sign that said "Twin Towers Overlook."
   c. I then beheld one of the most striking and magnificent views I have ever seen in my life.

3. a. Bright, warm sunlight filters through eucalyptus trees and presses against my shoulders.
   b. An old man greets me with a warm smile.
   c. The old man is raking leaves in the middle of the yard.

4. a. My grandfather sits on an old rust-covered metal stool.
   b. The stool used to be painted yellow.
   c. He tells me stories about my father's boyhood.

5. a. I have visited my grandparents' house many times during my childhood.
   b. I have not fully appreciated it until recently.

B. Revise each of the following sentences by changing one of the main clauses to a subordinate clause.

1. Justin entered the room, and everyone became silent.

2. We hiked up Mt. Whitney in one day, for we wanted the challenge.

3. Sonia likes peanut butter and chocolate ice cream, so that is the flavor she always orders.

4. Yosemite Valley is an amazing place, and it features incredible rock formations and beautiful waterfalls.

5. The outdoor location of the play was gorgeous, but the acting was mediocre.

C. Now examine your own draft. Identify any main clauses that would work better as subordinate clauses. Consider changing some of your compound sentences to complex sentences. If you have a series of short sentences, combine them by changing some of the short main clauses to subordinate clauses.

Proofreading

When you are finished, proofread your paper. Check the spelling of words you are uncertain about. Examine each sentence closely to be sure it is not a **fragment, comma splice,** or **fused sentence.** If it is, repair the error using the techniques you have studied in this chapter. Once you have a draft you are satisfied with, prepare a clean final draft, following the format your instructor has asked for.

Chapter 2 Practice Test

I. Review of Chapter One

A. In the following sentences, identify the underlined words by writing one of the following abbreviations above the words: noun (N), pronoun (Pro), verb (V), adjective (Adj), adverb (Adv), conjunction (Conj), or preposition (Prep).

1. <u>Toyota</u> was proud of its <u>new</u> cars.

2. The man <u>behind</u> the curtain did not <u>really</u> look like a wizard.

3. Louis Armstrong always <u>liked</u> to cook his special red beans and rice after a good jam <u>session</u>.

4. The <u>concept</u> of Pangea was dismissed at first, <u>but</u> now it is widely accepted.

5. Persephone ran <u>away</u> from the magic stairs because they led to <u>hell</u>.

6. Almost <u>everyone</u> in the theater was in tears when Rodney offered to read another one <u>of</u> his poems.

7. Dante could <u>not</u> believe Virgil was down there, <u>nor</u> did he believe Virgil could never leave.

8. As the Martians looked up at the <u>blue</u> earth, they <u>wondered</u> what to name it.

9. Irene had <u>always</u> thought *carpe diem* was an <u>orange</u> fish.

10. The candidates immediately <u>began</u> arguing about <u>their</u> religions.

B. For the following sentences, underline all subjects once and all complete verbs twice. Place parentheses around all prepositional phrases.

11. From a thousand contestants, Frank was named most jovial and practical.

12. Behind the wall Stephen Crane listened to the battle and wrote in his journal.

13. Jack did not worry about earthquakes, but he stocked his emergency pantry just in case.

14. Chelsea's candy from Halloween has disappeared because her father ate it.

15. The uprisings in the Middle East, which were reported in all of the papers, have encouraged the American students.

continued

C. In the following sentences, correct any errors in the use of adjectives and adverbs (or in the use of *then* or *than*) by crossing out any incorrect words and writing the correct words above them.

16. Clark liked it when the wind blew more harder then when there was barely a breeze.

17. Arbuelita's chicken tamales tasted badly, but she is a much better cook then anyone

    else I know.

18. The worse day of my life also turned out to be the most funniest day.

19. The director shouted real loud at the actors because they didn't perform good.

20. Of the two comments on my sister's blog, Mary's was the most vicious and it was

    real untrue.

Chapter 2 Practice Test

II. Chapter Two

A. Underline the subordinate clauses and identify the type of clause (adjective or adverb) in the space provided.

1. The sculpture that you see above the steps is the Nike of Samothrace.   _____

2. Until Amy would say "Beatles," Landry wouldn't let her play Lady Gaga.   _____

3. After Nashville, we visited Tupelo, Mississippi, where Homer's favorite

   singer was born.   _____

4. Anne would lose her head if she did not have a good excuse for the king.   _____

5. When jazz first appeared, the greatest performers came from New Orleans.   _____

B. To the main clauses below, add the types of subordinate clauses indicated in parentheses. Add your clause at any place in the sentence that is appropriate.

6. (adverb clause) The Wicked Witch of the West always carried an umbrella.

   _____

   _____

7. (adjective clause) In the Alamo waited James Bowie and Davy Crockett.

   _____

   _____

8. (adjective clause) Brent got a chance to face Kobe Bryant.

   _____

   _____

9. (adverb clause) Winnie the Pooh never says no to honey.

   _____

   _____

10. (adverb clause) Charlie Brown tried to kick the football one more time.

    _____

    _____

continued

C. In the spaces provided, identify the following sentences as simple, compound, complex, or compound-complex.

   11. If the creek rises, Tupelo is done for.   _____

   12. Piles of books filled the office; however, Barb knew her computer was in there somewhere.   _____

   13. Before the ice cream store with the crazy picture of an angel talking to Humphrey Bogart stood Steve with just enough money for a triple decker.   _____

   14. Josefina liked to visit Mexico, where she was born, but she enjoyed the United States just as much.   _____

   15. Ed took out his wallet after the game ended.   _____

D. Compose sentences of your own according to the instructions.

   16. Write a simple sentence that contains two prepositional phrases.

_____

_____

   17. Write a compound sentence. Use a coordinating conjunction and appropriate punctuation to join the clauses.

_____

_____

   18. Write a compound sentence. Use a transitional word or phrase and appropriate punctuation to join the clauses.

_____

_____

   19. Write a complex sentence. Use *until* as the subordinator.

_____

_____

continued

20. Write a compound-complex sentence. Use the subordinator *although*.

_____

_____

E. Identify each of the following sentences as correct (C), fused (F), comma splice (CS), or fragment (Frag). Then correct any errors by using the methods discussed in Chapter Two.

_____ 21. Before John Coltrane raised his saxophone.

_____

_____

_____ 22. The snake rubbed its nose against the tree, then it began to shed its skin.

_____

_____

_____ 23. Correct the punctuation first.

_____

_____

_____ 24. Oswald, wishing he had more time for the test.

_____

_____

_____ 25. Roger Clemens was accused of using steroids he was found innocent in court.

_____

_____

Chapter 2 Practice Test

continued

_____ **26.** When he placed his hand on his heart, the senator started lying, it was a good trick.

_____

_____

_____ **27.** Before the wedding could begin.

_____

_____

_____ **28.** Frieda was certain that jacaranda trees bloomed only in her neighborhood, however, Owen was not so sure.

_____

_____

_____ **29.** By wearing a hat with candles on it, Goya was able to paint at night.

_____

_____

_____ **30.** Frodo entered the dark cave he did not know Shelob was waiting.

_____

_____

Improving Sentence Patterns

Now you have a fundamental knowledge of the sentence patterns of English. Although sentences may fall into four broad categories according to the number and types of clauses, the ways to express any thought in a sentence are almost infinitely variable.

You may make a sentence short and to the point:

> Eniko sold her netsuke collection.

Or, through the addition of modifying words, phrases, and additional clauses, you can expand it.

> After much soul searching and after seeking the advice of her mother, her brother, and her best friend, Eniko, a person who always carefully considered important decisions, sold her netsuke collection, which was worth several thousand dollars, but she kept one special carving of a frog and a sacred bird.

The essential idea—*Eniko sold her netsuke collection*—is the same for both sentences. Sometimes you will want to be short and to the point, and a five-word sentence will serve your purpose best. Other times you will want to be more explanatory, and then you may need to use more words.

The difference between the five words of the first sentence and the fifty words of the second one is the addition of modifying words, phrases, and clauses. These modifiers can help you write more clearly and vividly. The second sentence, though admittedly a bit overdone, tells a story or paints a picture. Modifying words, phrases, and clauses can be overused and should never be substituted for strong verbs and nouns, but most writers err in the opposite direction, leaving their writing limp and colorless.

You need to follow certain guidelines when you use the various modifying phrases and clauses. First we will discuss the most effective ways to use phrases and clauses in your sentences, and then we will discuss how to avoid the typical errors that writers make in using these devices. We hope that by the end you will have gained an appreciation of the wonderful flexibility of the English sentence and that you will have acquired more tools for making your own writing more interesting and effective.

Modifying with Participial and Infinitive Phrases

You can use **participial and infinitive phrases** as modifiers in your sentences. These phrases can help you streamline your sentences and achieve sentence variety. In most cases, participial and infinitive phrases take the place of subordinate clauses.

⊚⊚ EXAMPLES   (subordinate clause)   **As he drove to work,** Harry saw a black cat run in front of his car.

                (participial phrase)   **Driving to work,** Harry saw a black cat run in front of his car.

As you already know, **a clause is a word group that contains a subject and a verb. A phrase, on the other hand, is a word group that does not contain a subject and a verb.** You are already aware of prepositional phrases. Other phrases, generally called verbal phrases, include **present participial phrases, past participial phrases,** and **infinitive phrases.**

Present Participial Phrases

As we mentioned in Chapter One, the present participle is a verbal. It is the form of the verb that ends in "ing" (*running, typing, looking*). Without a helping verb it cannot be used as the verb of a sentence. Instead, it is used as an adjective. For example, you can use it as a one-word adjective.

⊚⊚ EXAMPLE   The **running** man stumbled as he rounded the corner.

In this sentence, the present participle *running* modifies the noun *man*.
     You can also use the present participle as part of a phrase that functions as an adjective. Such a phrase is called a **participial phrase,** and it is often used to begin sentences.

⊚⊚ EXAMPLE   **Rounding the corner,** the running man stumbled.

In this sentence, the present participial phrase *Rounding the corner* is an adjective phrase modifying the noun *man*. The present participle is *Rounding*.
     The present participial phrase, then, is an adjective phrase consisting of the present participle plus any other words attached to it. When a present participial phrase introduces a sentence, it is always followed by a comma.

Past Participial Phrases

The past participle is the form of the verb that you use with the helping verbs *have, has,* or *had* (*have eaten, has defeated, had bought*). Like the present participle, the past participle is a verbal when used without a helping verb. And, like the present participle, it is used as an adjective.

You can use a past participle as a single-word adjective.

EXAMPLE   The **defeated** army retreated into the mountains.

In this sentence, the past participle *defeated* modifies the noun *army.*

Or you can use the past participle as part of a past participial phrase.

EXAMPLE   **Pursued by the enemy,** the army retreated into the mountains.

In this sentence, the past participial phrase *Pursued by the enemy* modifies the noun *army.* Notice that it is followed by a comma. As with the present participial phrase, when the past participial phrase introduces a sentence, you should place a comma after it.

Participial phrases make good introductions to sentences, but you can use them anywhere. To avoid confusion, though, you should place them as closely as possible to the words they modify.

EXAMPLES   All of the students **submitting essays for the contest** used word processors.

The man **bitten by the rattlesnake** walked ten miles to the hospital.

The present participial phrase *submitting essays for the contest* modifies the noun *students.* The past participial phrase *bitten by the rattlesnake* modifies the noun *man.*

PRACTICE   Underline the participial phrases in the following sentences and circle the words they modify.

1. Put into the game in the last ten minutes, Zoila scored twelve points for her team.

2. Reading the instructions closely, he was still unable to figure out all the functions on his new smartphone.

3. Eating with determination, he would not allow three slices of New York cheesecake to defeat him.

4. I drove to San Francisco with a car made in Germany.

5. The firefighter, standing in the large library, knew that 451 degrees Fahrenheit was the temperature at which paper ignites, and he hesitated.

6. The woman dressed in a blue gown attracted attention when she began to speak.

7. Surprised by the Book-of-the-Month Club's decision, Richard Wright knew that many more people would read his novel.

8. Writing a book by candlelight, Cervantes could not have realized that people would still know of him hundreds of years later.

9. Looking at the river, Lao Tzu understood that words could never fully describe reality.

10. Goose liver, produced through a harsh process, is disliked by people who are concerned about cruelty against animals.

Infinitive Phrases

The infinitive is a verbal that you can use as a noun, an adjective, or an adverb. You form the infinitive by adding *to* to the present tense form of the verb (*to write, to run, to listen*).

You can use the infinitive by itself.

EXAMPLE   **To fly, you must first take lessons and get a license.**

Or you can use the infinitive to form an infinitive phrase.

EXAMPLE   **To play the saxophone well, you must practice often.**

Notice that the infinitive phrase consists of the infinitive plus any words attached to it. Like the two participial phrases, it is followed by a comma when it introduces a sentence. However, when you use the infinitive as a noun, it can act as the subject of a sentence. In this case, you do not use a comma.

EXAMPLE   **To be a good husband was Clint's ambition.**

The infinitive phrase *To be a good husband* is the subject of the verb *was*.

Generally, like the two participial phrases, the infinitive phrase can appear in a variety of places in a sentence.

EXAMPLE   **Carla's motives were hard to understand at first.**

Here the infinitive phrase *to understand at first* acts as an adverb to modify the adjective *hard*.

EXAMPLE   **Eduardo liked having a sister to talk to even though she teased him constantly.**

Here, the infinitive phrase *to talk to* acts as an adjective to modify the noun *sister*.

PRACTICE Underline the modifying participial and infinitive phrases in the following sentences and circle the words they modify.

1. Mahdieh finally found a (pot) to hold her geraniums.

2. Hiding his criticism with irony, Molière hoped he would not get into trouble with the king.

3. Constructed all over Central America, magnificent but empty Maya cities impress many visitors today.

4. Without the ability to support an ever-growing population, the Maya left their cities before the Europeans arrived.

5. The most recent actor to appear on *Dancing with the Stars* hoped his performance would reinvigorate his career.

6. Expecting no profit from his action, the business owner contributed an enormous amount of money to the politician's campaign.

7. The first person to contribute to the politician's campaign hoped that he would be rewarded in the future.

8. Shocked by the sudden attention, the texting student did not know the answer to the question.

9. Picasso made an appointment to visit an African art exhibit.

10. Impressed by what he had seen, Picasso changed his style.

Section One Review

1. The **present participle** is a verbal that ends in "ing" and that is used as an adjective. (When the "ing" form is used as a noun, it is called a **gerund**.)

2. A **present participial phrase** consists of the present participle plus any words attached to it.

3. A comma follows a **present participial phrase** that introduces a sentence.

4. The **past participle** is the form of the verb used with the helping verbs *have*, *has*, and *had*.

5. The **past participle** is a verbal used as an adjective.

6. A **past participial phrase** consists of the past participle plus any words attached to it.

7. A comma follows a **past participial phrase** that introduces a sentence.

8. An **infinitive** is formed by adding *to* to the present tense of a verb.

9. The **infinitive** is a verbal that can be used as a noun, an adjective, or an adverb.

10. An **infinitive phrase** consists of the infinitive plus any words attached to it.

11. A comma follows an **infinitive phrase** that introduces a sentence and acts as a modifier.

Exercise 1A

From a magazine, newspaper, book, or online source (such as *Wikipedia*), copy three sentences that contain an infinitive phrase, three that contain a present participial phrase, and three more that contain a past participial phrase. Underline the phrase in each sentence.

A. Sentences with infinitive phrases:

1. _____

_____

2. _____

_____

3. _____

_____

B. Sentences with present participial phrases:

4. _____

_____

5. _____

_____

6. _____

_____

C. Sentences with past participial phrases:

7. _____

_____

8. _____

_____

9. _____

_____

Exercise 1B

Underline all participial and infinitive phrases. Circle the words that they modify. In the space at the end of each sentence, identify the phrase as present participle (Pres P), past participle (Past P), or infinitive (Inf).

A.

1. In Roman times, the intersection of three roads was used as a (place) to stop and talk. *Inf*

2. Sharing the events of the day, Roman travelers would rest for a few minutes. _____ **3.** Farmers, concerned about their crops, would discuss the weather or the land. _____ **4.** This kind of place was called a *trivium*, meaning a "three-road intersection." _____ **5.** Found in words like *triple, trinity,* and *tricycle, tri* means "three." _____ **6.** A common Spanish word to refer to a street or road is *via* (from the Latin *vium*). _____ **7.** "Trivial" conversation, referring to discussions of unimportant matters, really means "three-road" conversation. _____

B.

1. According to legend, tea, now drunk by hundreds of millions of people, was discovered by accident almost five thousand years ago. _____ **2.** Liking his water very clean, Shen Nun, a Chinese emperor, made his servants boil it. _____ **3.** To rest from a long day's march, the emperor and his army stopped for a day. _____ **4.** His servants built a fire to heat the emperor's water. _____ **5.** Unnoticed by anyone, a leaf from a tea bush fell into the water. _____ **6.** The servants, disregarding the water's changed color, brought the boiled water to the emperor. _____ **7.** The emperor, surprised by the flavor of the water, was pleased by its taste and drank water with tea leaves from then on. _____

Exercise 1C

In the places indicated by ^, add your own participial or infinitive phrases to the following sentences. Use the verbs in parentheses. Be sure to place a comma after any phrase that introduces a sentence.

1. ^ Chenelle bought groceries, beverages, and decorations. (prepare)

   To prepare for her birthday party, Chenelle bought groceries, beverages, and decorations.

2. Steve thought he would have more time in his retirement ^ . (play)

   _____

   _____

3. The car ^ was the most environmentally friendly car on the road. (make)

   _____

   _____

4. ^ The minister decided to put something in the church bulletin regarding turning off cell phones during service. (annoy)

   _____

   _____

5. At the boxing match, the audience did not expect to see the athletes ^. (laugh)

   _____

   _____

6. An aquarium is a place elementary school classes go ^. (see)

   _____

   _____

7. ^ The Central Africans wondered why Livingston thought they needed help. (stare)

   _____

   _____

Exercise 1C

continued

8. ^ Buddha slowly reached enlightenment. (meditate)

_____

_____

9. The shoppers ^ hoped to get the best bargains for more things they did not need. (fight)

_____

_____

10. ^ The teenager wanted to gain instant fame and fortune. (sing)

_____

_____

11. The Silk Road consisted of a number of trade routes ^. (link)

_____

_____

12. ^ Moses was brought up in an Egyptian household. (find)

_____

_____

13. Michael Jackson was the first person to perform the Moonwalk, but Neil Armstrong was the first person ^. (walk)

_____

_____

Exercise 1C

continued

14. ^ Muslims fast during the month of Ramadan. (learn)

_____

_____

15. The dangers were great and the odds overwhelming, but everyone knew the superheroes would not fail ^. (rescue)

_____

_____

Underline all infinitive and participial phrases and circle the words that they modify.

1. Jackie Robinson, the first (African American) to play baseball in the major leagues, has been honored in many cities across the United States and Canada. **2.** For instance, a statue honoring Jackie stands outside Olympic Stadium in Montreal, Quebec, where Jackie played for a Dodger farm club. **3.** In addition, Daytona, Florida, is home to Robinson Stadium, named after this great player. **4.** Jersey City, New Jersey, dedicating a bronze plaque to Jackie at Society Hill, has also honored Robinson. **5.** Of course, New York, home of the Brooklyn Dodgers, showed its appreciation to Jackie when it made the decision to change the name of Interboro Parkway to Jackie Robinson Parkway. **6.** In Los Angeles, UCLA has honored Jackie, who was the first UCLA athlete to star in four sports. **7.** UCLA baseball teams now play at Jackie Robinson Stadium, named after the legendary player. **8.** Erected at the stadium in 1985, a statue of Robinson was generously paid for by Jackie's brother, Mack Robinson. **9.** Pasadena, California, is another city showing its appreciation for Jackie's accomplishments. **10.** Moving to the city when they were young, Jackie and Mack grew up in Pasadena. **11.** On New Year's Day, 1997, the grateful city honored Robinson with a beautiful Rose Parade float donated by the Simon Wiesenthal Center. **12.** Naming a youth center, a post office, a park, and a baseball field after Jackie, Pasadena further showed its respect for the famous baseball player. **13.** Lately, the school board of Grady County, Georgia, which is near Jackie's birthplace, unanimously passed a motion to change the name of the Cairo High School baseball field to Jackie Robinson Field. **14.** Featuring a granite marker and bronze plaque, the field is dedicated to Jackie. **15.** Jackie Robinson, recognized by all as a brave man and gifted player, richly deserves all of these honors.

Modifying with Adjective Clauses and Appositives

Adjective Clauses

We discussed adjective clauses earlier in a section on subordinate clauses. An adjective clause is an important option when you want to modify a noun or pronoun in a sentence. Using an adjective clause instead of single-word adjectives or modifying phrases tends to place more emphasis on what you are saying about the noun or pronoun you are modifying. Consider the following sentences, for instance.

◎◎ EXAMPLES   (adjective)   **My insensitive neighbor plays his trombone all night long.**

(adjective clause)   **My neighbor, who is insensitive, plays his trombone all night long.**

Using the adjective clause *who is insensitive* places more importance on the neighbor's insensitivity. Sometimes you need only single-word modifiers, but it is good to be aware of all your choices for modifying words.

Here is a brief review of adjective clauses.

1. Adjective clauses follow the noun or pronoun they modify.

2. Adjective clauses begin with the relative pronouns *who, whom, whose, which, that* (and sometimes *when* or *where*).

◎◎ EXAMPLES   We returned the money to the *person* **who had lost it.** (*Who* introduces an adjective clause that modifies the noun *person*.)

I remember the *time* **when Homer and Hortense were married at the Spam factory.** (*When* introduces an adjective clause that modifies the noun *time*.)

Sidney decided to move to *Colorado,* **where his family used to spend summer vacations.** (*Where* introduces an adjective clause that modifies the noun *Colorado*.)

3. If the adjective clause provides information that is necessary to identify the noun or pronoun, do not set it off with commas.

◎◎ EXAMPLE   **The man who was sitting next to my uncle at the banquet is a famous sportswriter.**

The information in this adjective clause is necessary to identify which man at the banquet is the famous sportswriter.

4. If the adjective clause provides information that is merely descriptive and is not necessary to identify the noun or pronoun, then set off the clause with commas.

⊙⊙ EXAMPLE

Merlin Olsen, **who was an all-pro football player,** became a famous sportscaster.

Merlin Olsen's name already identifies him, so the adjective clause contains added but unnecessary information. Therefore, you need the commas.

We will discuss the rules for the use of commas with adjective clauses again in Chapter Five.

⊙⊙ PRACTICE

Underline all adjective clauses and circle the words they modify. For further practice, try to determine which clauses need commas and add them where necessary.

1. The (woman) who developed the new microchip was from Vietnam.

2. *Beowulf* which is an Old English epic poem was written about 1000 AD.

3. Someone who is not presently looking at the professor is texting furiously.

4. Hurling which is a sport played primarily in Ireland is being considered for future Olympics.

5. Maurice Ravel who was a famous French composer wrote *Bolero* which became one of the most popular concert pieces of the twentieth century.

6. She could not immediately remember the name of her classmate whom she had not seen in ten years.

7. Someone asked Toots Thielemans who is a famous harmonica player to perform *Bolero* for the crowd.

8. The women who were arguing about the baby decided to ask Solomon for advice.

9. The plane that Chelsea had jumped from was circling 13,500 feet above Chula Vista where she went to high school.

10. Wolf Moonglow who was an exceptionally hirsute man was telling us about the time when he first began to study lycanthropy.

Appositives

Appositives give you another option for adding descriptive detail. An **appositive** is a noun or pronoun, along with any modifiers, that **renames** another noun or pronoun. The appositive almost always follows the word it refers to, and it is usually set off with commas.

Note how the following two sentences can be combined not only by adding an adjective clause but also by adding an appositive:

My neighbor plays the trombone all night long.

He is an insensitive man.

EXAMPLES (adjective clause) My neighbor, **who is insensitive**, plays his trombone all night long.

(appositive) My neighbor, **an insensitive man**, plays his trombone all night long.

In the appositive, the noun *man* renames the noun *neighbor*.

EXAMPLES The wedding <u>ring</u>, **a <u>symbol</u>** of eternal love, dates back to 2800 BC in Egypt. (The noun *symbol* renames the noun *ring*.)

The huge <u>trout</u>, **the <u>one</u> still in the river**, would have made an impressive trophy on the wall of Harold's den. (The pronoun *one* renames the noun *trout*.)

The <u>honeymoon</u>, **a popular marriage <u>custom</u>**, comes from an ancient northern European practice of stealing brides. (The noun *custom* renames the noun *honeymoon*.)

PRACTICE Underline the appositives and circle the nouns or pronouns that the appositives rename.

1. The (cell phone) <u>a product of modern technology</u>, is an indispensable tool of many businesses.

2. Gothic cathedrals are often ornamented with gargoyles, grotesque sculptures of evil spirits.

3. Remus and Romulus, the mythical founders of Rome, survived their infancy by being suckled by a wolf.

4. John Brown, a man devoted to ending slavery, was hanged for attacking a weapons arsenal in Harpers Ferry, Virginia.

5. Istanbul, a famous city in Turkey, was once called Constantinople.

6. Jules Verne, author of *Twenty Thousand Leagues under the Sea* and *A Journey to the Center of the Earth,* predicted a number of technological developments in some of his science fiction novels.

7. Martin recently introduced me to Emma and Scott, physicians from Rhode Island.

8. The djembe, a West African drum, can produce many different tones.

9. Miles Davis's *Kind of Blue,* perhaps the most famous jazz album, has just been reissued in a box that contains a tee shirt showing Miles.

10. Two thousand Cleveland teenagers demonstrated for a skate park, a necessity for any practicing skateboarder.

PRACTICE — Add an appositive or an adjective clause to each of the following sentences. Use commas when they are needed.

1. The sports car was parked near the school.

   The sports car that had been stolen last week was parked near the school.

2. Indira Gandhi, Golda Meir, and Angela Merkel all were leaders of their countries.

   _____

   _____

3. In the 1980s, Prince and Michael Jackson produced a lot of popular dance music.

   _____

   _____

4. Jeremy asked Diane to pass him another hot dog.

_____

_____

5. The wolf asked Romulus and Remus to take turns.

_____

_____

6. Chinese and Irish laborers laid a lot of railroad track.

_____

_____

7. Johnny Cash was born in Arkansas, but he later moved to Nashville.

_____

_____

8. Among the Navajo, paintings made with sand could be produced only by medicine men.

_____

_____

9. In Hinduism, the god Ganesh is depicted as having the head of an elephant.

_____

_____

10. In 1869, the Cincinnati Red Stockings became the first professional baseball team.

_____

_____

Section Two Review

1. **Adjective clauses** modify nouns and pronouns.

2. **Adjective clauses** follow the nouns or pronouns they modify.

3. **Adjective clauses** begin with *who, whom, whose, which, that* (and sometimes *when* or *where*).

4. **Adjective clauses** that contain information necessary to identify the words they modify are not set off with commas.

5. **Adjective clauses** that do not contain information necessary to identify the words they modify are set off with commas.

6. **Appositives** are words or word groups containing a noun or pronoun that renames another noun or pronoun in a sentence.

7. **Appositives** usually follow the nouns or pronouns they rename.

8. **Appositives** are usually set off with commas.

Exercise 2A

Get a local paper of any kind. That may be a campus newspaper, a city magazine, a neighborhood paper, or any paper readily available to you that contains at least some articles and not only advertisements. Find ten sentences in that paper that contain at least one adjective clause each and five sentences that contain appositives.

A. Ten adjective clauses:

1. _____

   _____

2. _____

   _____

3. _____

   _____

4. _____

   _____

5. _____

   _____

6. _____

   _____

7. _____

   _____

8. _____

   _____

9. _____

   _____

10. _____

   _____

Exercise 2A

continued

B. Five appositives:

11. _____

_____

12. _____

_____

13. _____

_____

14. _____

_____

15. _____

_____

Exercise 2B

Underline all adjective clauses and appositives. Circle the words they modify or rename. Indicate whether the modifier is an appositive (AP) or an adjective clause (Adj). Add commas where necessary.

1. The body of (Abraham Lincoln) who was assassinated in 1865 was almost stolen from its grave in 1876. _*Adj*_ **2.** Big Jim Kenealy the leader of an Illinois counterfeiting gang had recently been put out of business by the U.S. Secret Service. _____ **3.** Secret Service agents had arrested key members of his gang as well as the engraver who did Kenealy's most important work. _____ **4.** Kenealy developed a plan that would force the government to release his men. _____ **5.** He decided to kidnap Lincoln's body which was buried two miles outside of Springfield, Illinois. _____ **6.** After his death, Mary Todd Lincoln had taken her husband's body to Oak Ridge Cemetery where he was buried in an unguarded grave. _____ **7.** Kenealy who knew there was no Illinois law against stealing a body considered his plan foolproof. _____ **8.** However, Kenealy made one blunder a very serious mistake. _____ **9.** To steal the body, he recruited a helper an undercover agent of the Secret Service. _____ **10.** He decided upon November 7 the night after the national elections as the best time to dig up Lincoln's body. _____ **11.** He planned to use the excitement that accompanies all elections to cover his activities. _____ **12.** On November 8 his arrest was reported in the *Chicago Tribune* which ran the full story of his plot. _____ **13.** Robert Todd Lincoln the president's oldest son hired attorneys to prosecute Jim Kenealy. _____ **14.** The only crime that they were able to charge him with was conspiracy to steal a coffin. _____ **15.** Kenealy who almost succeeded in stealing the body of President Lincoln received a sentence of one year in the state penitentiary. _____

Exercise 2C

A. Add adjective clauses of your own to each of the sentences below. Make sure you use commas where necessary.

1. Chris likes to work on his old motorcycle.

Chris likes to work on his old motorcycle, which he purchased last year from his brother.

2. The president of the United States appoints judges to the Supreme Court.

_____

_____

3. However, these judges have to be confirmed by the Senate.

_____

_____

4. In the days of the old wooden sailing ships, drinking too much alcohol in a bar was risky if one lived in a port city.

_____

_____

5. When a sailing ship pulled into the harbor and did not have enough seamen, recruiters would sometimes go to the local bars.

_____

_____

6. In those bars, they would treat people to drinks.

_____

_____

7. Since the drinks were free, some people drank far too much and would pass out.

_____

_____

continued

8. The next morning, these lovers of free drinks would find themselves on the ocean on board a ship.

_____

_____

B. Add appositives of your own to the sentences below. Make sure you use commas where necessary.

9. The pilot landed the burning airplane in a muddy field.

The pilot, an eighty-five-year-old grandmother, landed the

burning airplane in a muddy field.

10. Nagadya was bored by *Titanic*.

_____

_____

11. College students should know where Brunei is.

_____

_____

12. Lesotho is a place that many college professors have never heard of.

_____

_____

13. Among the most popular sports in China, table tennis is also widely played in Europe.

_____

_____

14. Carpaccio is a dish served in many restaurants in Italy.

_____

_____

Exercise 2C

continued

   15. The conquistadores from Spain never found Machu Picchu.

      _____

      _____

Exercise 2D

Underline all adjective clauses and circle the words they modify. Underline all appositives and circle the words they rename. Add commas where necessary.

1. Many English-speaking people are surprised when they discover the number of everyday (words) that are drawn from different mythologies.   2. For example, the names of several of our weekdays—Tuesday, Wednesday, Thursday, and Friday—derive from Norse mythology.

3. Tuesday and Thursday refer to Tiu the Norse god of war and Thor the Norse god of thunder.

4. Wednesday refers to Woden who was the king of the Norse gods and Friday refers to Frigga the Norse goddess of love.   5. Other common words are derived from Greek mythology.   6. For instance, the word *tantalize* refers to Tantalus who was a king condemned to Hades as a punishment for his crimes.   7. In Hades he was forced to stand below fruit that was just beyond his reach and in water that he could not drink.   8. Another common Greek word in our language is *atlas* which refers to a map of the world.   9. As a mythological figure, Atlas was a Titan who was condemned to support the heavens on his shoulders.   10. Finally, Roman mythology which in many ways parallels Greek mythology is another source of many English words.   11. For example, the month of January is named after Janus the Roman god with two faces.   12. Janus whose two faces allowed him to watch two directions at once was the Roman god of doorways.   13. June another of the many months that refer to Roman mythology is named after Juno the goddess of marriage and childbirth.   14. These examples are just a few of the hundreds of English words that reflect the many mythologies of the world.

Misplaced and Dangling Modifiers

In Chapter Two, when you combined clauses to form various sentence types, you learned that joining clauses improperly can lead to comma splices and fused sentences. As you can probably guess, adding modifiers to sentences leads to an entirely new set of problems. In some cases, these problems are a bit more complicated than those caused by comma splices and fused sentences, but with a little practice, you should have no trouble at all handling them.

Misplaced Modifiers

Misplaced modifiers are exactly what their name says they are—modifiers that have been "misplaced" within a sentence. But how is a modifier "misplaced"? The answer is simple. If you remember that a modifier is nearly always placed just before or just after the word it modifies, then a misplaced modifier must be one that has been mistakenly placed so that it causes a reader to be confused about what it modifies. Consider the following sentence, for example:

EXAMPLE   Albert said **quietly** to move away from the snake.

Does the modifier *quietly* tell us how Albert said what he said, or does it tell us how we should move away from the snake? Changing the placement of the modifier will clarify the meaning.

EXAMPLES   Albert **quietly** said to move away from the snake. (Here, the word modifies the verb *said*.)

Albert said to move **quietly** away from the snake. (Here the word modifies the verbal *to move*.)

Sometimes finding the correct placement of a modifier can be a bit difficult. Let's look at a few other typical examples.

Misplaced Words

Any modifier can be misplaced, but one particular group of modifiers causes quite a bit of trouble for many people. These words are *only, almost, just, merely,* and *nearly.* Consider, for example, the following sentences:

EXAMPLES   By buying her new computer on sale, Floretta **almost** saved $100.

By buying her new computer on sale, Floretta saved **almost** $100.

As you can see, these sentences actually make two different statements. In the first sentence, *almost* modifies *saved*. If you *almost* saved something, you did *not* save it. In the second sentence, *almost* modifies *$100*. If you saved *almost* $100, you saved $85, $90, $95, or some other amount close to $100.

Which statement does the writer want to make—that Floretta did *not* save any money or that she *did* save an amount close to $100? Because the point was that she bought her computer on sale, the second sentence makes more sense.

To avoid confusion, be sure that you place all of your modifiers carefully.

EXAMPLES

(incorrect)	Her piano teacher encouraged her **often** to practice.
(correct)	Her piano teacher **often** encouraged her to practice.
(correct)	Her piano teacher encouraged her to practice **often**.
(incorrect)	Sophia **nearly** drank a gallon of coffee yesterday.
(correct)	Sophia drank **nearly** a gallon of coffee yesterday.

PRACTICE   Underline and correct any misplaced words in the following sentences. Some of the sentences may be correct.

1. During breakfast, Marshall ~~nearly~~ drank ^*nearly*^ a whole quart of orange juice.

2. The gamer staring at his computer sadly noticed that his results were not improving.

3. The bullfighter knew that he had only one chance to win the heart of the señorita.

4. The sinister-looking man who had been sitting in the corner silently got up and left the room.

5. When Fidel Castro and Che Guevara landed in Cuba, they almost had no chance of succeeding in their attempt to overthrow the Batista government.

6. Many soft drinks nearly contain enough sugar to be used as hummingbird food.

7. South Korea just had a low per-capita income in the 1950s, not in the decades after that.

8. Because she was worried about her health, Shawna asked Fernando frequently to take her to the gym.

9. The world-famous prevaricator would only invite the gullible to his dinner

party.

10. She had almost tried everything to convince him to attend the demolition derby.

Misplaced Phrases and Clauses

The phrases and clauses that you studied earlier in this chapter are as easily misplaced as individual words. Phrases and clauses often follow the words they modify.

EXAMPLES

(prepositional phrase)	The driver **in the blue sports car** struck an innocent pedestrian.
(present participial phrase)	The dog **chasing the car** barked at the bewildered driver.
(past participial phrase)	They gave the bicycle **donated by the shop** to the child.
(adjective clause)	Lucia gave the money **that she had borrowed from her sister** to the homeless woman.

In each of the above sentences, the modifier follows the word it modifies. Notice what happens when the modifier is misplaced so that it follows the wrong word.

EXAMPLES

The driver struck an innocent pedestrian **in the blue sports car.**

The dog barked at the bewildered driver **chasing the car.**

They gave the bicycle to the child **donated by the shop.**

Lucia gave the money to the homeless woman **that she had borrowed from her sister.**

Obviously, misplaced phrases and clauses can create rather confusing and sometimes even humorous situations. Of course, not all phrases and clauses follow the words they modify. Many occur before the word they refer to.

EXAMPLES

(past participial phrase)	**Angered by the umpire's poor call,** Dana threw her bat to the ground.
(present participial phrase)	**Hoping to win the debate,** Cyrus practiced three hours every day.

Regardless of whether the modifier appears before or after the word it modifies, the point is that you should place modifiers so that they clearly refer to a specific word in the sentence.

◎◎ PRACTICE   Underline and correct any misplaced phrases and clauses in the following sentences. Some of the sentences may be correct.

1. The doctor set the leg of the dog <u>that had been broken in the accident.</u>

   The doctor set the dog's leg that had been broken in the accident.

2. Marco Polo presented the golden chest to the pope filled with exotic spices.

   _____

   _____

3. Desperate to make an impression, the singer failed to convince the judges reaching for a high note.

   _____

   _____

4. The astronauts were monitored by personnel at NASA who were sitting in a space rover on the surface of Mars.

   _____

   _____

5. Sitting at his desk, Natsume sensed that his cat would try to interrupt his writing, which had a tendency to scratch.

   _____

   _____

6. Alisha noticed that she had left her favorite novel at her friend's house down the street with many handwritten comments in it.

   _____

   _____

7. Naomi was sure she had left her wallet in the restaurant thinking back over her day.

_____

_____

8. The alien mothership crashed from the sky, which was disabled by a computer virus.

_____

_____

9. My mother loved the film *Milk*, but my uncle did not, praising its honest handling of the life of a brave man.

_____

_____

10. The Lewis and Clark expedition finally arrived at the Pacific Ocean, which had been gone for months.

_____

_____

Dangling Modifiers

A **dangling modifier** is an introductory phrase (usually a verbal phrase) that lacks an appropriate word to modify. Since these modifiers usually represent some sort of action, they need a **doer** or **agent** of the action represented.

For example, in the following sentence the introductory participial phrase "dangles" because it is not followed by a noun or pronoun that could be the doer of the action represented by the phrase.

EXAMPLE   **Driving madly down the boulevard,** the horse just missed being hit and killed.

The present participial phrase *Driving madly down the boulevard* should be followed by a noun or pronoun that could logically do the action of the phrase. Instead, it is followed by the noun *horse,* which is the subject of the sentence. Was the horse "driving"? Probably not. Therefore, the modifying phrase "dangles" because it has no noun or pronoun to which it can logically refer. Here are some more sentences with dangling modifiers.

EXAMPLES

Nearly exhausted, the game was almost over.
(Was the *game* exhausted?)

After studying all night, the test wasn't so difficult after all.
(Did the *test* study all night?)

To impress his new girlfriend, Dominic's Chevrolet was polished.
(Did the *Chevrolet* want to impress Dominic's girlfriend?)

As you can see, you should check for dangling modifiers when you use introductory phrases.

PRACTICE

In the following sentences, indicate whether the modifying phrases are correctly used by writing either "C" for correct or "D" for dangling modifier in the spaces provided.

_____D_____ **1.** Rushing into the club, Angelica's earrings fell onto the floor.

_____ **2.** Putting the finishing touches on his manuscript, Kalidasa had a good feeling that it would be a success.

_____ **3.** Confused by the differences between hip hop and crumping, Shawn's decision to focus on the Electric Slide was a good one.

_____ **4.** To become proficient at the game, a lot of hours of practice had to be put in.

_____ **5.** Seated in the restaurant, both the tabouli and the baba ghanoush looked delicious.

Correcting Dangling Modifiers

You can correct a dangling modifier in one of two ways.

1. Rewrite the sentence so that the introductory modifier logically refers to the subject of the sentence it introduces.

EXAMPLES

Nearly exhausted, **I** hoped the game was almost over.
(*I* was nearly exhausted.)

After studying all night, **Lucilla** passed the test easily.
(*Lucilla* studied all night.)

To impress his new girlfriend, **Dominic** polished his Chevrolet.
(*Dominic* wanted to impress his girlfriend.)

2. Change the introductory phrase to a clause.

EXAMPLES

Because I was nearly exhausted, I hoped the game was almost over.

After Lucilla had studied all night, she passed the test easily.

Dominic wanted to impress his girlfriend, so he polished his Chevrolet.

NOTE: Do not correct a dangling modifier by moving it to the end of the sentence or by adding a possessive noun or pronoun to a sentence. In either case, it will still "dangle" because it lacks a **doer** or **agent** that could perform the action of the modifier.

EXAMPLES

(incorrect)	After searching for three weeks, the lost watch was finally found. (There is no doer for *searching*.)
(still incorrect)	The lost watch was finally found **after searching for three weeks.** (There still is no logical doer.)
(still incorrect)	After searching for three weeks, Alfredo's lost watch was finally found. (Adding the possessive form *Alfredo's* does not add a doer of the action.)
(correct)	After searching for three weeks, Alfredo finally found his watch. (The noun *Alfredo* can logically perform the action—*searching*—of the modifying phrase.)
(correct)	**After Alfredo had searched for three weeks,** he finally found his watch. (Here again, the doer of the action is clear.)

PRACTICE

Underline and correct any dangling modifiers in the following sentences. Some of the sentences may be correct.

1. Delighted by the victory, the champagne and caviar were quickly

consumed.

Delighted by the victory, the coach and her team quickly

consumed the champagne and caviar.

2. Disappointed by his 3,098th failure, the rock of Sisyphus rolled back down the hill.

   _____

   _____

3. After drinking the magic potion, his expectations were disappointed.

   _____

   _____

4. To make his ideas clear, Plato decided on the cave metaphor.

   _____

   _____

5. Examining their hearts, the lives of the newly dead were judged by Osiris.

   _____

   _____

6. Concerned about missing the bus, Fatima's running speed increased considerably.

   _____

   _____

7. To balance the stone at the top of the hill, it was secured with duct tape by Sisyphus.

   _____

   _____

8. Huffing and puffing up the stairs, the Eiffel Tower still seemed high.

_____

_____

9. Orbited by sixty-two moons, the speed of wind on Saturn can be as fast as

1,100 miles per hour.

_____

_____

10. To survive in the Kalahari Desert, ostrich egg shells were used by the San

people as water containers.

_____

_____

Section Three Review

1. A **misplaced modifier** is a modifier that has been mistakenly placed so that it causes the reader to be confused about what it modifies.

2. Commonly misplaced words are *only, almost, just, merely,* and *nearly.*

3. Place modifying phrases and clauses so that they clearly refer to a specific word in a sentence.

4. A **dangling modifier** is an introductory phrase (usually a verbal phrase) that lacks an appropriate word to modify. Since these modifiers usually represent some sort of action, they need a **doer** or **agent** of the action represented.

5. You can correct a dangling modifier in one of two ways.

    a. Rewrite the sentence so that the introductory modifier logically refers to the subject of the sentence it introduces.

    b. Change the introductory phrase to a clause.

6. Do not correct a dangling modifier by moving it to the end of the sentence or by adding a possessive noun or pronoun.

Exercise 3A

A. Underline and correct any misplaced words in the following sentences. Some sentences may be correct.

1. After <u>nearly</u> chasing Trigger for four hours, Roy was almost out of breath.

   After chasing Trigger for nearly four hours, Roy was

   almost out of breath.

2. Richard merely noticed that one of his five hundred books was missing.

3. Though we only invited ten people to dinner, we cooked as if thirty might come.

4. We decided to stay at the beach a little longer because just the sun was beginning to set.

5. When Priyanka noticed that the desert was delicious, she almost ate a pound of it.

B. Underline and correct any misplaced phrases or clauses in the following sentences. Some of the sentences may be correct.

6. As Elise sat down in the bus, she looked over at the man in the next seat <u>with the huge ears</u>.

   As Elise sat down in the bus, she looked over at the

   man with the huge ears in the next seat.

continued

7. Percival found the grail but failed to ask the right question that everyone was looking for.

   _____

   _____

8. The basketball players became frustrated as they watched the game sitting on the bench.

   _____

   _____

9. The taxi driver saw the police officer stop a jaywalker who had just written him a ticket

   for speeding.

   _____

   _____

10. Sundiata knew that he would be able to uproot the tree aware of his growing strength.

    _____

    _____

C. Underline and correct any dangling modifiers in the following sentences. Some of the sentences may be correct.

11. <u>Angered by the booing of the fans,</u> bats and helmets came flying out of the Dodger

    dugout.

    Angered by the booing of the fans, the Dodger players threw bats and helmets

    out of the dugout.

    _____

Exercise 3A

continued

12. After leaving class, deposit the plastic bottles in the recycling bin.

_____

_____

13. Visiting Graceland for the tenth time, Homer's belief that Elvis was still alive grew even stronger.

_____

_____

14. To purchase the new software for my iMac, a trip to the Apple website is required.

_____

_____

15. Visiting the island, Prospero's hope was for a brave new world.

_____

_____

Exercise 3B

Underline and correct any misplaced or dangling modifiers in the following sentences. Some of the sentences may be correct.

1. <u>Before leaving for their cross-country trip,</u> the silver was placed in their safety deposit box.

   Before leaving for their cross-country trip, the McDonalds put their silver in their safety deposit box.

2. Rob barbecued the yellowtail and then took a drink from a bottle of Gatorade that he had caught on his fishing trip.

   _____

   _____

3. Marley wagged his tail and looked up lovingly at his master hanging his tongue out.

   _____

   _____

4. Drinking the cup of hemlock, Socrates accepted the verdict of the Athenian jury.

   _____

   _____

5. Although Peter Piper had hoped to pick a bushel of pickled peppers, he merely picked a peck of them.

   _____

   _____

6. A grizzly bear stood on its hind legs with yellow fangs and roared at us.

   _____

   _____

Exercise 3B

continued

7. Sherrie only asks her daughter to change the cat litter if the stink becomes too extreme.

_____

_____

8. After memorizing the manual for your new laptop, send me your apology by e-mail.

_____

_____

9. The bodybuilder stopped to look at the Monarch butterfly lifting weights in his backyard.

_____

_____

10. Refusing to give up her seat, Rosa Parks's actions helped start the civil rights movement of the 1950s and 1960s.

_____

_____

11. Diana gave the cute rabbit to her favorite wood nymph that she had found nesting in her garage.

_____

_____

12. To get to the cabin, you only need to follow a few simple directions.

_____

_____

13. Intrigued by her coy smile, the *Mona Lisa* is viewed by thousands of tourists every year.

_____

_____

continued

14. Bruno almost had given away all of his gold chains before he realized how valuable they were.

_____

_____

15. Armand drove his new Italian sports car wearing a red beret to his French girlfriend's house to impress her.

_____

_____

Exercise 3C

Correct any dangling or misplaced modifiers in the following paragraph.

1. My last trip to Germany <u>almost</u> was the best trip I have ever taken to that country because it acquainted me better with rural and small-town Germany. **2.** Taking day trips to small towns rather than to the big cities, my car took me through a lush, green countryside and along picturesque roads. **3.** Driving along quiet but well-paved country roads, a deep relaxation and calm came over me, and I wondered why I had not done this more often on previous trips.

4. One of the places I visited was Bad Bergzabern, a town of only 8,000 inhabitants. **5.** Like many German towns, this one has a "pedestrian zone," a central shopping and entertainment district that just allows pedestrians, not cars. **6.** Bustling with people out to shop, the town center's quaint old buildings created a charming atmosphere. **7.** All of the many street cafés almost were full with customers sipping coffee or eating cake. **8.** Gleiszellen-Gleishorbach was the next little town I visited neighboring Bad Bergzabern. **9.** Nestled among hills covered with vineyards, hiking is a favorite activity for tourists visiting this town. **10.** As in other towns in the region, there were many more cafés, restaurants, and stores than one would expect in a place that only has a few thousand inhabitants. **11.** These shops, cafés, and restaurants serve the needs of the local populace and tourists, who thus do not have to drive to the bigger cities, visiting from other parts of Germany, France, Austria, the Netherlands, and other neighboring countries.

12. Returning to the city of Kaiserslautern, where I was staying, a stop at Annweiler proved to be a good idea. **13.** The little town sits just below the ruin founded approximately 1,200 years ago of a fortress. **14.** To walk around in the old part of town, several bridges had to be crossed because a river flows through the middle of town. **15.** The three- to four-story buildings built directly along the river were nicely renovated to modern standards and, though they stood in the river, had been preserved for centuries. **16.** The old watermills just had been restored recently and were now used to generate electricity. **17.** At the end of the day, having visited several towns, my appreciation for the southwestern part of Germany had increased considerably.

Sentence Practice: Using Participial and Infinitive Phrases, Appositives, and Adjective Clauses

In this chapter, you have become aware of the many choices you have when you want to modify words in your sentences. Your options range from single-word modifiers to modifying phrases to subordinate clauses. Let's explore some of the possibilities with the following sentence.

> The beautiful dalmatian looked hungrily at the thick steaks cooking on the grill and quietly begged the chef for a bite.

By changing various modifiers, you can express the sentence in several other ways. For instance, *The beautiful dalmatian,* with its single-word modifier *beautiful* describing *dalmatian,* could be changed into an appositive.

> The dog, **a beautiful dalmatian,** looked hungrily at the thick steaks cooking on the grill and quietly begged the chef for a bite.

This version tends to emphasize the beauty of the dog.

If you change the part of the sentence that contains the verb *looked* to a present participial phrase, you will get a different effect.

> **Looking hungrily at the thick steaks cooking on the grill,** the beautiful dalmatian quietly begged the chef for a bite.

This version places a bit more emphasis on the dog's hungry look.

Another alternative is to change the present participial phrase *cooking on the grill* to an adjective clause.

> The beautiful dalmatian looked hungrily at the thick steaks **that were cooking on the grill** and quietly begged the chef for a bite.

As you can see, the choices are many, and good writers often try several versions of a sentence before deciding on the one that best expresses their ideas. Experimenting with your sentences in this way is part of the fun and the challenge of writing.

The exercises in this section are designed to give you practice in using various types of modifiers when you compose your sentences.

Sentence Combining Exercises

Using your knowledge of modifying phrases and clauses, combine the following lists of sentences according to the directions. Avoid dangling and misplaced modifiers. Add commas where necessary.

EXAMPLE   Combine these sentences into one sentence. Use sentence a as a present participial phrase. Use sentence b as an appositive.

   a. Elvira hoped to win the Los Angeles Marathon.
   b. Elvira is a world-class runner.
   c. Elvira practiced running on the sand dunes.
   d. The sand dunes were in the deserts of Southern California.

Hoping to win the Los Angeles Marathon, Elvira, a world-class runner, practiced running on the sand dunes in the deserts of Southern California.

1. Combine the following sentences into one sentence. Use sentence a as an appositive. Use sentence c as an adjective clause.

   a. Tinnitus is a constant ringing sensation in the ear.
   b. Tinnitus is the result of a disturbed auditory nerve.
   c. The auditory nerve sends sound signals to the brain.

   _____

   _____

   _____

2. Combine the following sentences into one sentence. Use sentence a as a present participial phrase. Use sentence c as an adjective clause.

   a. Halley's comet passes close to the earth every seventy-six years.
   b. Halley's comet is a ball of rock and ice.
   c. Halley's comet has been recorded by historians since 240 BCE.

   _____

   _____

   _____

Sentence Combining Exercises

continued

3. Combine the following sentences into one sentence. Use sentence a as an appositive. Use sentence c as an appositive. Use sentence d as an adjective clause. Use sentence e as an adverb clause.

   a. "The real McCoy" is an expression meaning "the real thing."
   b. "The real McCoy" most likely comes from Kid McCoy.
   c. Kid McCoy was the welterweight champion boxer in 1898.
   d. He started to call himself Kid "the Real" McCoy.
   e. He called himself Kid "the Real" McCoy because he had so many imitators.

   _____

   _____

   _____

4. Combine these sentences into one sentence. Use sentence c as an appositive. Use sentence d as a present participial phrase.

   a. All cultures play the flute.
   b. These cultures are on almost all continents.
   c. It is a wind instrument carved out of wood.
   d. Those continents include Africa, Asia, Europe, North and South America, and Australia.

   _____

   _____

   _____

5. Combine the following sentences into one sentence. Use sentence b as an adjective clause. Use sentence c as an introductory adverb clause.

   a. Percussion instruments can be found everywhere in the world as well.
   b. They can be made from almost any hard natural material.
   c. Percussion enables dancing, communication, and self-expression.

   _____

   _____

   _____

Sentence Combining Exercises

continued

6. Combine the following sentences into one sentence. Use sentence a as an introductory infinitive phrase. Use sentence b as an adjective clause. Use sentence c as an adverb clause. Add sentence d as another main clause.

   a. When one wants to play percussion, one has to invest a lot of time.
   b. Playing percussion is more difficult than many people think.
   c. Each percussion instrument requires a proper technique.
   d. It takes some time to internalize that technique.

   _____

   _____

   _____

7. Combine the following sentences into one sentence. Use sentence c as an appositive phrase. Use sentence d as an adjective clause.

   a. Gamelan music is highly complex.
   b. Gamelan music comes from Indonesia.
   c. Gamelan is a rhythmic music utilizing a variety of percussion instruments.
   d. Indonesia is a country in Southeast Asia.
   e. Gamelan music is deeply rooted in Indonesian culture.

   _____

   _____

   _____

8. Combine the following sentences into one sentence. Use sentence a as an introductory past participial phrase. Combine sentences c and d into one adjective clause.

   a. Africa is known for its many different kinds of drums.
   b. Africa has some of the most developed rhythmic traditions.
   c. These traditions vary from region to region.
   d. These traditions are difficult to learn.

   _____

   _____

   _____

Sentence Combining Exercises

continued

9. Combine these sentences into one sentence. Use sentence a as an infinitive phrase. Use sentence c as an adjective clause.

a. One can illustrate the difficulty of African drumming.
b. One can turn to the talking drum.
c. The talking drum originated in West Africa.
d. The talking drum can be held and squeezed in such a way that its sounds resemble words, phrases, and melodies.

_____

_____

_____

10. Combine the following sentences into one sentence. Use sentence a as an introductory prepositional phrase. Use sentence c as a present participial phrase.

a. It is played in Ghana, Mali, Nigeria, Senegal, and other West African countries.
b. The talking drum is often used in African pop music.
c. African pop music is playing on many radio stations today.
d. Some of these radio stations are in the United States.
e. One finds such stations especially in college towns and large cities.

_____

_____

_____

Essay and Paragraph Practice: Using Examples

Assignment

In the first two chapters of this text, you have written paragraphs about an event and a place. Such writing is usually called "narrative" or "descriptive" because it either narrates (tells about) an event or describes a place. In this chapter you will write an **expository** paragraph or essay (your instructor will decide which one). Expository writing **explains** a topic or idea to a reader, or it **informs** the reader about a topic or idea. Expository writing is not all that different from narrative writing: like a narrative, an expository piece of writing also has a beginning, a middle, and an ending. Thus, exposition and story telling are more closely related to one another than many people think. The topic of an expository paragraph or essay can range from explaining how to conduct an experiment in chemistry to analyzing the causes of World War II. In fact, most of the writing you will do in college classes will be expository.

One common type of expository writing is the paragraph or essay that relies on examples to make its point. If you look at Exercises 1D (page 164), 2D (page 177), and 3C (page 194) of Chapter Three you will see that they all rely on examples to support the statements made in the topic sentences. Exercise 1D gives examples of cities that have honored Jackie Robinson. Exercise 2D gives examples of English words that are drawn from mythology. And Exercise 3C gives examples of small towns in Germany.

Supporting your ideas with examples is a powerful way to help your readers understand your point. Examples allow your readers to see your topic at work in real-life situations, and they show your readers that your topic is based on reality. Of course, examples are also important when you take tests. Your ability to back up general answers with specific examples can show an instructor that you have understood and mastered the material you have been studying.

For this chapter, your assignment is to write a paper that uses several *specific examples* to support a statement made in a topic sentence or a thesis statement. Develop your paper from one of the following prewriting suggestions or from an idea suggested by your instructor.

Prewriting to Generate Ideas

Whether you are writing a paragraph or an essay, the prewriting techniques are the same. Use freewriting, brainstorming, and clustering to develop ideas from the topic suggestions that follow. Look for topics that you can illustrate with specific, detailed examples of your own.

Prewriting Application: Finding Your Topic

Read the following topic suggestions before you begin to prewrite. Not all of them will apply to you. Find the suggestions that interest you the most and then spend five or ten minutes freewriting on each of them. Try not to settle for a topic that seems only mildly interesting. Instead, look for that "Aha!" experience, the emotional reaction that identifies a topic that really moves you.

1. Give examples of *one* particular personality characteristic of your own. Are you a hard-working, "Type A" personality? Do you overeat when you experience stress, anger, or boredom? Are you sometimes too outspoken? Are you overly impulsive? Choose <u>one</u> personality characteristic of your own and illustrate it with examples.

2. Select one specific behavior that you admire and then give examples of incidents of people engaging in that behavior. You could describe acts of generosity, courage, selflessness, or any other behavior you find admirable.

3. Have you ever found that at times telling a lie is the ethical, responsible thing to do? Have you ever told a lie to protect someone from danger or from unnecessary pain? Use specific examples to illustrate times when lying seemed to you to be the correct, responsible behavior.

4. Take any simple statement that you know to be true and illustrate it with specific examples. Consider ideas like these:

   The fact that a restaurant is expensive does not guarantee that the food served there is good.

   Not getting enough sleep tends to lead to problems.

   Driving a car seems to bring out the worst in some people.

   The Sun City Senior Center is full of people who have led exciting, adventurous lives.

   If one spends time around animals, one recognizes that they, too, have personalities.

5. Have you ever experienced intolerance or bigotry because of your race, gender, religious beliefs, or age? Write a paper in which you use specific examples to illustrate what has happened to you.

6. People sometimes say that the simplest things in life are the most valuable. If you agree, use specific examples to illustrate the truth of that statement in your own life.

7. Think of a road trip or a vacation you have taken and focus on a specific location or experience on that trip or vacation. Give examples of what made that location or experience memorable.

8. What makes a piece of music, an artwork, or a book good? Choose one specific piece of music, book, or artwork and give examples of why you think it is good.

9. Choose a statement that people commonly believe to be true and use examples to show why it is or is not true in your life. Here are some examples:

Good and bad things always happen in threes.

Sometimes help can come from the most unlikely places.

You can become anything you want.

Friends and money do not mix.

10. Choose a technological device—smartphones, laptops, tablets, i-Pods, and so on—and use examples to illustrate how that device is changing how people relate to one another.

Choosing and Narrowing the Topic

As you choose your topic, remember that a more specific focus will result in a better paper than a more general focus. For example, don't try to give examples of a topic as general as *problems in the United States*. There are hundreds of possible examples of such a general topic, so all you would be able to do is briefly list a few of them, without going into detail about any. On the other hand, a more focused topic, such as *problems caused by my father's excessive drinking*, could certainly be supported by several detailed, descriptive examples.

Writing a Topic Sentence

If your assignment is to write a single paragraph, use your prewriting to decide upon a narrowed topic and a limited central point. Then write a topic sentence that can be supported with examples. Examine your topic sentence closely. Not all statements suggest that examples will follow. Consider the following sentences. Which would cause a reader to expect examples as support? Which would not?

EXAMPLES

1. Last summer I had a chance to visit Toronto, Canada.

2. Many people on the corner of Queen and Peter Streets in Toronto, Canada, looked as if they had stepped directly out of the 1960s.

Sentence 1 merely states a fact. It does not cause one to expect examples. Sentence 2 would cause a reader to expect examples of the people on Queen and Peter Streets.

EXAMPLES

3. Some of my best friends today used to be some of my worst enemies.

4. One of my best friends recently made a very unwise decision.

Sentence 3 causes one to expect examples of friends who used to be enemies. Sentence 4 would cause a reader to expect an explanation of the decision and why it was unwise, but it does not suggest that several examples will follow.

Prewriting Application: Working with Topic Sentences

Identify the topic sentences in Exercises 1D (page 164), 2D (page 177), and 3C (page 194). Then identify the topic and the central point in each topic sentence.

Prewriting Application: Evaluating Topic Sentences

Write "No" before each sentence that would not make a good topic sentence *for this assignment*. Write "Yes" before each sentence that would make a good one. Using ideas of your own, rewrite the unacceptable topic sentences into topic sentences that might work.

_____ **1.** I have many different personality characteristics.

_____

_____

_____ **2.** Laptops are very convenient, but visit any coffee shop and you will see that laptops also build walls between people.

_____

_____

_____ **3.** I have lent money to a lot of people, and they are still my friends.

_____

_____

_____ **4.** One reason that some of Prince's music is so good is that it does not merely follow popular trends.

_____

_____

_____ **5.** After having had a dog for several years, I realize that my dog has trained me far better than I have trained him.

_____

_____

_____ **6.** Whenever I go to a garage sale or a swap meet, I end up buying some absolutely useless item.

_____

_____

_____ **7.** My paragraph is about why Idaho holds such pleasant memories for so many people.

_____

_____

_____

_____ **8.** One sees a lot of bad drivers on the road these days.

_____

_____

_____ **9.** Our country is a wonderful place to live, but it has many serious problems that need to be resolved.

_____

_____

_____ **10.** My father believes that we should never lie, but sometimes his honesty is so painful it is almost cruel.

_____

_____

Prewriting Application: Talking to Others

Once you have decided on a topic and a preliminary topic sentence, you need to develop your examples. A good way to do so is to tell three or four other members of your class why your topic sentence is true. Think of yourself as an attorney before a jury. You must provide the evidence—the examples—to support the central idea in your topic sentence.

For example, if your topic is that your father's honesty borders on cruelty, convince the other people in your group with brief, specific examples. Consider these questions as you discuss your topics.

1. Exactly where and when does each example occur? Have the place and time of each instance been clearly identified?

2. Can you visualize the examples? Are the people mentioned in the example identified by name or by relationship? Are physical features specifically named or described?

3. What point do these examples reveal? Should the topic sentence be revised to express that point more clearly?

4. Are you convinced? Have enough examples been provided to illustrate the topic idea? Should any of the examples be more convincing?

5. Which example should be used first in the paper? Last?

Organizing Examples

Examples can be organized a number of ways. Sometimes a **chronological order** is best, arranging examples according to *when* they occurred. Sometimes a **spatial order** would work well, arranging examples by *physical location*. Many times an **emphatic order** should be used, arranging examples from *least to most important* (or, sometimes, from most to least important).

Prewriting Application: Organizing Examples

First, arrange the following examples in chronological order, numbering them 1, 2, 3, 4, 5. Next, arrange them in spatial order. Finally, arrange them in emphatic order. If you prefer one arrangement over another, explain why.

Topic Sentence: My father thinks that the junk items he buys at swap meets and garage sales make terrific household decorations.

_____ He bought a warped wooden tennis racket a few months ago for five dollars and nailed it above our front door. He thinks it makes our house look "sporty."

_____ On the hallway wall is a cuckoo clock that he bought last Saturday. The bird is missing one of its wings, and the clock will not keep correct time anymore. He thought it was a real bargain because he got the clock for one dollar.

_____ Upstairs in our guest bedroom is a faded velvet picture of Elvis Presley and another one of some dogs playing poker. He bought them last year for ten dollars each.

——————— When we used to live in Big Bear, California, he spent $75 for a huge moth-eaten moose head that turned out to be crawling with bugs that infested our whole house. It's now mounted over the fireplace in the living room.

——————— Two plastic pink flamingos are stuck into our front lawn. Dad bought them the weekend we moved into this house. He says they add "character" to our home.

Writing the Paragraph

Write the first draft of your paragraph. Your first sentence should be your preliminary topic sentence. After writing the topic sentence, write the examples that illustrate your point. Devote several sentences to each example and be as specific and as detailed as you can in each of those sentences.

Using Transitions

Transitions are words, phrases, or clauses that let the reader know when you are moving from one idea or example to another. They are essential for clear writing because they help your readers follow your train of thought. Since you will be writing several examples in one paragraph for this assignment, you need to let your readers know when one example has ended and another is beginning. Use common transitional phrases such as those below to introduce each new example:

for example   to illustrate
for instance   another example of

Notice how transitional words and phrases are used to introduce examples in Exercise 2D, page 177.

EXAMPLES **For example,** the names of several of our weekdays—Tuesday, Wednesday, Thursday, and Friday—derive from Norse mythology.

Other common words derive from Greek mythology.

For instance, the word *tantalize* refers to Tantalus, who was a king condemned to Hades as a punishment for his crimes.

Finally, Roman mythology, which in many ways parallels Greek mythology, is another source of many English words.

For example, the month of January is named after Janus, the Roman god with two faces.

Writing Application: Identifying Transitional Sentences

Examine Exercises 1D (page 164) and 3C (page 194). In each paragraph, identify the transitions that introduce each example.

Rewriting and Improving the Paragraph

1. Once your first draft is complete, read it over to determine how you can improve the examples you have used. In particular, try to make the examples as specific and as concrete as you can. Use actual names of people and places and refer to specific details whenever possible.

2. As you read your draft, make sure you can tell where each of your examples ends and the next begins. Revise your transitional sentences as needed to make them clearer.

3. If your preliminary topic sentence can be improved so that it more accurately states the central point of your paragraph, change it now.

4. Examine your draft for sentences that can be combined using participial phrases, appositives, infinitive phrases, or adjective clauses. Combine such sentences the way you did in the Sentence Combining Exercises.

Rewriting Application: Responding to Writing

Read the following paragraph. Then respond to the questions following it.

I Enjoy H_2O to Relax

Whenever I feel stressed, I find that I can relax best if I am near the water. For example, as a teenager living in San Bernardino, I would drive many miles into the local foothills of the mountains, where a small river or a large stream called Lytle Creek was located in the little town of Applewhite. I would walk down between the trees and then over all of the rocks to find a place where I would sit for hours. I enjoyed watching the water rush by because it made me become very relaxed. Then, in the late 1980s, I moved to San Diego County. My first apartment was in Escondido, and times were troubled and stressful nearly every day, yet I was able to find comfort by driving to Lake Dixon. After several weekend trips I began taking this drive at all different times of the week. Usually alone, but sometimes with my boys, I would go to the lake and feed the ducks or just fish from the shore. Now, living in San Marcos, I prefer the ultimate water

---

experience by relaxing at the beach. During most of my quick trips, I drive down Del Dios Highway and across the railroad tracks into Solana Beach parking lot. I walk down the large ramp and sit on the sand or walk along the shoreline to the cave. Watching the water really washes away any troubles that I brought with me. It seems to clear my head and to bring a warm feeling of contentment to my soul. In conclusion, no matter whether the water is a stream, lake, or ocean, its appearance and its soothing sounds take away all of my stress and troubles.

1. Identify the topic sentence. State its topic and central idea. Is it an effective topic sentence? Why or why not?

2. Identify the transitional sentences that introduce each example.

3. Are the examples specific? Point out which words in each example identify specific places or things.

4. Which words in each example would you make still more specific?

5. Which example is the most effective? Why? Which one would you improve? How?

Proofreading

Before you do the final editing of your paper, revise it one more time. If the topic sentence needs work, improve it now. Check the examples. Are they as specific and descriptive as they can be? Add transitional sentences between examples. Wherever you can, combine related sentences using subordinate clauses as well as participial and infinitive phrases.

Now edit the paper. Check your draft for any of the following errors:

- Sentence fragments
- Comma splices
- Fused sentences
- Misplaced modifiers
- Dangling modifiers
- Misspelled words

Prepare a clean final draft, following the format your instructor has requested. Before you turn in your final draft, proofread it carefully and make any necessary corrections.

Moving from Paragraph to Essay

All of the assignments so far have asked you to write single paragraphs, but most college classes will ask you to produce essays consisting of several paragraphs.

Writing an essay is not really much different from writing a paragraph. An essay focuses on and develops one central idea, just as a paragraph does. The central idea of an essay is called its **thesis statement**.

The main difference between an essay and a paragraph is that the supporting material in an essay is longer and more complicated, so it needs to be separated into different body paragraphs, each with its own **topic sentence.**

Recognizing Essay Form

An essay consists of an introductory paragraph, one or more body paragraphs, and a concluding paragraph.

- The *introductory paragraph* includes the **thesis statement** (usually as the last sentence of the first paragraph).

- Each *body paragraph* starts with a **topic sentence** that supports the thesis statement. The central idea of each body paragraph is supported with **facts, examples, and details.**

- The *concluding paragraph* brings the essay to a close, often by restating the central idea of the essay.

Introductory Paragraph

Introductory sentences
ending with a
thesis statement

Body Paragraphs

Topic sentence
supported with
facts, examples, and details

Topic sentence
supported with
facts, examples, and details

> **Topic sentence**
>
> supported with
>
> facts, examples, and details

Concluding Paragraphs

> Concluding sentences
>
> bringing the essay
>
> to a close

Choosing and Narrowing a Thesis Statement

A **thesis statement** states the topic and the central idea of an entire essay, just as a topic sentence states the topic and central idea of a paragraph. Like a topic sentence, a thesis statement needs to be narrowed and focused so that it does not try to cover too much material in a short essay.

Consider the following sentences. Which is narrowed enough to function as a thesis statement in a brief essay?

EXAMPLES

1. Many people have problems when they move to a new place.

2. Immigrants face many obstacles when they move to the United States.

3. Immigrants who do not yet speak English will encounter several obstacles when they try to get a job in the United States.

Sentence 1 is much too broad for any essay. Both sentences 2 and 3 could work as thesis statements, but sentence 3 will work better in a brief essay because it is narrowed to the topic of *Immigrants who do not yet speak English,* and its central point is focused on *obstacles when they try to get a job.* An essay with this thesis statement would devote a separate body paragraph to each obstacle to getting a job. Each body paragraph would then include examples of one or more immigrants who encountered that obstacle.

Writing the Essay

An essay takes more time to write than a paragraph, but the writing process itself is very similar.

- Generate topic ideas as well as supporting material by freewriting, brainstorming, and clustering.

- Focus your material on one central idea, expressed in a thesis statement.

- Divide your supporting material (examples, facts, details) into separate body paragraphs.

- Arrange your body paragraphs into a logical order, such as a chronological, spatial, or emphatic order.

- Write your first draft without worrying too much about the quality of your writing. Focus more on getting your ideas onto paper. You can improve them later.

Rewriting and Improving the Essay

Once you have a complete draft, consider these questions as you revise your paper.

- Do your opening sentences introduce the topic in a way that will interest a reader?

- Is your thesis sufficiently narrowed? Is it placed at the end of the introductory paragraph?

- Does each paragraph open with a topic sentence that clearly supports the thesis statement?

- Are the supporting facts and examples in each paragraph specific and clear?

- Does each paragraph contain enough examples?

- Are transitions used to move clearly from one idea to another?

- Does the conclusion close the essay in an interesting way?

Application: Working with Essay Form

Read the following student essay and answer the questions at the end.

Lying

My parents are two of the most honest people I have ever met. Ever since I can remember, they have told me that "Honesty is the best policy." My father says that lying leads only to more lying and that telling the truth is exactly the right thing to do. The problem is that I don't think they are right. There are times when the right thing to do is to tell a lie.

For example, sometimes lying can mean the difference between survival and disaster. I have a friend with two daughters, ages three and five. When her husband deserted her, she needed to find a job fast. But there was one problem. Every place where she applied asked if she had ever been convicted of a crime. She told the truth that she had been convicted of selling marijuana years ago, and she was politely shown out the door at Sears, Target, and Walmart. It didn't matter that she hasn't used drugs or alcohol now for over seven years. She needed to feed her children, so on her next job application she lied and got the job. I would have lied too.

Lying is also the right thing to do when you need to spare people any unnecessary pain in an emotional time. For instance, when I was in high school, a friend of mine named Melody died in a car accident, and the police believed drugs were involved. The parents refused to believe that their little girl would ever have taken drugs, but they didn't know everything about their daughter. Several of her friends and I knew that Melody had been using marijuana for a while. She had even tried cocaine a few times, but when her parents talked to us, we told them that she had never tried drugs. What good would telling the truth have done? It would only have hurt her parents more. So we lied.

I've also found that telling the truth can sometimes cause trouble among friends. There have been plenty of times when I have prevented a fight by not telling one friend what another one said about him or her. I've prevented these situations when I felt that the argument between the two was not worth fighting over.

I know that lying is not usually the right answer to a problem. But sometimes honesty isn't either. It seems to me that a person has to think about each situation and not live his or her life by general rules that don't always apply.

1. Underline the thesis statement. Is it sufficiently narrowed for a brief essay? Explain your response.

2. Now underline each topic sentence. Each topic sentence should clearly refer to and support the thesis statement. Explain how each one does so.

3. Look at the introductory sentences before the thesis statement. What function do they serve?

4. Look at the examples in each body paragraph. Which examples are the strongest? Why? Which are the weakest? Why?

5. Consider the organization of the three body paragraphs. Should it be changed at all? Explain why or why not.

6. Look at the concluding paragraph. Does it close the essay effectively? Why or why not?

Proofreading

As with all of your papers, proofread your essay carefully before you submit it.

I. Review of Chapters One and Two

A. In the following sentences, identify the underlined words by writing one of the following abbreviations above the words: noun (N), pronoun (Pro), verb (V), adjective (Adj), adverb (Adv), conjunction (Conj), or preposition (Prep).

1. I wish more restaurants <u>would</u> use Nutella instead of some cheap <u>substitute</u>.

2. The shoebill is a <u>unique</u> bird found <u>in</u> Uganda.

3. The <u>cloud</u> forests in Costa Rica grow on mountains that are almost <u>always</u> covered with clouds.

4. Many nurses work long hours, <u>yet</u> they need to fully concentrate <u>on</u> the job at hand.

5. A nurse <u>who</u> takes his or her job seriously knows that concentration and professionalism <u>are</u> necessary to avoid mistakes.

B. In the following sentences, underline the subjects once and the complete verbs twice. Put parentheses around all prepositional phrases.

6. Albert Einstein never liked his mathematics classes during his time in school.

7. Can Rafael Nadal or Roger Federer toss the ball to the umpire?

8. Captain Ahab came on deck and addressed his crew.

9. In our English classes, we study irregular verbs; however, linguists call them "strong" verbs.

10. After Thetis dipped her son in the river, she dried him with a towel.

C. Compose sentences of your own according to the instructions.

11. Write a simple sentence with one subject, two verbs, and at least one prepositional phrase.

_____

_____

12. Write a compound sentence. Use a coordinating conjunction and appropriate punctuation to join the two clauses.

_____

_____

continued

13. Write a complex sentence that starts with a subordinate clause. Use appropriate punctuation.

_____

_____

14. Write a complex sentence that uses the subordinator *who*.

_____

_____

15. Write a compound-complex sentence. Use the conjunction *yet* and the subordinator *after*.

_____

_____

D. Identify the following items as being correct (C), fused (F), comma splice (CS), or fragment (Frag). Then correct the errors. If a sentence is correct, do nothing to it.

_____ 16. The famous American writer John Updike died this year, appropriately, *The New Yorker* devoted an entire issue to him.

_____

_____

_____ 17. *Game of Thrones*, which is almost as good as *The Wire*.

_____

_____

_____ 18. When she looked into Krishna's mouth, she saw the entire universe.

_____

_____

continued

_____ **19.** There are many vampire movies, however, none is as good as Bram Stoker's novel *Dracula*.

_____

_____

_____ **20.** Ishmael was baffled he could not see the relationship between a coffee shop and *Moby Dick*.

_____

_____

II. Chapter Three

A. Underline all infinitive and participial phrases and circle the words that they modify.

1. Rounding the tip of South America, Magellan headed into the Pacific.

2. In celebration of his new position, Steve's wife and daughters bought a gift certificate to give to him after dinner.

3. During the Beijing Olympics, one could see many impressive buildings built for that event.

4. The student dancing in the hallway has just received a scholarship.

5. We have written a manual to accompany the new pool skimmer.

B. Add infinitive or participial phrases to the following sentences at the places indicated. Use the verbs in parentheses.

6. The treasure map ^ was almost impossible to read. (discover)

   _____

   _____

7. ^ Dr. Faustus signed the contract. (tremble)

   _____

   _____

8. The political ads ^ cost a great deal of money. (criticize)

   _____

   _____

9. Clyde thought that Bonnie's plan ^ was a good one. (steal)

   _____

   _____

10. ^ Serena knew she would be remembered as one of the greatest tennis players. (win)

    _____

    _____

continued

C. Underline the adjective clauses and appositives in the following sentences and circle the words they modify.

11. Fritz Perls, a famous psychotherapist, developed the concept of Gestalt therapy.

12. The diamond that she wore was mined in Namibia.

13. Cochise, who was a great Apache leader, resisted attempts to move his tribe from

Arizona to New Mexico.

14. Fernando realized he should not have used this particular stamp, a rare blue Mauritius.

15. *Slumdog Millionaire*, which was filmed in Mumbai, won an Oscar for best picture.

D. Add adjective clauses or appositives to the following sentences and punctuate them correctly.

16. August Wilson wrote many plays, and they were performed on many stages.

_____

_____

17. Mount Vesuvius has erupted many times since its lava and ash covered Pompeii.

_____

_____

18. DNA analysis has helped solve many crimes.

_____

_____

19. George Clooney reportedly hangs out with Brad Pitt and Angelina Jolie.

_____

_____

continued

20. Sophocles discussed his new play with his wife.

_____

_____

E. Underline and then correct any dangling or misplaced modifiers in the following sentences. Do nothing if a sentence is correct.

21. Marie was still thinking about the play and recommended it to her cousin that had

premiered last night.

_____

_____

22. When Tranh slammed the door, his anger was almost obvious to everyone in the room.

_____

_____

23. Digging deep into his demented memory, the crucial turning point came to The Joker.

_____

_____

24. To get from here to there, using an electronic navigation system is recommended.

_____

_____

25. Because of the divorce, she only sold the Porsche for one dollar.

_____

_____

continued

26. Hitting the snooze button one too many times, the test was missed.

_____

_____

27. Their oldest friend surprised Aisha and Luigi, showing up on their doorstep, who had already packed their suitcases.

_____

_____

28. Scratching his head in frustration, Aesop's imagination could not think of a tale to tell.

_____

_____

29. Writing letter after letter, Celie began to wonder whether she would ever hear from Nettie again.

_____

_____

30. A group of students who were talking to each other quietly approached their classroom.

_____

_____

Lining Up the Parts
of a Sentence

The Careful Writer

As you have probably already noticed, effective writing is less a matter of inspiration and more a matter of making innumerable choices and paying careful attention to detail. Strictly speaking, every word in each of your sentences represents a specific choice on your part. Good writers carefully choose words and their positions in sentences, not only to be grammatically correct but also to make their writing clear and concise.

Although close attention to detail alone will not ensure good writing, it does have a number of advantages. The most important reason for you to take care in your writing is to make certain that you communicate your ideas clearly. As you can see from having worked through the last chapter, if your sentences contain misplaced or dangling modifiers, your reader will sometimes be confused about what you mean. In addition, a clear and careful piece of writing in itself creates a good impression, just as a well-tended lawn does. You have probably already found that people are often judged by their writing. If your writing is carefully thought out and presented with an attention to correctness and detail, it will be taken seriously.

Making sure that your sentences are correctly constructed and checking to see that your modifiers clearly and logically modify the right words are two ways of taking care in your writing. In this chapter we will discuss a few others: paying attention to the special relationship between those two most important parts of your sentences, the subjects and verbs; making sure that the pronouns you use are in their correct forms; and checking the connection between your pronouns and the words they stand for.

Subject–Verb Agreement

One reason you need to be able to identify subjects and verbs accurately is that the form of the verb often changes to match the form of its subject. If the subject of your sentence is singular, your verb must indicate singular. If the subject is plural, your verb must indicate plural. This matching of the verb and its subject is called **subject–verb agreement.**

You need to pay special attention to subject–verb agreement when you use present tense verbs. **Most present tense verbs that have singular subjects end in "s." Most present tense verbs that have plural subjects do not end in "s."** Here are some examples.

Singular	*Plural*
The dog bark**s.**	The dogs bark.
He walk**s.**	They walk.
It i**s.**	They are.
The man ha**s.**	The men have.
She doe**s.**	They do.

Notice that in each case the verb ends in "s" when the subject is singular. This rule can be confusing because an "s" at the end of a <u>noun</u> almost always means that the noun is plural, but **an "s" at the end of a <u>verb</u> almost always means it is singular.**

👓 PRACTICE

Change the subjects and verbs in the following sentences from singular to plural or from plural to singular. You may need to add *a, an,* or *the* to some of the sentences.

1. In spring, my wisteria smells wonderful.

   In spring, my wisterias smell wonderful.

2. The toy poodle escapes from the yard nearly every day.

3. The goalie always blocks my shots.

4. Tim's text message infuriates his teachers every time.

5. Ahmed's answers are usually thoughtful.

Identifying Subjects: A Review

1. Make sure you accurately identify the subject. Sentences usually contain several nouns and pronouns.

EXAMPLE   The **boys** from the private **school** on the other **side** of **town** often use our **gymnasium.**

This sentence contains five nouns, but only *boys* is the subject.

2. Remember that a noun or pronoun that is part of a prepositional phrase cannot be the subject.

EXAMPLE   **Each** of the children takes a vitamin with breakfast.

The subject is *Each*, not *children*, because *children* is part of a prepositional phrase.

3. Indefinite pronouns can be subjects. The indefinite pronouns are listed on page 5.

EXAMPLE   **Everyone** sitting at the tables under the trees has a picnic lunch.

Subject–Verb Agreement: Points to Know

1. Two subjects joined by *and* are plural.

EXAMPLES
     S   S   V
The **boy** <u>and</u> his **dog were** far from home.

   S   S   V
Ham <u>and</u> **rye make** a delicious combination.

2. However, if a subject is modified by *each* or *every*, it is singular.

EXAMPLES
     S   S   V
<u>Every</u> **boy** and **girl** at the party <u>**was**</u> given a present to take home.

    S   S   V
<u>Each</u> **envelope** and **piece** of paper <u>**has**</u> the name of the company on it.

3. The following indefinite pronouns are singular.

EXAMPLES

anybody	either	neither	one
anyone	everybody	nobody	somebody
anything	everyone	no one	someone
each	everything	nothing	something

EXAMPLES

S   V

Each of the band members **has** a new uniform.

S   V

Everyone sitting under the trees **is** part of my family.

4. A few nouns and indefinite pronouns, such as *none, some, all, most, more, half,* or *part,* may sometimes be considered plural and sometimes singular, depending on the prepositional phrases that follow them. If the object of the preposition is singular, treat the subject and verb as singular. If the object of the preposition is plural, treat the subject and verb as plural.

EXAMPLES

                      S   V

(singular)   **None** of the cake **is** left.

                      S   V

(plural)   **None** of the people **are** here.

PRACTICE

Place an "S" above the subjects and underline the correct verb form in parentheses.

                           S   S

1. In the writing lab, a teacher and a student (was <u>were</u>) working on a piece of writing.

2. The marine always (enjoy enjoys) the packages that he receives from his mother.

3. Every firefighter and police officer in the city (has have) brought an item to the auction.

4. My professor and his assistant from the graduate school usually (arrive arrives) at the same time.

5. All of the sailors and officers in the submarine (was were) rescued.

6. Each glass bottle and plastic container (was were) recovered from the trash and recycled.

7. Somebody from one of our local schools (has have) won the prestigious

   Peacock scholarship.

8. The war's length and cost (have has) worried the citizens of that country.

9. A squirrel with two cats chasing it (was were) running down the street.

10. Few of the ants ever (escape escapes) that aardvark.

---

5. When subjects are joined by *or* or *nor,* the verb agrees with the closer subject. If one subject is singular and one is plural, place the plural subject closer to the verb to avoid awkwardness.

EXAMPLES

(singular subjects)

               S   S   V

Neither **Alberto** nor his **brother knows** what to do.

(plural subjects)

               S   S   V

Either the **actors** or the **screenwriters have decided** to strike.

(singular and plural subjects)

               S   S   V

Neither **Alberto** nor his **sisters were** at last night's concert.

NOTE: When you have helping verbs in a sentence, the helping verb—not the main verb—changes form.

EXAMPLES

HV   S   S   MV

Does Alberto or his **brother** want to go fishing?

HV   S   S   MV

Have the **actors** or **screenwriters** decided to strike?

6. Collective nouns usually take the singular form of the verb. Collective nouns represent groups of people or things, but they are considered singular. Here are some common collective nouns.

audience	crowd	herd
band	family	jury
class	flock	number
committee	government	society
company	group	team

EXAMPLES

          S   V

The **audience was** delighted when the curtain slowly rose to reveal the orchestra already seated.

          S   V

My **family goes** to Yellowstone National Park every summer.

7. The relative pronouns *that, which,* and *who* may be either singular or plural. When one of these pronouns is the subject of a verb, you will need to know which word it refers to before you decide whether it is singular or plural.

EXAMPLES

(singular)   I bought the <u>peach</u> **that was** ripe.

(plural)   I bought the <u>peaches</u> **that were** ripe.

(plural)   Colleen is one of the <u>students</u> **who are** taking flying lessons.

(singular)   Colleen is the only <u>one</u> of the students **who is** taking flying lessons.

PRACTICE   Place an "S" above the subjects and underline the correct verb forms in parentheses.

1. Neither the money nor my excuses for the accident (pleases / <u>please</u>)

   Mr. Hernandez.

2. A squad of soldiers (has / have) entered the village.

3. Rory is one of the dogs that (plays / play) Frisbee in the park every Sunday.

4. Neither Angelina nor her cousins (knows / know) that Madonna plans to

   adopt a child.

5. Her long wait for a raise or benefits (frustrates / frustrate) Josefina.

6. That crowd of people at the end of the pier (belongs / belong) to the Polar

   Bear Club.

7. That citizen from Liberty is the only person who gladly (pay / pays) taxes

   each year.

8. (Does / Do) Guinevere or Galahad regret what the two of them have done?

9. The speeches that Senator Cassius makes (impress / impresses) the people

   each time.

10. Carlos, among all of the other sailors, (was / were) chosen to find the

    left-handed pipe wrench.

8. A few nouns end in "s" but are usually considered singular; they take the singular form of the verb. These nouns include *economics, gymnastics, mathematics, measles, mumps, news, physics,* and *politics.*

EXAMPLES

                   S   V

World **economics** <u>has</u> been an important international issue for years.

     S   V

Gymnastics <u>is</u> one of the most popular events in the Olympics.

9. When units of measurement for distance, time, volume, height, weight, money, and so on are used as subjects, they take the singular verb form.

EXAMPLES

         S   V

Two **teaspoons** of sugar **was** all that the cake recipe called for.

     S   V

Five **dollars** **is** too much to pay for a hot dog.

10. In a question or in a sentence that begins with *there* or *here,* the order of the subject and verb is reversed.

EXAMPLES

    V   S

Was the **bus** on time?

    V   S

Is there a squeaking **wheel** out there somewhere?

       V   S

There **is** an **abundance** of wildflowers in the desert this spring.

      V   S

Here **are** the **keys** to your car.

11. The verb must agree only with the **subject**.

EXAMPLE

         S   V

Our biggest **problem** **is** termites in the attic.

The singular verb form *is* is correct here because the subject is the singular noun *problem.* The plural noun *termites* does not affect the form of the verb.

PRACTICE

Place an "S" above the subjects and underline the correct verb forms in parentheses.

      S

1. Mathematics (<u>remains</u> remain) one of the hardest subjects for students.

2. Ten ounces of sugar (is are) usually enough for a lemon icebox pie.

3. The subject of Miles's dissertation (was were) three obscure Croatian poets.

4. The news of Demeter's missing daughter (has have) cast a shadow across the land.

5. (Does Do) gymnastics interest Antonio as much as competitive ice fishing?

6. The committee for the abolishment of dangling modifiers (meet meets) Fridays.

7. Twenty-five dollars (is are) too much to pay for a bacon and cheese hamburger.

8. Here, alive and well fed, (is are) the two-headed horned toad and the legless lizard from the pet store down the street.

9. Esther's favorite hobby (requires require) paperclips and pots of glue.

10. Ten miles of unpaved road (lies lie) between my house and the beach.

Section One Review

1. In the present tense, when the subject is a singular noun or a singular pronoun, the verb form usually will end in "s."

2. Subject–verb agreement:

   a. Two subjects joined by *and* are plural.

   b. If a subject is modified by *each* or *every*, it is singular.

   c. Indefinite pronouns are usually singular.

   d. Sometimes indefinite pronouns like *some, half,* or *part* are considered plural, depending on the prepositional phrases that follow them.

   e. When subjects are joined by *or* or *nor,* the verb agrees with the closer subject. If one subject is singular and one is plural, place the plural subject closer to the verb to avoid awkwardness.

   f. When a collective noun, such as *family* or *group,* is the subject, the singular form of the verb is used.

   g. The relative pronouns *that, which,* and *who* may be either singular or plural, depending upon the word the pronoun refers to.

   h. A few nouns, such as *economics* or *news,* end in "s" but are usually considered singular.

   i. When the subject is a unit of measurement, such as distance, weight, or money, the singular form of the verb is used.

   j. In a question or in a sentence that begins with *there* or *here,* the verb will often come before the subject.

   k. The verb must agree only with the **subject.**

Exercise 1A

Circle the subjects and underline the correct verb forms in parentheses.

1. (Anyone) with plaid pants and pink shoes (<u>was</u> were) let into the golf tournament free.

2. Neither the police officer nor the two firefighters (knows know) what to do with the Cheshire cat in the tree.

3. Both his mother and his uncle (has have) been puzzled by Hamlet's behavior.

4. On the shore of the lake (stand stands) Okonkwo's wife and his children.

5. College mathematics taught by Dr. Jones (have has) continued to frustrate Sandy.

6. A trailer carrying several Volkswagens (sit sits) near the gas station.

7. Six hundred tons of wheat (was were) not enough to feed the victims of the drought.

8. A little pig with two of his friends (loves love) his new house of straw.

9. (Has Have) the jury voted on the damages that the company will pay for the lost pension funds?

10. Every lost boy and evil pirate in Neverland (enjoys enjoy) the stories that Wendy reads.

11. According to the report, high school gymnastics (cause causes) more injuries than football.

12. Anyone in the two villages who (live lives) in the path of the volcano will be relocated.

13. Two weeks with his daughter Regan (was were) too much for Lear and his men.

14. The wolf pack, consisting of an alpha male and various other wolves, (roam roams) in the upper part of Yellowstone Park.

15. Anyone at the proceedings (has have) the right to express an opinion.

Exercise 1B

Correct any subject–verb agreement errors in the following sentences. If a sentence is correct, do nothing to it. To check your answers, circle the subjects.

1. Neither (Horatio) nor (Fortinbras) ~~want~~ *wants* to clean up the mess.

2. By Friday, everyone in the class who have not completed the test will drop out.

3. Each mountain and river were surveyed by Lewis and Clark.

4. Women's rights in all areas of life is a major concern of the president's wife.

5. The winged statue with no head and the portrait of the woman with the enigmatic smile appears in the museum.

6. Mrs. Hutchinson is one of the villagers who supports the lottery.

7. A flock of Canada geese visit Yellowstone National Park each season.

8. Do either Cupid or Eros plan to attend the Valentine's Day party?

9. Romeo and his friend Mercutio hopes the Montagues will be at the party.

10. Benedict Arnold is one of the colonists who has secretly decided to support the British.

11. Wayne's reading group in the Twin Cities discusses books about the history of the automobile.

12. Pretty soon, anyone in the church who had not signed up for the lecture series were out of luck.

13. Two hundred yards of line connect Moby Dick and Ishmael's whaleboat.

14. Here is the sacred medal and the cape with symbols that you ordered.

15. Six pounds of hot chili peppers have been added to the hot sauce for our neighborhood block party.

Exercise 1C

Correct all subject–verb agreement errors. Not all sentences will contain errors.

1. One divorce in our family ~~have~~ *has* had many unpleasant consequences. 2. Everyone in my family, including my aunts and uncles, were affected when my grandparents decided to divorce. 3. One of the most glaring effects of their divorce are my grandparents' financial difficulties. 4. Now that the divorce is final, the assets that once belonged to both of them has been divided. 5. As a result, both my grandmother and my grandfather struggles to pay rent on separate apartments. 6. My grandmother, who hasn't worked in years, now work as a secretary for a realty company. 7. These financial problems causes bitterness between my grandmother and grandfather. 8. Another unfortunate result of their divorce are the many awkward situations at family get-togethers. 9. Today my grandmother won't even come to a family event if my grandfather plan to attend. 10. Without both of them there, everybody feel rather sad. 11. Finally, their divorce seem to have created dissension in the family. 12. When my grandparents argue, my grandfather always ask my mother and her brothers and sisters to agree with him. 13. If some of them takes the other side, he feels angry. 14. There has been many instances when he even yells at some of them. 15. Clearly, my grandparents' divorce have damaged our family. 16. I hope there is no future separations among my family members.

Pronoun Agreement and Reference

Pronoun–Antecedent Agreement

Because pronouns stand for or take the place of nouns, it is important that you make it clear in your writing which pronouns stand for which nouns. The noun that the pronoun takes the place of is called the **antecedent**. **Pronoun–antecedent agreement** refers to the idea that a pronoun must match or "agree with" the noun that it stands for in **person** and in **number**.

Person

Person in pronouns refers to the relationship of the speaker (or writer) to the pronoun. There are three persons: **first person**, **second person**, and **third person**.

1. **First person** pronouns refer to the person speaking or writing:

Singular	*Plural*
I	we
me	us
my, mine	our, ours

2. **Second person** pronouns refer to the person spoken or written to:

Singular	*Plural*
you	you
your	your
yours	yours

3. **Third person** pronouns refer to the person or thing spoken or written about:

Singular	*Plural*
he, she, it	they
him, her, it	them
his, her, hers, its	their, theirs

Because nouns are always in the third person, pronouns that refer to nouns should also be in the third person. Usually this rule poses no problem, but sometimes writers mistakenly shift from third to second person when they are referring to a noun.

EXAMPLE   When a new **student** first enters the large and crowded registration area, **you might** feel confused and intimidated.

In this sentence, *you* has mistakenly been used to refer to *student*. The mistake occurs because the noun *student* is in the third person, and the pronoun *you* is in the second person. There are two ways to correct the sentence:

1. You can change the second person pronoun *you* to a third person pronoun.

EXAMPLE   When a new **student** first enters the large and crowded registration area, **he or she** might feel confused and intimidated.

2. You can change the noun *student* to the second person pronoun *you*.

EXAMPLE   When **you** first enter the large and crowded registration area, **you** might feel confused and intimidated.

Here's another incorrect sentence.

EXAMPLE   Most **people** can stay reasonably healthy if **you** watch **your** diet and exercise several times a week.

One way to correct this sentence is to change *you* to *they* and *your* to *their* so that they agree with *people*.

EXAMPLE   Most **people** can stay reasonably healthy if **they** watch **their** diets and exercise several times a week.

PRACTICE   Correct any errors in pronoun person in the following sentences. When you correct the pronoun, you also may need to change the verb.

1. When a person first attends a college class, ~~you~~ *he or she* might feel nervous.

2. Many students feel anxious when facing your first orientation.

3. A student coming to a large campus for the first time should bring a parent or a friend if you want help registering.

4. When my daughter left home for her first class, you could see she was worried.

5. In a very short time, you will find that the campus becomes familiar.

Number

Errors in number are the most common pronoun–antecedent errors. To make pronouns agree with their antecedents in **number,** use singular pronouns to refer to singular nouns and plural pronouns to refer to plural nouns. The following guidelines will help you avoid errors in number.

1. Use plural pronouns to refer to words joined by *and* unless the words are modified by *each* or *every.*

@@ EXAMPLE   **General Ulysses S. Grant and General Dwight D. Eisenhower** led **their** armies to victory.

2. Use singular pronouns to refer the following indefinite pronouns.

anybody	either	neither	one
anyone	everybody	nobody	somebody
anything	everyone	no one	someone
each	everything	nothing	something

@@ EXAMPLES   **Everything** was in **its** place.

Neither of the girls wanted to give up **her** place in line.

One of the fathers was yelling loudly at **his** son throughout the game.

NOTE: In spoken English, the plural pronouns *they, them,* and *their* are often used to refer to the antecedents *everyone* or *everybody.* However, in written English, the singular pronoun is still more commonly used.

@@ EXAMPLE   **Everybody** at the game cheered for **his** or her favorite team.

3. In general, use singular pronouns to refer to collective nouns.

@@ EXAMPLE   The **troop** of soldiers had almost reached **its** camp when the blizzard started.

4. When antecedents are joined by *or* or *nor,* use a pronoun that agrees with the closer antecedent.

@@ EXAMPLE   Neither **Chris** nor **Craig** wanted to spend his Saturday mowing the lawn.

NOTE: If one antecedent is singular and one is plural, place the plural antecedent last to avoid awkwardness. If one antecedent is female and one is male, rewrite the sentence to avoid awkwardness.

⊙⊙ EXAMPLES   (awkward)   **Either the members of the council or the mayor will send his regrets.**

(rewritten)   **Either the mayor or the members of the council will send their regrets.**

(awkward)   **Either Mary or Ruben will lend you his watch.**

(rewritten)   **You may borrow a watch from either Mary or Ruben.**

⊙⊙ PRACTICE   Correct any pronoun–antecedent errors in the following sentences. When you correct a pronoun, you may also need to change the verb.

he or she needs

1. When a hiker comes upon a wolf in the wild, ~~you need~~ to stay very still and hope that the animal will just go on its way.

2. Somebody in one of the nearby condominiums plays their trumpet late into the evenings.

3. When parents read a story by the Brothers Grimm, you might scare your children.

4. The school with the Native American mascot was worried about having to change their team name.

5. Neither Galileo nor Copernicus could keep their eyes focused on the ground.

6. Someone with gray hair wants to read their poetry at the department meeting.

7. No one could tell us where the dog had misplaced its tail.

8. When a visitor plans to visit Yellowstone, you should check on the schedule for Old Faithful.

9. Either Croesus or the Rockefellers left their dinner plates in my sink.

10. One group of indigenous people in New Guinea burns all of their possessions at a certain time each year.

Sexist Language

In the past it was traditional to use masculine pronouns when referring to singular nouns whose gender could be either masculine or feminine. A good example is the sentence *A **person** should stop delivery of **his** newspaper before **he** leaves on a trip of more than a few days.* Although the noun *person* could be either masculine or feminine, masculine pronouns like *he* or *his* tended to be used in a case like this one.

Because women make up over 50 percent of the English-speaking population, they have been justifiably dissatisfied with this tradition. The problem is that the English language does not contain a singular personal pronoun that can refer to either sex at the same time in the way that the forms of *they* can.

The solutions to this problem can prove awkward. One of the solutions is to use feminine pronouns as freely as masculine ones to refer to singular nouns whose gender could be masculine or feminine. Either of the following sentences using this solution is acceptable.

EXAMPLES A **person** should stop delivery on **her** newspaper before **she** leaves on a trip of more than a few days.

A **person** should stop delivery on **his** newspaper before **he** leaves on a trip of more than a few days.

Another solution is to change *his* to *his or her* and *he* to *he or she*. Then the sentence would look like this:

EXAMPLE A **person** should stop delivery on **his or her** newspaper before **he or she** leaves on a trip of more than a few days.

As you can see, this solution does not result in a very graceful sentence. An alternative is to use *her/his* and *she/he*, but the result would be about the same. Sometimes a better solution is to change a singular antecedent to a plural one and use the forms of *they*, which can refer to either gender. That would result in a sentence like this:

EXAMPLE **People** should stop delivery of **their** newspapers before **they** leave on a trip of more than a few days.

This sentence is less awkward and just as fair. Finally, in some situations, the masculine pronoun alone will be appropriate, and in others the feminine pronoun alone will be. Here are two such sentences:

EXAMPLES Each of the hockey players threw **his** false teeth into the air after the victory. (The hockey team is known to be all male.)

The last runner on the relay team passed **her** opponent ten yards before the finish line. (All members of the relay team are female.)

Whatever your solutions to this problem, it is important that you be logical and correct in your pronoun–antecedent agreement in addition to being fair.

Unclear Pronoun Reference

Sometimes, even though a pronoun appears to agree with an antecedent, it is not clear exactly which noun in the sentence is the antecedent. And sometimes a writer will use a pronoun that does not clearly refer to any antecedent at all. The following two points will help you use pronouns correctly.

1. A pronoun should refer to a specific antecedent.

EXAMPLE **Mr. Mellon** told **Larry** that **he** could take a vacation in late August.

In this sentence, *he* could refer to *Mr. Mellon* or to *Larry*. To correct this problem, you can eliminate the pronoun.

EXAMPLE Mr. Mellon told Larry that **Larry** could take his vacation in late August.

Or you can revise the sentence so that the pronoun clearly refers to only one antecedent.

EXAMPLES Mr. Mellon told **Larry** to take **his** vacation in late August.

OR

Mr. Mellon told Larry, "Take your vacation in late August."

Here is another example:

EXAMPLE Every time **Patricia** looked at the **cat, she** whined.

In this sentence, the pronoun *she* could refer to *Patricia* or the *cat*. The pronoun reference needs to be clarified.

EXAMPLES **Patricia** whined every time **she** looked at the cat.

OR

The **cat** whined every time Patricia looked at **her**.

PRACTICE Revise the following sentences so that each pronoun refers to a specific antecedent.

1. Julio told his roommate that his new contact lenses were at the optometrist's office.

Julio said to his roommate, "Your new contact lenses are at the optometrist's office."

2. When Abbott was trying to explain to Costello the positions of the baseball players, he became very confused.

_____

_____

3. As Peyton Manning was showing the equipment manager how his uniform should be fitted, he seemed impatient.

_____

_____

4. When Jennifer Aniston discussed her new film with Meg Ryan, she offered her some good advice.

_____

_____

5. The famous archer shot an arrow through the apple on his son's head and then sold it on eBay.

_____

_____

---

2. <u>Pronouns should not refer to implied or unstated antecedents.</u> Be especially careful with the pronouns *this, that, which,* and *it.*

EXAMPLE   My baseball coach made us go without dinner if we lost a game; **this** was unfair.

In this sentence, there is no specific antecedent for the pronoun *this* to refer to. The following sentence clarifies the pronoun reference.

EXAMPLE   My baseball coach made us go without dinner if we lost a game; **this punishment** was unfair.

Sometimes a pronoun refers to a noun that is implied only in the first part of the sentence.

EXAMPLE   Mrs. Brovelli is a poet, **which** she does some of every day.

In this sentence, *which* apparently stands for "writing poetry," which is implied in the noun *poet*; however, there is no specific noun for the pronoun *which* to stand for. The faulty pronoun reference can be cleared up in several ways.

◎ EXAMPLES   Mrs. Brovelli is a poet, and **she writes** poetry every day.

Mrs. Brovelli is a poet **who writes** poetry every day.

◎ PRACTICE   Revise the following sentences so that each pronoun refers to a specific, not an implied or unstated, antecedent. To correct the sentence, you may have to eliminate the pronoun altogether.

1. I have always resisted learning how to serve oysters, which annoys my roommate.

   My resistance to learning how to serve oysters annoys

   my roommate.

2. The king shepherd barked all night when our neighbors were having a party, which made me call the police.

   _____

   _____

3. There were many pieces of glass on the kitchen floor, but Ibrahim had not broken it.

   _____

   _____

4. Rafiki was looking forward to watching the Padres play the Angels, but this wasn't what happened.

   _____

   _____

5. It rained all day Friday and then cleared up on Saturday, which ruined our plans.

   _____

   _____

Reflexive and Intensive Pronouns

The reflexive and intensive pronouns are those that end in *self* or *selves*. The singular pronouns end in *self,* and the plural ones end in *selves.*

Singular	*Plural*
myself	ourselves
yourself	yourselves
himself	themselves
herself	
itself	
oneself	

<u>These are the only reflexive and intensive forms.</u> Avoid nonstandard forms like *hisself, ourselfs, theirselves,* or *themselfs.*

The **reflexive pronouns** are used to reflect the action of a verb back to the subject.

@@ EXAMPLE Amos gave **himself** a bloody nose when he tried to slap a mosquito.

The **intensive pronouns** emphasize or intensify a noun or another pronoun in the sentence.

@@ EXAMPLE Let's have **Estella Cordova herself** show us how to cross-examine a witness in court.

To help you use intensive and reflexive pronouns correctly, remember these three points.

1. <u>Do not use a reflexive pronoun unless it is reflecting the action of a verb back to a subject.</u>

2. <u>Do not use an intensive pronoun unless the sentence contains a noun or pronoun for it to emphasize or intensify.</u>

3. <u>In general, do not use a reflexive or intensive pronoun where a personal pronoun is called for.</u> For example, reflexive and intensive pronouns are never used as subjects.

@@ EXAMPLES

(incorrect)	Tim's mother and **myself** often go shopping together on Saturdays.
(correct)	Tim's mother and **I** often go shopping together on Saturdays.
(incorrect)	The other employees at the restaurant gave Carmen and **myself** large bouquets of flowers on the anniversary of our first year there.
(correct)	The other employees of the restaurant gave Carmen and **me** large bouquets of flowers on the anniversary of our first year there.

⊚⊚ PRACTICE   Correct any errors in the use of reflexive or intensive pronouns in the following sentences.

                                          ourselves.

1. We decided to redecorate the den ~~ourself.~~

2. Lorenzo, a misanthrope, prefers to spend his days by hisself.

3. Several members of the congregation enjoyed theirselves as they discussed *The Hunger Games.*

4. Whenever Fergal and myself have time, we meet for lunch at the Market Street Café.

5. In Europe we entertained ourselfs by listening to the music of Miles and Thelonious.

⊚⊚ PRACTICE   Correct any errors in pronoun reference or in the use of reflexive and intensive pronouns in the following sentences.

                                    painting them

1. I used to paint landscapes, but I do not like ~~it~~ anymore.

2. Fergal wondered if his fellow teacher and hisself should return to Galway this summer.

3. My accountant filled in my tax return in pencil, and he took a large deduction for jelly doughnuts. This made the IRS suspicious.

4. Jose Luis apologized to his brother, but he still was still angry.

5. When Thor himself arrived at the scene, a bolt of lightning fell from the clouds.

6. She wanted to show her new painting in the gallery, but it was not ready.

7. Robert Hughes reviewed paintings by David Hockney and Patti Smith, which I did not enjoy.

8. The pope and one of the Vatican cardinals recently watched *The DaVinci Code,* but he did not appreciate it.

9. Bean stuck a peppermint stick in his nose and broke it.

10. Charlotte Brontë told Emily that Anne's new novel was not as well written as hers.

Section Two Review

1. The **antecedent** is the word a pronoun stands for.

2. A pronoun must agree with its **antecedent** in **person** and in **number.**

3. Use a plural pronoun to refer to antecedents joined by *and*.

4. Use a singular pronoun to refer to an **indefinite pronoun.**

5. Use a singular pronoun to refer to a **collective noun.**

6. When antecedents are joined by *or* or *nor*, use a pronoun that agrees with the closer antecedent.

7. Make sure a pronoun refers to a specific antecedent in its sentence or in the previous sentence.

8. Be sure that your pronoun does not refer to an implied or unstated antecedent.

9. A **reflexive pronoun** reflects the action of a verb back to the subject.

10. An **intensive pronoun** emphasizes or intensifies a noun or pronoun in the sentence.

11. Do not use a reflexive or intensive pronoun when a personal pronoun is called for.

Exercise 2A

Underline the correct pronouns in parentheses.

1. Ms. Pelican likes to watch the 11 o'clock news, but Mr. Pelican doesn't consider (<u>it</u>/them) interesting.

2. Everybody gripes about taking off (his or her / their) shoes at the airport.

3. The senator argued that his state would not be able to meet (its / their) obligation to care for the needy if the tax cuts passed.

4. Either the *Niña*, the *Pinta*, or the *Santa Maria* had used up all of (its/their) fresh water.

5. Anyone who wants a scholarship or grant should return (his or her / their) application as soon as possible.

6. Even though my brother offered to help, we decided to build the sand castle by (ourself/ ourselfs/ourselves).

7. If a driver sees another car attempting to merge onto a freeway, (you / he or she / they) should slow to allow the car room to merge.

8. Carly and her husband have two Priuses, but neither the 2010 model nor the 2013 one has achieved (its / their) advertised mileage.

9. Someone had told us that Mammoth Mountain was situated near a volcano, but we did not take (her/their) warning seriously.

10. As every viewer entered the theater, an usher handed (him or her / them) a program.

11. Icarus had tried to find a way out of the labyrinth by (hisself/himself) many times.

12. When a traveler passes the House of Usher, (you/he or she/they) should ignore the horrible shrieks coming from the second-story windows.

13. Mireya's laptop or her desktop computer will need (its / their) memory increased soon.

14. As the boat crossed the River Lethe, one of the passengers lost (his/their) memory.

15. Every American fencer's sword needed to have (its / their) tip adjusted at the end of the ceremony.

Exercise 2B

Correct all errors in pronoun usage in the following sentences. Do nothing if the sentence is correct.

1. As a visitor enters the hospital, ~~you~~ *he or she* should use the hand sanitizer.

2. When AIG offered large bonuses to their top-performing employees, the public was outraged.

3. Everyone in our small village casts their vote at the fire station.

4. A colony of beavers is doing their best to build a dam across Murrieta Creek.

5. Neither Pinocchio nor Cyrano knew if their nose would keep growing.

6. As contestants pass through the turnstyle, you are asked to turn off all cell phones.

7. Ashley and Conrad found theirselfs in complete darkness in the middle of a huge Walmart.

8. Lance Armstrong used to be considered a great cyclist, which is my favorite sport.

9. The volcanologist asked my brother and myself if we had ever heard of Pompeii.

10. Abel told Cain that his father was in big trouble.

11. The stock market fell 400 points, and two unions threatened to strike, but this did not worry our CEO.

12. The ancient culture completely disappeared in one day, which is an enduring mystery.

13. If a person approaches that rat terrier too quickly, you might get bitten.

14. Elton John, Eminem, and Dolly Parton performed together at the concert, which confused many people.

15. When Dante saw the sign above the entrance, he knew that Virgil and himself were in trouble.

Exercise 2C

Correct any errors in pronoun agreement or reference in the following paragraph.

1. Over many years, the wolf has found that ~~their~~ *its* amazing reputation has become tarnished.

2. One reason is that wolves live in such remote locales that you hardly ever see them. **3.** Many folktales express that fear of the unknown, revealing itself in stories such as *Peter and the Wolf, The Three Little Pigs* (featuring "The big bad wolf"), and *Little Red Riding Hood.* **4.** And a person who finds themselves in the woods at night will even fear that they might meet a werewolf.

5. Every day, the bad reputation of wolves is reinforced when it kills sheep or cattle. **6.** Surprisingly, a person will not hear of a wolf killing someone like theirself. **7.** The truth is that the wolf is a more intelligent and useful animal than people give them credit for. **8.** You probably don't know that wolves are not only fairly harmless but also immensely important to the other animals it shares its territory with. **9.** For instance, the wolf occupies the top point or apex of their food chain. **10.** If the wolf is eliminated from a habitat, nearly every other animal will find themselves in danger of elimination. **11.** Wolves prey on elk, caribou, deer, rabbits, and other animals.

12. This makes sure that those animals don't destroy their own food source by overgrazing.

13. In other words, an animal may lose their food source if the wolves are killed. **14.** You would miss wolves for many other reasons, including the very interesting lifestyle it leads. **15.** Just like you, wolves mate for life and raise their families together. **16.** In fact, a wolf will recognize and welcome a member of their family that has been gone for years, which is similar to humans.

17. Also, wolves employ complex strategies as they hunt as a unit. **18.** In fact, Genghis Khan studied the wolves' habits as it hunted. **19.** This helped him use what he learned in his own war strategies. **20.** For many reasons, we would be doing ourself a favor by ensuring that wolves thrive, not just survive.

Pronoun Case

Pronouns, like verbs, can appear in a variety of different forms, depending on how they function in a sentence. For example, the pronoun that refers to the speaker in a sentence may be written as *I*, *me*, *my*, or *mine*. These different spellings are the result of what is called **pronoun case.**

The three pronoun cases for English are the **subjective,** the **objective,** and the **possessive.**

Subjective Case

Singular	Plural
I	we
you	you
he, she, it	they
who	who

Objective Case

Singular	Plural
me	us
you	you
him, her, it	them
whom	whom

Possessive Case

Singular	Plural
my, mine	our, ours
your, yours	your, yours
his, her, hers, its	their, theirs
whose	whose

Subjective Pronouns

The subjective pronouns are *I*, *we*, *you*, *he*, *she*, *it*, *they*, and *who*. They are used in two situations.

1. Subjective pronouns are used as subjects of sentences.

EXAMPLES

S
I will return the car on Monday.

S
They are trying to outwit me.

247

2. Subjective pronouns are used when they follow linking verbs. Because the linking verb <u>identifies</u> the pronoun after it with the subject, the pronoun must be in the same case as the subject.

EXAMPLES

S

It was **she** who won the award for being the best-dressed mud wrestler. (The subjective pronoun *she* is <u>identified</u> with the subject *it* by the linking verb *was*.)

S

That was **I** you saw rowing across the lake yesterday.

S

It was **they** who caused the huge traffic jam.

Objective Pronouns

The **objective pronouns** are *me, us, you, him, her, it, them,* and *whom.* They are used in three situations.

1. <u>Objective pronouns are used as objects of prepositions.</u>

EXAMPLES

Sally loved the chrysanthemums that Mr. Kim had given <u>to her</u>.

The difficulties <u>between Samantha and me</u> continued into the fall.

2. <u>Objective pronouns are used as direct objects of action verbs.</u> The noun or pronoun that receives the action of the action verb is called the **direct object.**

For example, in the simple sentence *Tuan visited Serena yesterday,* the verb is *visited,* an action verb. The direct object of *visited* is *Serena* because *Serena* receives the action of the verb *visited.* If you substitute a pronoun for *Serena,* it must be the objective pronoun *her—Tuan visited **her** yesterday.*

EXAMPLES

Brenda married **him** on March 7, 1987.

Last summer Joan beat **me** at tennis every time we played.

Both classes helped clean up the park, and the city rewarded **them** with a picnic.

3. <u>Objective pronouns are used as indirect objects.</u> The **indirect object** indicates **to whom or for whom (or to what or for what) an action is directed,** but the prepositions *to* and *for* are left out.

EXAMPLES

(prepositional phrase)   He threw the ball **to her.**

(indirect object)   He threw **her** the ball.

In the first sentence, *her* is the object of the preposition *to*. In the second sentence, the *to* is omitted and the pronoun is moved, making *her* the indirect object. In both sentences, the direct object is *ball*. Here are other examples.

◎◎ EXAMPLES   She had already given **me** two chances to make up for my mistakes.

The architect showed **them** a picture of how the new city hall would look.

◎◎ PRACTICE   In the blanks, identify the underlined pronouns as subjective (sub) or objective (obj).

*sub*   **1.** During last night's party, <u>we</u> could not agree on the meaning of *mendacity*.

_____   **2.** Many words of praise were offered to <u>him</u> after his performance.

_____   **3.** Could <u>he</u> have prevented the debt crisis?

_____   **4.** Emily felt lonely and left out, so Esteban gave <u>her</u> his seat.

_____   **5.** Will you send <u>them</u> your email address and telephone number?

_____   **6.** The Loch Ness Monster was on their minds as <u>they</u> submerged.

_____   **7.** She is the one <u>whom</u> everyone copies when it comes to style.

_____   **8.** For six months Ceres had to wait for <u>her</u>.

_____   **9.** Because <u>he</u> was a quadruped, he had to buy two pairs of shoes.

_____   **10.** Persephone told <u>us</u> that hell was not so hot.

Possessive Pronouns

The **possessive pronouns** are *my, mine, our, ours, your, yours, his, her, hers, its, their, theirs,* and *whose.* They are used in two situations.

1. <u>Possessive pronouns are used as adjectives to indicate possession.</u>

◎◎ EXAMPLES   The old sailor had turned up **his** collar against the wind.

The weary travelers shuffled off to **their** rooms.

The polar bear constantly paced up and down **its** enclosure.

NOTE: The contraction *it's* means "it is." The word *its* is the only possessive form for *it*. (In fact, you do not use apostrophes with any of the possessive pronouns.)

2. <u>Some possessive pronouns indicate possession without being used as adjectives.</u> In this case, they may be used as subjects or objects.

EXAMPLE   I had to borrow Zan's flashlight because **mine** was lost.

Here the possessive pronoun *mine* is the subject of its clause.

EXAMPLE   The Chin house is large, but **yours** is cozy.

In this example, *yours* is the subject of its clause.

EXAMPLE   He didn't have any change for a phone call because he had given **his** to the children begging on the street.

Here the possessive pronoun *his* is a direct object.

Common Sources of Errors in Pronoun Case

Compound Constructions

Compound subjects and objects often cause problems when they include pronouns. If your sentence includes a compound construction, be sure to use the correct pronoun case.

EXAMPLES

(compound subject)	Sandra and <u>she</u> will return the car on Monday.
(compound after linking verb)	That was **my friend and I** whom you saw on the news.
(compound object of a preposition)	They awarded first-place trophies **to both Dolores and me.**
(compound direct object)	Julio's boss fired **Mark and <u>him</u>** yesterday.
(compound indirect object)	She had already given <u>him and me</u> two chances to make up our minds.

In most cases, you can use a simple test to check whether you have chosen the right pronoun case when you have a compound construction. Simply remove one of the subjects or objects so that only one pronoun is left. For example, is this sentence correct? *Our host gave **Erin and I** a drink.* Test it by dropping **Erin and.** *Our host gave I a drink.* Now you can see that the *I* should be *me* because it is an object (an indirect object). The correct sentence should read: *Our host gave **Erin and me** a drink.*

⚙️ PRACTICE   Underline the correct pronoun in parentheses.

1. My family and (<u>I</u> / me) attended the London Olympics.

2. Just between you and (I / me), Kendal is worried about the John Coltrane CD.

3. Without Dionysius and (she / her), the party won't be any fun.

4. Aritakis enjoyed the gyros that Placido and (he / him) had made.

5. The Scarecrow told Dorothy and (I / me) that Toto was afraid of the monkeys.

6. Barbara recommended the film *Hugo* to Carlton and (she / her).

7. The vice squad stopped Manuela and (he / him) for interdigitation.

8. The culprits who used all of the pencils were Brent and (she / her).

9. Chuck Berry smiled when Keith Richards and (she / her) asked him for an autograph.

10. At the end of the war, Victor Frankl and (he / him) were released from the concentration camp.

Who and Whom

When to use *who* or *whom* is a mystery to many writers, but you should have no problem with these pronouns if you remember two simple rules.

1. Use the subjective pronoun *who* or *whoever* if it is used as the subject of a verb.

2. Use the objective pronoun *whom* or *whomever* if it is not used as the subject of a verb.

⚙️ EXAMPLES   After leaving the airport, I followed the man **who** had taken my bags. (*Who* is the subject of *had taken*.)

The letter was sent to the person **whom** we had decided to hire. (*Whom* is not the subject of a verb.)

Please give the money to **whoever** needs it. (*Whoever* is the subject of *needs*.)

PRACTICE   Underline the correct pronoun in parentheses.

1. The actor (who / whom) played Richard III was adept at depicting his physical problems.

2. Leonardo is painting a woman (who / whom) he has described as having a very subtle smile.

3. Richard claimed he loved his cousin Clarence, (who / whom) he had ordered drowned in a keg of wine.

4. Charles Darwin would explain his theory to (whoever / whomever) would listen.

5. Martha was quick to blame anyone (who / whom) was close at hand.

Comparisons

When a pronoun is used in a comparison, you often need to supply the implied words in order to know what pronoun case to use. For example, in the sentence *My brother cannot skate as well as I,* the implied words are the verb *can skate: My brother cannot skate as well as I [can skate].*

EXAMPLE   The police officer allowed my friend to leave the scene sooner than **me.**

You can tell that *me* is the correct case in this sentence when you supply the implied words:

The police officer allowed my friend to leave the scene sooner than [**she allowed**] me [**to leave**].

PRACTICE   Underline the correct pronoun in parentheses.

1. Michelle always eats more slowly than (I / me).

2. I love my mother dearly, but she always serves my brother a bigger slice of pie than (I / me).

3. Chris thought she was as triskaidekaphobic as (he / him).

4. When it came to hustling Popsicles, no one did it better than (she / her).

5. When they became engaged, the happy couple told William sooner than (I / me).

Appositives

As you will remember from Chapter Three, an appositive is a word group containing a noun or pronoun that renames another noun or pronoun. When the appositive contains a **pronoun** that does the renaming, be sure that the pronoun is in the same case as the word it renames.

EXAMPLE   Some team members—Joe, Frank, and I—were late for practice.

Here *I* is in the subjective case because the appositive *Joe, Frank, and I* renames the word *members*, the subject of the sentence.

EXAMPLE   When the show is over, please send your review to the producers, Mark and **her**.

Here *her* is in the objective case because the appositive *Mark and her* renames *producers*, the object of the preposition *to*.

PRACTICE   Underline the correct pronoun in parentheses.

1. Dietrich was thrilled with the new trio—Helmut, Natasha, and (he / <u>him</u>).

2. The winners, Cuthbert and (I / me), were cleared of fibbing about our weights.

3. Kalisha was disappointed that her teammates, Cameron and (he / him), had given up.

4. The curry was cooked by the three roommates—Inder, Sara, and (she / her).

5. The last people to arrive—Celeste, Annamaria, Lawrence, and (I / me)— were told to sit in the back of the room.

PRACTICE   Underline the correct pronoun form in parentheses.

1. We will send the news of the battle to (<u>whoever</u> / whomever) is on duty at the time.

2. Do you really think that Maria is humbler than (I / me)?

3. Exhibition of the truth is at (its / it's) lowest when (its / it's) election time.

4. The new Thai student and (she / her) agreed not to use too many hot spices in their cooking.

5. Petra decided that she would marry (whoever / whomever) her astrologer recommended.

6. Before the wedding, she also consulted two palm readers, Madame Sosostris and (he / him).

7. Send Narcissus and (he / him) this invitation to the self-reflection workshop.

8. Aphrodite worried that Ares was more attracted to Artemis than to (she / her).

9. Charlie used a can of Spam to depict the conductor Neville Mariner, (who / whom) he knew personally.

10. During the war in Pakistan, Ricardo and (she / her) were separated for more than a year.

Section Three Review

1. The **subjective pronouns** are used in two ways:

    a. As the subjects of sentences

    b. After linking verbs

2. The **objective pronouns** are used in three ways:

    a. As objects of prepositions

    b. As direct objects of action verbs

    c. As indirect objects

3. The **possessive pronouns** are used in two ways:

    a. As adjectives to modify nouns to indicate possession

    b. As subjects and objects

4. Some common sources of errors in pronoun case:

    a. Pronouns in compound constructions

    b. The use of the pronouns *who, whom, whoever,* and *whomever*

    c. Pronouns in comparisons

    d. Pronouns in appositives

Exercise 3A

Underline the correct pronoun form in parentheses.

1. The Batmobile stalled when (its / it's) Battank ran out of Batgas.

2. A special sense of cooperation and respect exists between Coral and (I / me).

3. The $64,000 challenge for Eric and (she / her) was to name the thirteen original colonies.

4. Was it (she / her) (who / whom) lifted the Lexus SUV off the child?

5. No one was more surprised than (I / me) to see Neptune rise from the waves in Ocean Beach.

6. Tell General Lee and (they / them) that Cemetery Ridge cannot be taken by General Pickett.

7. The fellows (who / whom) the Earps met at the OK Corral were soon sorry they had come.

8. Did Ahab ever explain to you and (she / her) why he was chasing the whale?

9. Walking through the maze, the Minotaur lost (its / it's) way.

10. It was (she / her) who started the movement to end the war.

11. The gold medal will go to (whoever / whomever) is able to parallel park perfectly five times in a row.

12. Loren was certain he had seen Meryl Streep and (she / her) on the Sunset Strip.

13. Two poets, T. S. Eliot and (she / her), discussed the merits of "The Love Song of J. Alfred Prufrock."

14. (Its / It's) hard to believe that your pet parrot can spell (its / it's) own name.

15. The study group and (he / him) decided to present a paper on the symptoms of autism.

Exercise 3B

Correct any pronoun errors in the following sentences. Some sentences may not contain errors.

1. Alice likes mushrooms and white rabbits more than ~~me~~ *I*.

2. Do you think that the CEO and he will ever agree on the design of the next Leaf?

3. Was that Dr. Frankenstein and his monster who you invited for dinner?

4. The ranger told my brother and I that we could not take even an acorn from the national park.

5. The Mad Hatter sadly told his friends, the hedgehog and she, that he could no longer wear his favorite hat.

6. When your condition is at it's worst, Dr. Freud will give you a call.

7. Plato smiled philosophically at Bill and I as we stared at the shadows flickering across the screen.

8. For a week, Dr. Scarpetta and she studied the DNA tests.

9. The 2012 American gymnastics team visited the children who the Ronald McDonald House had recently admitted.

10. Her fellow marines had started up the mountain an hour before she, but she reached the top sooner than them.

11. Between Horace and me was a deep chasm.

12. It's food was covered with ants, so it's not surprising the dog started to howl.

13. The first- and second-place ribbons for hallway whistling were awarded to Bruce and him.

14. The iconoclasts whom were bothering Pollyanna and her were finally asked to leave.

15. At Orca's Revenge beachside café, Jack and me always order fish and chips.

Exercise 3C

Correct any errors in pronoun case in the following paragraph.

1. Urban legends—ironic, supernatural, or unbelievable accounts of real-life events—may be the result of the ordinary human emotions of the people ~~whom~~ *who* tell them. **2.** For example, one of my favorite urban legends clearly finds it's origin in the desire to get something for nothing. **3.** It was originally told to my brother and I by a local bank manager. **4.** Someone whom she knows has a friend who says that his wife and him paid only $15,000 for a $100,000 Porsche 911 Turbo. **5.** They paid so little because it had sat in the Mojave Desert for two weeks with the body of it's owner in it. **6.** My brother is more skeptical than me, but even he would like to believe that such an event could happen to him. **7.** Another urban legend is probably caused by our fear of the unknown, especially in dark, lonely places. **8.** According to this legend, a boy and a girl whom have parked in the woods are talking about a rumor that a one-armed man has been seen nearby. **9.** Friends have told the boy and she that he has attacked several people with his hook in the past few weeks while frothing at the mouth and yelling, "Bloody murder!" **10.** Frightened, the two leave the woods, but when they arrive home and get out of the car, they find a hook dangling from it's right front door. **11.** They are both terrified, but the boy is determined to find the man who tried to attack his girlfriend and he. **12.** He drives back to the woods and is never heard from again. **13.** Finally, an urban legend that my wife and me have heard several different versions of must be caused by a need to see people get what they deserve. **14.** In this one, an elderly woman whom lives in a downtown apartment with her blind husband finds her beloved cat dead one day. **15.** The old woman puts the body into a shopping bag, and her husband and her tearfully take a bus across town to a pet cemetery. **16.** On the trip, a teenage gang member, who is much stronger than them, grabs the bag, laughs at the woman, and jumps off the bus. **17.** According to almost every version told to my wife and I, when the thief looks into the bag, he is so startled that he falls backward into the path of a car. **18.** Clearly, urban legends like these are repeated because they express many of our unspoken desires and fears.

Sentence Practice: Using Transitions

Writers use certain words and phrases to indicate the relationships among the ideas in their sentences and paragraphs. These words and phrases provide links between ideas, leading a reader from one idea to another smoothly. They show relationships like time, addition, or contrast. Consider this paragraph from Rachel Carson's *Edge of the Sea*:

> **When** the tide is rising the shore is a place of unrest, with the surge leaping high over jutting rocks **and** running in lacy cascades of foam over the landward side of massive boulders. **But** on the ebb it is more peaceful, **for then** the waves do not have behind them the push of the inward pressing tides. There is no particular drama about the turn of the tide, **but presently** a zone of wetness shows on the gray rock slopes, **and** offshore the incoming swells begin to swirl **and** break over hidden ledges. **Soon** the rocks that the high tide had concealed rise into view and glisten with the wetness left on them by the receding water.

Because she is writing about a process, most of Rachel Carson's transitional words indicate a relationship in time (*when, then, presently, soon*). But she also uses transitional words that indicate contrast (*but*), cause (*for*), and addition (*and*). As you can see, she uses these expressions to lead her readers smoothly from one idea to another.

The sentence combining exercises in this chapter are designed to give you practice in using transitional words and phrases to link your ideas. Try to use as many different ones as you can. For your convenience, here is a list of commonly used transitional words and phrases.

- Time: *then, soon, first, second, finally, meanwhile, next, at first, in the beginning*

- Contrast: *yet, but, however, instead, otherwise, on the other hand, on the contrary*

- Addition: *and, also, besides, furthermore, in addition, likewise, moreover, similarly*

- Cause–effect: *for, because, consequently, so, therefore, hence, thus, as a result, since*

- Example: *for example, for instance, that is, such as*

- Conclusion: *thus, hence, finally, generally, as a result, in conclusion*

◎◎ PRACTICE   Add transitions to the following sentences.

1. Sometimes I am indecisive about the most trivial things. _____, this morning I spent fifteen minutes trying to decide whether to buy a cinnamon roll or a jelly doughnut.

2. People love Paris for its many excellent art museums. _____, it has world-renowned restaurants.

3. Barbara and Greg have been very successful in their real estate careers. _____, they have raised five well-adjusted, happy children.

4. Eight of the Lonewolves defensive starters were unable to play. _____, they lost the game against the Meatpackers by a lopsided score.

5. Tonight I might stay home and worry and feel sorry for myself. _____, maybe I will meet some friends, have dinner, and see a movie.

Sentence Combining Exercises

Combine the following sentences, using transitions as indicated in the directions.

◎◎ EXAMPLE Combine these sentences into two sentences. Use transitions that indicate contrast, example, and addition. Underline your transitions.

a. Herman knows he needs to lose weight.
b. He is unable to resist the urge to eat ice cream.
c. Yesterday he drank a low-fat fiber shake for lunch.
d. After work he stopped at a 31 Flavors ice cream store.
e. He ate a large chocolate sundae.

Herman knows he needs to lose weight, <u>but</u> he is unable to resist the urge to eat ice cream. <u>For example,</u> yesterday he drank a low-fat fiber shake for lunch, <u>but</u> after work he stopped at a 31 Flavors ice cream store <u>and</u> ate a large chocolate sundae.

1. Combine the following sentences into two sentences. Use transitions that indicate time and addition. Underline your transitions.

   a. At the bowling alley, Sarah pays for a lane.
   b. She rents some bowling shoes.
   c. She meets her friends.
   d. They order some pizza, sandwiches, and drinks.

   _____

   _____

   _____

   _____

2. Combine the following sentences into two or three sentences. Use transitions that indicate addition and result. Underline your transitions.

   a. Cameron's Restaurant has too many choices on the menu.
   b. People end up ordering food they do not like.
   c. There are too many fatty selections.
   d. There are no small selections for children.
   e. People often return their food.
   f. Cameron's is losing money.

   _____

   _____

   _____

   _____

Sentence Combining Exercises

continued

3. Combine the following sentences into two sentences. Use transitions that indicate cause–effect. Underline your transitions.

   a. Horse-drawn covered wagons used to be called "Conestogas."
   b. Conestogas were originally built in the Conestoga Valley of Pennsylvania.
   c. The Conestogas supplied cigars, among other things, to the pioneers.
   d. Cigars came to be called "stogies."

   _____

   _____

   _____

   _____

4. Combine the following sentences into three sentences, using transitions that show time, contrast, and cause–effect relationships. Underline your transitions.

   a. Finals were approaching.
   b. Cally was reviewing her biology notes from the semester.
   c. Cally became sleepy.
   d. Cally brewed some coffee.
   e. Cally felt alert.
   f. Cally was bored with studying.
   g. Cally called her boyfriend Nat.
   h. They decided to pop some popcorn.
   i. They decided to rent a movie from Amazon.

   _____

   _____

   _____

   _____

Sentence Combining Exercises

continued

5. Combine the following sentences into two or three sentences. Use transitions that indicate cause–effect, example, and contrast. Underline your transitions.

   a. Kelly has decided to break up with Armando.
   b. Armando has started drinking too much.
   c. Armando has bad breath.
   d. He has gained twenty pounds.
   e. Kelly is afraid of how Armando will react.
   f. Armando might become depressed.
   g. He might drop out of college.
   h. He might even become violent.

   _____

   _____

   _____

   _____

6. Combine the following sentences into three or four sentences, using transitions that show time and cause–effect relationships. Underline your transitions.

   a. The holes in bread are made by bubbles of gas.
   b. Flour and water are mixed to form dough.
   c. A small amount of yeast is added.
   d. The yeast grows.
   e. The yeast gives off a gas.
   f. The gas bubbles up through the dough.
   g. The dough expands.

   _____

   _____

   _____

   _____

Sentence Combining Exercises

continued

7. Combine the following sentences into two sentences. Use transitions that indicate cause–effect and contrast. Underline your transitions.

   a. In ancient times, wedding guests threw wheat at a new bride.
   b. Wheat was a symbol of fertility and prosperity.
   c. In the first century BCE, Roman bakers began to cook the wheat into small cakes.
   d. Wedding guests did not want to give up the custom of throwing wheat.
   e. They threw the wedding cakes instead.

   _____

   _____

   _____

   _____

   _____

8. Combine the following sentences into three sentences. Use transitions that indicate cause–effect and contrast. Underline your transitions.

   a. Many drunk people drive home.
   b. They believe that drinking coffee before they leave will sober them up.
   c. Drinking coffee will do nothing to make a drunk person less drunk.
   d. A good sleep, plenty of liquids, and enough time will remedy the effects of alcohol.

   _____

   _____

   _____

   _____

Sentence Combining Exercises

continued

9. Combine the following sentences into three sentences. Use transitions that show contrast and addition.

    a. The song "Chopsticks" was not named after the Chinese eating implement.
    b. It was named after the chopping motions the hands have to make to play it.
    c. A Chinese composer did not write the little waltz.
    d. A British girl wrote it.
    e. She made up the instructions to play it with both hands turned sideways to imitate a chopping motion.

_____

_____

_____

_____

_____

10. Combine the following sentences into three sentences. Use transitions that indicate example, cause–effect, and addition. Underline your transitions.

    a. Many superstitions have unusual origins.
    b. It is considered bad luck to walk under a ladder.
    c. A ladder leaning against a wall forms a triangle.
    d. Many ancient societies believed that a triangle was a place sacred to the gods.
    e. Walking through a triangle defiled that space.

_____

_____

_____

_____

Essay and Paragraph Practice: Explaining Causes and Effects

Assignment

In Chapter Three you wrote an expository paper that used examples as support. Such an organization—one that calls for a listing of examples to support an idea—is very common in college papers and tests. Another common assignment is one that asks you to explain the **causes** or the **effects** of something. In an American history class, for example, you might be asked to explain the causes of the South's failure to win the Civil War. Or in a psychology class you might be asked to explain the long-term effects that physical abuse can have on children.

A paper that focuses on causes explains *why* a certain event might have occurred or why people do what they do. On the other hand, a paper that focuses on effects explains what has *resulted* or might result from an event, action, or behavior. In this chapter, Exercise 1C (page 232) explains the effects of a divorce in the family; Exercise 2C (page 246) explains causes and effects of the wolf's reputation; and Exercise 3C (page 258) explains the causes of some urban legends. Each of these paragraphs states the purpose of the paragraph (to explain causes or effects) in a topic sentence and then presents several specific causes or effects.

Your assignment is to write a paper that explains *either* the causes *or* the effects of a topic with which you are personally familiar. Develop your paper from one of the suggestions below or from an idea suggested by your instructor.

Prewriting to Generate Ideas

Prewriting Application: Finding Your Topic

Use prewriting techniques of freewriting, brainstorming, or clustering to decide which of the following topic ideas interests you. Write for five or ten minutes on several of these suggestions. Don't stop writing once you find one topic that might work. Try out several of them before you make a decision.

Analyzing Causes

1. Why do you or do you not admire, respect, or trust a particular person?

2. Why are you doing well or poorly in a particular course?

3. Why did your or your parents' marriage or relationship fail, or why is it a success?

4. Why was your childhood or some other period the best or worst time of your life?

5. Why did you move from one place to another?

6. Why did you buy the particular car or other item that you did?

7. Why are you attending a particular college?

8. Why did you make an important decision?

9. Why did a particular experience affect you the way it did?

10. Why will you never go to *that* restaurant, hotel, beach, or lake again?

Analyzing Effects

1. What were the effects of an important decision that you made?

2. What were the effects of your move to a new place?

3. What were the effects of your being an only child, or an oldest child, or a youngest child, or of growing up in a large family?

4. What are the effects of stress upon the way you act, feel, or think?

5. What were the effects upon you of a major change in your life—having a child? getting married? changing jobs? experiencing a divorce?

6. What have been the effects of a serious compulsion or addiction to drugs, alcohol, gambling, or overeating upon someone you know or upon his or her loved ones?

7. What have been the effects of mental, emotional, or physical abuse upon you or someone you know?

8. What have been the effects of discrimination or prejudice upon you or someone you know? (Discrimination might involve race, gender, age, sexuality, or religion.)

9. What have been the effects upon you and/or upon your family of working and/or raising a family and attending school at the same time?

10. What have been the effects upon you of some major change in your lifestyle or values?

Choosing and Narrowing the Topic

Once you have settled on several possible topics, consider these points as you make your final selection.

- Choose the more limited topic rather than the more general one.

- Choose the topic about which you could develop several causes or effects. Avoid topics that involve only one or two causes or effects.

- Choose the topic about which you have the most experience or knowledge.

- Choose the topic in which you have the most personal interest. Avoid topics about which you don't really care.

Writing a Thesis Statement or Topic Sentence

If your assignment is to write a single paragraph, you will open it with a topic sentence. If you are writing a complete essay, you will need a thesis statement at the end of your introductory paragraph. In either case, you will need a clear statement of the topic and central idea of your paper.

Prewriting Application: Working with Topic Sentences

Identify the topic sentences in Exercises 1C (page 232), 2C (page 246), and 3C (page 258). Then identify the topic and the central point in each topic sentence.

Prewriting Application: Evaluating Thesis Statements and Topic Sentences

Write "No" before each sentence that would not make an effective thesis statement or topic sentence for a paper explaining causes or effects. Write "Yes" before each sentence that *would* make an effective one. Identify each effective sentence as introducing a paper about causes or effects. Using ideas of your own, rewrite each ineffective sentence into one that might work.

_____ **1.** My father's generosity, sensitivity, and openness have made him into the most important person in my life.

_____

_____

_____ **2.** I divorced my husband on June 30 of last year.

_____

_____

_____

_____ **3.** Although I loved living in Boulder, Colorado, several events over the past few years helped me decide that it was time to move.

_____

_____

_____ **4.** Whenever I let myself worry too much about my job, school, or family responsibilities, everyone that I love is affected by my strange behavior.

_____

_____

_____ **5.** My life has changed in many ways since I was young.

_____

_____

_____

_____ **6.** Many students at our local high school use marijuana, methamphetamines, and even cocaine.

_____

_____

_____ **7.** Telling my parents that I was gay was one of the best decisions that I ever made.

_____

_____

_____ **8.** Growing up as an only child helped me become an independent, decisive, and responsible person.

_____

_____

_____ **9.** My new computer, which uses all the latest technology, came loaded with my favorite games and word processing software.

_____

_____

_____

_____ **10.** Attending a college away from home has caused me to become a much better person in a number of ways.

_____

_____

_____

Prewriting Application: Talking to Others

Form a group of three or four people and tell one another what topic you have chosen and whether you plan to discuss causes or effects. Use the following guidelines to discuss your papers.

1. What is the topic of the paper? Will the paper focus on causes or effects?

2. What causes or effects will be included? Can they be more specific and descriptive? Can they be explained more clearly?

3. What other causes or effects could be included? Are there any less obvious but more interesting ones?

4. Are you convinced? Have enough causes or effects been provided to illustrate the topic idea? Should any of them be explained or described more thoroughly?

5. Which cause or effect should the paper open with? Which should it close with?

Organizing Causes and Effects

Chronological and **emphatic** arrangements are perhaps the most common ways to organize several causes or effects. If you are explaining what caused you to stop smoking, a chronological arrangement would list the most remote causes first and move to the most recent causes. On the other hand, an emphatic arrangement would involve deciding which cause was the most significant one and saving it until last.

Writing the Essay

If your assignment is to write a complete essay:

- Place your **thesis statement** at the end of the introductory paragraph.

- Write a separate **body paragraph** for each cause or effect that you intend to discuss.

- Open each body paragraph with a **topic sentence** that identifies the specific cause or effect.

- Within each body paragraph, use **specific facts and details** to explain and support your ideas.

Writing the Paragraph

If your assignment is to write a single paragraph:

- Open it with a **topic sentence** that clearly identifies the topic and central idea of the paragraph.

- Use **clear transitions** to move from one cause or effect to the next.

- Use **specific facts and details** to explain and support your ideas.

Writing Application: Identifying Transitional Words, Phrases, and Sentences

Examine Exercises 1C (page 232), 2C (page 246), and 3C (page 258). Identify the transitions that introduce each new cause or effect. Then identify any other transitions that serve to connect ideas between sentences.

Rewriting and Improving the Paper

1. Revise your sentences so that they include specific and concrete details. As often as possible, use actual names of people and places. Refer to specific details whenever possible.

2. Add or revise transitions wherever doing so will help clarify your movement from one idea to another.

3. Improve your preliminary thesis statement (if you are writing an essay) or your preliminary topic sentence (if you are writing a single paragraph) so that it more accurately states the central point of your paper.

4. Examine your draft for simple sentences that can be combined to make compound, complex, or compound-complex sentences. Watch also for sentences that can be combined using participial phrases, appositives, infinitive phrases, or adjective clauses.

Rewriting Application: Responding to Paragraph Writing

Read the following paragraph. Then respond to the questions following it.

Changing Careers

Two years ago, after serving for over twenty-five years in the United States Navy, I decided that it was time to move on to new and better things, and I have never regretted that decision. One of the most pleasant effects of retiring from the military has been not having to endure any more family separations. While in the Navy, I spent most of my career aboard ship and made many six-month deployments or had to stand duty every four or five days when not on deployment. Now that I have more time to spend with my family, I have joined a family bowling league and have time to attend school events that my children are participating in. Another effect of leaving the military is that I am able to get involved with community activities because I know that I won't be moving to another city in two or three years. During one period of my career my family and I lived in San Francisco two years, Norfolk, Virginia, three years, and then San Diego. Now that I don't plan to move within two or three years, I have joined the Parent/Teachers' Association at my son's school, become an active member in the local Boy Scout troop, and become a board member of my homeowners' association. Finally, by working fewer hours than I did when I was in the Navy, I have the opportunity to go to school. I am able to use the Montgomery G.I. Bill to supplement my income while in school and obtain a degree in business management. My wife and I agree that we made the right decision to leave the military when I did. The week after I retired, the ship I had been stationed on made an unexpected nine-month deployment to Somalia. I obtained a good civil service job after I retired, and my supervisor allows me to attend school in the mornings and work in the afternoons and weekends.

1. Identify the topic sentence. State its topic and central idea. Is it an effective topic sentence? Can you tell whether the paper will focus on causes or effects?

2. How many causes or effects are mentioned in this paper? Identify them.

3. Identify the transitional sentences that introduce each cause or effect. What other transitions are used between sentences in this paragraph?

4. What parts of each cause or effect could be made still more specific?

5. Consider the organization of the paragraph. Would you change the order of the causes or effects? Explain why or why not.

Rewriting Application: Responding to Essay Writing

Read the following essay. Then respond to the questions at the end of it.

A New Person

I used to be the kind of person who thought only of herself. I wanted to make a lot of money, party every weekend, and just have fun. I was probably the most self-centered person you have ever met. But in the past two years I have really changed. I have started to think about other people before I think about myself. I am happy that I am becoming a different person, but the causes of my change have been painful.

I think my change started when my boyfriend left me last year. We had been together for five years, ever since we graduated from Oceanside High School. Even though we fought a lot, I was sure that we would eventually get married and be together forever. So I was stunned and really hurt when he told me goodbye. He told me I was the most selfish person he had ever met. I was furious for a long time after that, but I kept thinking about what he had said. I began to think that maybe he was right. Maybe I was selfish.

I have also changed because of people I have met at Palomar College. When I decided to go back to school, I just wanted to get my degree and be left alone. I thought I was smarter than everyone else, so I hardly ever talked to anyone in my classes. By the end of my first semester, I was really lonely. It seemed as if everyone but me had made friends and was having fun. So I tried an experiment. I started asking people around me in class how they were doing, and if they were having trouble I offered to help.

That was really a big step for me. By the end of the year, I had several new friends, and two of them are still my best friends today.

The biggest cause of my new attitude, however, came when I took a part-time job at Vista Convalescent Care. I had never worked with older people before, and I dreaded the idea of changing bedpans and cleaning up after them. But after a few weeks I really started to like the people I was taking care of, and I began to see that making them feel good made me feel good too. One older woman in particular became my friend. Her name was Rita Gonzalez, and she had Alzheimer's. Whenever I came into her room, she was always so happy because she thought I was her daughter. Her real daughter never visited her, so I took her place, and Rita and I spent lots of afternoons together. She taught me to forget about my own problems, so when she died last month, I was heartbroken, but I was also very grateful to her.

I think I am a much better person today than I used to be, and I hope I will not forget these experiences. They have been painful, but they have taught me how to think about other people before I think about myself. I like who I am today, and I could not say that a few years ago.

1. Identify the thesis statement. State its topic and central idea. Is it an effective thesis statement? Can you tell whether the paper will focus on causes or effects?

2. Identify each topic sentence. State its topic and central idea. Does each topic sentence clearly introduce one specific cause or effect?

3. What transitional words introduce each new body paragraph?

4. Does the essay use a chronological or emphatic organization? Would you change the order of the paragraphs? Why or why not?

5. Is each cause or effect explained clearly and fully? If you would improve any, explain how you would do so.

Proofreading

When proofreading your paper, watch for the following errors:

- Sentence fragments
- Comma splices
- Fused sentences
- Misplaced modifiers
- Dangling modifiers
- Incorrect subject–verb agreement
- Incorrect pronoun case
- Incorrect pronoun–antecedent agreement or pronoun reference
- Misspelled words

Prepare a clean final draft, following the format your instructor has requested. Before you turn in your final draft, proofread it carefully and make any necessary corrections.

Chapter 4 Practice Test

I. Review of Chapters One, Two, and Three

A. Underline all subjects once and complete verbs twice. Place all prepositional phrases in parentheses.

   1. The block of ice in the old freezer contained a frozen alien from outer space.

   2. After the romantic had praised the beauty of nature, the realist decided to mow the lawn.

   3. September had come to New Jersey, so it was time for flu shots.

   4. The marines loaded their weapons and dug trenches among the trees on the hill.

   5. Last Halloween some people gathered smelly material, placed it in a paper bag, and set it on fire on our front porch.

B. Correct any fragments, fused sentences, or comma splices in the following sentences. Do nothing if the sentence is correct.

   6. Persephone, asking her mother if she should eat the pomegranate.

   _____

   _____

   7. The moonshiners hated the revenuers they were scaring away their business.

   _____

   _____

   8. The salmon, swimming swiftly upstream, did not see the bear, which flicked many of them out of the water with its huge paw.

   _____

   _____

   9. The candidate expected applause, however, he did not realize that he had just insulted his opponent's mother.

   _____

   _____

continued

10. After Babe Ruth had eaten seven hotdogs and drunk a bucket of beer.

_____

_____

C. At the places indicated, add adjective clauses, appositives, infinitive phrases, or participial phrases to the following sentences as directed in parentheses. Use commas where they are needed.

11. The minnow stared at the barracuda ^ . (adjective clause)

_____

_____

12. The audience laughed at the clown ^ as he walked onto the stage. (appositive)

_____

_____

13. ^ The batter glared at the pitcher. (participial phrase)

_____

_____

14. Jenna trained her African gray parrot ^ whenever the doorbell would ring. (infinitive phrase)

_____

_____

15. The navy helicopter ^ almost collided with the marine jet. (participial phrase)

_____

_____

continued

D. Correct any dangling or misplaced modifiers in the following sentences. Do nothing if the sentence is correct.

16. Rocco saw his favorite kitten dash into the street while playing badminton with his daughter.

_____

_____

17. The tsunami was so devastating that it nearly covered the whole town.

_____

_____

18. Breathing the last of the air, the scuba diving session was almost over.

_____

_____

19. The man with no name ignored the stagecoach dreaming of the open prairie.

_____

_____

20. Surprised by the detective's flashlight, the diamonds dropped all over the marble staircase.

_____

_____

Chapter 4 Practice Test

II. Chapter Four

A. Underline the correct verb form in parentheses.

1. Each earthworm, cricket, and toad in our backyard (has/have) crawled or hopped into our family room.

2. During an election year, politics (seems/seem) to dominate the news.

3. There (is/are) the pen, paper, and folder that you ordered.

4. The panel of judges (decide/decides) which sculpture gets the prize.

5. Neither the surgeon nor the oncologist (want/wants) to deal with the pathologist's behavior.

B. Correct any subject–verb agreement errors in the following sentences. Do nothing if the sentence is correct.

6. A couple of raccoons and an opossum with its litter eats our cat's food some nights.

7. Anything you might need to buy and sell houses are easily found on the Internet.

8. One hundred dollars seems like a fair price for my collection of broken roof tiles.

9. Have Alfred Einstein or Robert Frost written anything about the source of human love?

10. The man wearing seven gold medals at the boys' swim meet remind me of someone famous, but I can't remember his name.

C. Underline the correct pronouns in parentheses.

11. Somebody dropped (her/their) bag of snacks in the laboratory.

12. If a fan wants to get tickets for the Beatles' revival concert, (you/he or she/they) should call the phone number in the Sunday paper.

13. For the rest of their lives, Hester and Dimmesdale kept their secret to (themself/theirselves/themselves).

14. The exploration party forded fifteen rivers on (its/their) way to the sea.

15. All the children in the audience clapped (his or her/their) hands enthusiastically.

continued

D. Correct any pronoun errors in the following sentences. Do nothing if the sentence is correct.

16. The Africanized honey bees have established a hive near the black bear's den, which worries Mark's mother.

17. Whenever Elvis visited Ringo, he complained about today's music.

18. The director was certain that his latest film would be nominated for an Oscar, but this failed to happen.

19. Everyone who heard about the "Orphan Train" wanted to know why they had never learned about it in history class.

20. Although many people wanted to know the name of the singer, the producers decided to keep his identity to theirselfs.

E. Underline the correct pronoun in parentheses.

21. Dirt-Be-Gone, the unbelievable stain remover, was awarded to Cherie and (him/he).

22. Jenna headed for San Francisco once Danny and (she/her) had loaded the U-Haul.

23. The salesman gave the instructions to the new car's owners, Shirley and (she/her).

24. Everyone was devastated when the trophy went to Kanga rather than (I/me).

25. Hester, (who/whom) borrowed some needles and thread from me, seems to be working hard on her project.

F. Correct any pronoun errors in the following sentences. Do nothing if the sentence is correct.

26. When the Mustang hit the ice, it's wheels began to slide.

27. The overconfident students could not spell as well as us, so they lost the spelling bee.

28. Do you want Tom and him to help you paint that fence?

29. Between Achilles and I, we met about thirty thousand Trojans that day.

30. When the wedding was over, my sister and me could not stop crying.

Using Punctuation and Capitalization

When we speak to people face to face, we have a number of signals, aside from the words we choose, to let them know how we feel. Facial expressions—smiles, frowns, grimaces—convey our emotions and attitudes. Tone of voice can tell a listener whether we feel sad or lighthearted or sarcastic about what we are saying. Hand gestures and other body language add further messages to the communication. In fact, experts tell us that these nonverbal communications make up over 80 percent of the messages in a conversation.

When we write in order to communicate with a reader, we must make up for that 80 percent of lost, nonverbal communication by using the writing signals that we know. Some of the most important signals in writing are the punctuation marks. They signal whether we are making a statement or asking a question. They indicate the boundaries of our sentences. They determine much of the rhythm and emotion of our writing.

If you are able to use punctuation effectively, you have a powerful tool to control how your writing affects your readers. If you do not know the basic rules of punctuation, you run the risk of being misunderstood or of confusing your readers. In this chapter we will discuss the essential rules of punctuation, not just so that your writing will be correct but, more importantly, so that you will be able to express your ideas exactly the way you want them to be expressed.

Using Commas

The comma gives writers more trouble than any of the other punctuation marks. Before printing was developed, commas came into use to tell readers when to put in a slight pause when they were reading aloud. Now, although the placement of the comma does affect the rhythm of sentences, it also conveys many messages that are more important than when to pause. Because the comma is such an important punctuation mark and because it can be troublesome to you if you don't know how to use it correctly, we take it up first. You are already familiar with several of its uses.

Comma usage can be explained by four general rules:

1. Use commas before coordinating conjunctions that join main clauses to form a compound sentence.

2. Use commas between elements in a series.

3. Use commas after introductory elements.

4. Use commas before and after interrupters.

Commas in Compound Sentences

1. When joining two main clauses with one of the coordinating conjunctions to form a compound sentence, use a comma before the conjunction.

EXAMPLES   I don't know her, **but** I like her already.

The tableware in the restaurant was exquisite, **and** the food was some of the best I have ever tasted.

We had to remove the huge eucalyptus tree, **or** its encroaching roots would have undermined our happy home.

2. When conjunctions join other parts of a sentence, such as two words, two phrases, or two subordinate clauses, do not put commas before the conjunctions.

EXAMPLE   Every morning that scoundrel has a drink **and** then thoroughly beats his poor dog.

No comma is needed before *and* because it does not join two main clauses. Instead, it joins the verbs *has* and *beats*.

EXAMPLE   I decided to visit France because I had never had a chance to see that country **and** because my travel agent was able to offer me a special discount on the trip.

No comma is needed before *and* because it joins two subordinate clauses, not two main clauses.

◎◎ PRACTICE   Add commas to the following sentences where necessary.

1. Roy brought out Dale's new horse,and she named it Buttermilk.

2. The jetliner crash-landed in the Hudson River but everyone was rescued.

3. The hounds searched under the dinner table but could find no hush puppies.

4. The giraffes would not come up to be fed for the Wild Animal Park had changed their feeding location.

5. One giraffe started toward the feeding station so the children cheered.

Commas with Elements in a Series

1. When listing three or more elements (words, phrases, clauses) in a series, separate them by commas. When the last two elements are joined by a coordinating conjunction, a comma before the conjunction is optional.

◎◎ EXAMPLES

(words)   The gazpacho was **cold, spicy, and fresh.**

(phrases)   In the mountains, he had been **thrown by his horse, bitten by a snake, and chased by a bear.**

(clauses)   To rescue the koala, the firefighters brought a ladder, the police brought a rope, and the mayor brought a speech.

2. When using two or more adjectives to modify the same noun, separate them with commas if you can put *and* between the adjectives without changing the meaning or if you can easily reverse the order of the adjectives.

◎◎ EXAMPLES

She eagerly stepped into the **comforting, cool water.**

A **stubborn, obnoxious** boll weevil is ruining my cotton patch.

Note that you could easily use *and* between the above adjectives. (The water is *comforting* and *cool*; the boll weevil is *stubborn* and *obnoxious*.) You could also reverse the adjectives (the *cool, comforting water* or the *obnoxious, stubborn* boll weevil).

3. On the other hand, if the adjectives cannot be joined by *and* or are not easily reversed, no comma is necessary.

⊙⊙ EXAMPLE

A bureaucrat wearing a **black leather jacket** and a smirk strode into the auditorium.

Notice how awkward the sentence would sound if you placed *and* between the adjectives (*a black and leather jacket*) or if you reversed them (*a leather black jacket*).

⊙⊙ PRACTICE

Insert commas between main clauses joined by a coordinating conjunction and between items in a series.

1. Adam bought a new 3-D television so he invited his friends over to watch the Final Four.

2. My red-beans-and-rice dish contains red beans a ham hock cayenne pepper tomato sauce and many other secret ingredients found only in New Orleans.

3. Martin finished the ninety-five items grabbed a hammer and nailed them to the church door.

4. The historical exciting opening of the London Olympics impressed millions of people from around the world.

5. Everyone is looking forward to New Year's Day for a holographic presentation of a Beatles concert is going to be shown.

6. The redesigned rebuilt football stadium has been chosen as the site of the 2016 Super Bowl.

7. Eeyore was good at fielding and hitting but not much fun in the dugout.

8. You may embrace a geocentric view of the universe if you wish or you may accept the heliocentric model.

9. Sam called Bill loaded his pickup with fishing gear stopped at Starbucks and then headed for the lake.

10. The courageous proud Cherokee Chief Tsali surrendered to save the rest of his people in the Smoky Mountains.

Commas with Introductory Elements

When you begin a sentence with certain introductory words, phrases, or clauses, place a comma after the introductory element.

1. Use a comma after the following introductory words and transitional expressions.

Introductory Words		Transitional Expressions
next	similarly	on the other hand
first	nevertheless	in a similar manner
second	therefore	in other words
third	indeed	for example
moreover	yes	for instance
however	no	in fact
		in addition
		as a result

EXAMPLES

First, we will strike at the heart of the matter and then pursue other clichés.

For example, let's all stand up and be counted.

2. Use a comma after introductory prepositional phrases of five or more words. However, you may need to use a comma after shorter introductory prepositional phrases if not doing so would cause confusion.

EXAMPLES

After a long and thrilling nap, Buster went looking for a cat to chase.

After dinner we all went for a walk around the lake.

In spring, time seems to catch up with small furry animals.

Without the comma, this last sentence might look as if it begins *In springtime*.

3. Use a comma after all introductory infinitive and participial phrases.

EXAMPLES

Blackened with soot, the little boy toddled out of the smoldering house.

Begging for her forgiveness, Homer assured Hortense that they would never run short of Spam again.

To break in your new car properly, drive at varying speeds for the first one thousand miles.

4. Use a comma after introductory adverb subordinate clauses.

⊚⊚ EXAMPLES

Because Umberto played the tuba so well, he was awarded a music scholarship.

As soon as he arrived on shore, Columbus claimed the land for Spain.

Although it was raining furiously, Freida ran six miles anyway.

⊚⊚ PRACTICE

Insert commas after introductory elements.

1. First, do not be standing in water when you turn the machine on.

2. On board the *Santa Maria* in 1492 Columbus and his crew were relieved to find that the world is not flat.

3. Waiting for a day and a half Chet finally boarded his jet out of Afghanistan.

4. While he was processing the transaction for the iPhone the Apple salesperson asked Gates for a picture identification.

5. Yes Freud named some of his psychological observations after people in Greek myths.

6. Walking down the aisle Barbara slowed and then unexpectedly stopped at the halfway mark.

7. As the artist looked up at the ceiling he hoped the pope would like it.

8. When learning how to parallel park try to avoid busy city streets.

9. In order to create a romantic atmosphere Juliet played Louis Armstrong's "A Kiss to Build a Dream On" for Romeo.

10. To determine whether to forgive Sir Lancelot King Arthur flipped a coin.

Commas with Interrupters

Sometimes certain words, phrases, or clauses will interrupt the flow of thought in a sentence to add emphasis or additional information. These interrupters are enclosed by commas.

1. Use commas to set off parenthetical expressions. Common parenthetical expressions include *however, indeed, consequently, as a result, moreover, of course, for example, for instance, that is, in fact, after all, I think,* and *therefore.*

EXAMPLES   The answer, **after all,** lay right under his left big toe.

That big blue bird by the feeder is, **I think,** one of those unruly Steller's jays.

She is, **moreover,** a notorious misspeller of the word *deceitful.*

NOTE: Whenever a parenthetical expression introduces a second main clause after a semicolon, the semicolon takes the place of the comma in front of it.

EXAMPLE   Yes, you may eat your snails in front of me; **after all,** we are old friends.

PRACTICE   Use commas to set off any parenthetical elements in the following sentences.

1. Each of the female gods, after all, wanted Paris to choose her as the most beautiful.

2. Wynton Marsalis on the other hand knows more about jazz than any other living person I know.

3. Marsalis went to Juilliard School of Music and plays trumpet; moreover he plays both classical and jazz trumpet excellently.

4. Wynton incidentally has a father who plays jazz piano, a brother who plays saxophone, and another brother who plays percussion.

5. Miles Davis loved playing his trumpet; for instance I once saw him keep playing in a rainstorm even though his trumpet had an electrical connection on it.

2. Use commas to set off nonrestrictive elements. Nonrestrictive elements are modifying words, phrases, or clauses that are not necessary to identify the words they modify. They include adjective subordinate clauses, appositives, and participial phrases.

Adjective Clauses

(See pages 85–89 if you need to review adjective clauses.) If the information in an adjective clause <u>is not necessary to identify the word it modifies</u>, it is called a **nonrestrictive clause**, and it is enclosed in commas.

EXAMPLE   Ms. Erindira Sanchez, **who is president of that company**, began twenty years ago as a secretary.

Because the name of the person is used, the adjective clause is not necessary to identify which woman began twenty years ago as a secretary, so the commas are needed.

However, if her name is not used, the adjective clause is a **restrictive** one <u>because the woman is not already identified</u>. In this case, the commas are not necessary.

EXAMPLE   The woman **who is president of that company** began twenty years ago as a secretary.

The following are additional examples of nonrestrictive clauses.

EXAMPLE   My oldest brother, **who is a park ranger**, showed me his collection of arrowheads.

Because a person can have only one oldest brother, the brother is already identified, and the adjective clause is <u>not needed to identify him</u>, making it nonrestrictive.

EXAMPLE   His hometown, **which is somewhere in northeastern Indiana**, wants him to return for its centennial celebration.

A person can have only one hometown, so the adjective clause is nonrestrictive.

PRACTICE   In the following sentences, set off all nonrestrictive clauses with commas.

1. Milan, which is the most famous place in the world for opera, is the first place I visited in Italy.

2. Aspirin which is not considered a performance-enhancing drug is used even by archery competitors.

3. Claudius who was the brother of the murdered King Hamlet met an ironic death.

4. The man who had poisoned his brother was poisoned himself.

5. Odysseus who is the hero of the *Iliad* did not know how to defeat the huge monster with one eye.

Participial Phrases

(See pages 154–155 if you need to review participial phrases.) Participial phrases that <u>do not contain information necessary to identify the words they modify</u> are nonrestrictive and are therefore set off by commas. Restrictive participial phrases do not require commas.

EXAMPLE   (nonrestrictive)   The president, **seeking to be reelected,** traveled throughout the country making speeches and kissing babies.

Because we have only one president, the participial phrase *seeking to be reelected* is nonrestrictive. It is not necessary to identify who is meant by *president.*

EXAMPLE   (restrictive)   The woman **sitting by the door** is a famous surgeon.

Sitting by the door is a restrictive participial phrase because it is necessary to identify which woman is the famous surgeon.

EXAMPLE   Foxworth, **discouraged by years of failure,** decided to buy a pet chimpanzee.

Discouraged by years of failure is a nonrestrictive past participial phrase. It is not necessary to identify Foxworth.

PRACTICE   In the following sentences, set off nonrestrictive participial phrases with commas.

1. Steven Tyler, concerned about Liv's behavior, banned her from going to the Aerosmith concert.

2. The man swimming in the public fountain was arrested as a public nuisance.

3. Rosa Parks determined not to sit at the back of the bus was instrumental in beginning the civil rights movement.

4. The Ultradome lying in the path of the tsunami was almost completely destroyed.

5. The jury awarded $50 million to the tourist injured by falling rocks.

Appositives

(See pages 167–169 if you need to review appositives.) Appositives usually contain information <u>not necessary to identify the words they modify</u> and are therefore nonrestrictive. Set them off with commas.

EXAMPLES   Natalie's mother, **a lawyer in Boston,** will be coming to visit her soon.

Kleenex, **a household necessity,** was invented as a substitute for bandages during World War I because of a cotton shortage.

Parker took his stamp collection to Mr. Poindexter, **a noted stamp expert.**

PRACTICE   In the following sentences, set off all appositives with commas.

1. The Tickled Trout, a nearby seafood restaurant, attracts many customers.

2. Lupita drove to the grocery store to buy a rib-eye steak her husband's favorite cut of beef.

3. Eros the son of the goddess Aphrodite plays all sorts of tricks on mortals.

4. On his way to Sacramento, Matthew stopped in Fresno the home of many well-known poets.

5. The cat in our backyard an orange-and-white tabby is stalking a robin.

3. Use commas to separate most explanatory words from direct quotations.

EXAMPLES   Mr. Jones asked, "Where are you going?"

"I will arrive before dinner is over," he remarked.

"Tonight's dinner," **he said,** "will be delayed."

NOTE: Do not use commas to separate explanatory words from a partial direct quotation.

EXAMPLE   He described the clouds as "ominous, dark, and threatening."

4. Use commas to set off words of direct addresses. If a writer addresses someone directly in a sentence, the word or words that stand for that person or persons are set off by commas. If the word or words in direct address begin the sentence, they are followed by a comma.

EXAMPLES   And now, **my good friends,** I think it is time to end this conversation.

Mr. Chairman, I rise to a point of order.

I would like to present my proposal, **my esteemed colleagues.**

5. <u>Use commas to set off dates and addresses.</u> If your sentence contains two, three, or more elements of the date or address, use commas to set off these elements. The following sentences contain two or more elements.

EXAMPLES   We visited Disneyland on **Monday, June 5,** in order to avoid the weekend rush.

We visited Disneyland on **Monday, June 5, 2013,** in order to avoid the weekend rush.

Celia has lived at **3225 Oliver Street, San Diego,** for five years.

Celia has lived at **3225 Oliver Street, San Diego, California,** for five years.

Celia has lived at **3225 Oliver Street, San Diego, California 92023,** for five years.

NOTE: The zip code is not separated from the state by a comma.

The following sentences contain only one element.

EXAMPLES   We visited Disneyland on **Monday** in order to avoid the weekend rush.

Celia has lived at **3225 Oliver Street** for five years.

PRACTICE   In the following sentences, use commas to set off explanatory words for direct quotations, words in direct address, and dates and addresses that have two or more elements.

1. Hester, have you lived at 4590 A Street, Salem, Massachusetts, for the past two years?

2. The computer that was mailed on October 21 2013 from Cupertino California arrived in Santa Fe New Mexico the next day.

3. Each of the presidential candidates smiled and said "I will make your life better."

4. The multicolored togas arrived at The Debauchery 415 Cicero Street Rome Arkansas on the day before Saturnalia began.

5. Hit the road Jack.

⊚⊚ **PRACTICE** Use commas to set off parenthetical expressions, nonrestrictive elements, explanatory words for direct quotations, words in direct address, and dates and addresses that have two or more elements.

1. Starbucks, for example, is one of Michelle's favorite places to study.

2. A misanthrope who is a person who dislikes other people is usually not well liked.

3. *The Tell-Tale Tart* a novel by Dulcinea Baker will soon be a movie.

4. Christine how effective do you think the newly elected president will be?

5. This year Easter occurs on April 20 2014 which is the first Sunday after the first full moon after the vernal equinox.

6. The missing coprolite was found on August 10 1954 in Rome Georgia.

7. Clare Danes playing a CIA agent stars in the series *Homeland*.

8. "The spiders have arrived" said Harker "and I'm ready."

9. Steven Spielberg for example directed *E.T.*

10. Clark please tell Scarlett who is a sensitive Southern belle that you apologize for using the word *damn*.

Section One Review

Rules for the Use of the Comma

1. <u>Use a comma before a coordinating conjunction that joins two main clauses</u>.

2. <u>Use commas to separate elements in a series</u>.

   a. Elements in a series may be words, phrases, or clauses.

   b. Two or more adjectives that modify the same noun may need to be separated with commas.

3. <u>Use a comma after an introductory element.</u> Introductory elements include:

   a. Introductory words

   b. Transitional expressions

   c. Prepositional phrases

   d. Verbal phrases

   e. Adverb clauses

4. <u>Use commas to separate interrupters from the rest of the sentence</u>. Interrupters include:

   a. Parenthetical expressions

   b. Nonrestrictive clauses

   c. Nonrestrictive participial phrases

   d. Appositives

   e. Explanatory words for direct quotations

   f. Words in direct address

   g. Dates and addresses with two or more elements

Exercise 1A

Add commas to the following sentences where necessary.

1. Bill's sciatic nerve is giving him pain, and his brother-in-law is also.

2. Arachna had long thin arms and legs but never considered herself unattractive.

3. She was however embarrassed about her red hourglass birthmark.

4. Lady Gaga my brother's favorite singer-songwriter will perform at Cricket Amphitheater this fall.

5. Sir William Rootes said "No other man-made device since the shields and lances of the ancient knights fulfills a man's ego like an automobile."

6. If you want to find a witty quotation look up Oscar Wilde who was famous for his satirical wit.

7. On the aging soiled sign was a warning about the depredations of aging.

8. Stations KPJO and WFHI suffering from low ratings have decided to add 3-D.

9. Coming from the humblest of Irish conditions Seamus Heaney a contemporary poet was awarded the Nobel Prize for Literature.

10. Alice you should leave that rabbit alone and you should pay no attention to the cat with the big smile.

11. Before Virgil entered the room full of geeks he checked his pocket protector.

12. The fearsome belligerent crowd on December 8 1857 supported slavery but that did not deter Abraham Lincoln who gave one of the most powerful speeches of his career.

13. Johansen was clever with his hands; however he could not assemble the table from IKEA.

14. Yes the new national health program did help the people of Malady Tennessee.

15. CVS which is a large drugstore chain has had a hard time procuring earplugs lately.

Exercise 1B

Add commas to the following paragraph where necessary.

1. During last night's storm, I had a dream that I was taken back to September 6, 1963, the start of my first year in high school. **2.** I won't say it was a nightmare but the differences between the very early sixties and today were somewhat of a shock. **3.** For instance the fashions were much more conservative; as I looked around I saw students wearing white bucks saddle shoes Keds and penny loafers. **4.** To my surprise most of the boys wore chinos or blue jeans but no shorts; in addition the girls all wore dresses or skirts and none of them wore long pants. **5.** Drug and alcohol use among teens also seemed different from today. **6.** In the early sixties I was not aware of drug use in high school except for some rumors of a few renegade students smoking pot. **7.** Like today however high school students could always find a way to acquire alcohol whether through an older acquaintance a fake ID or the parents' liquor cabinet. **8.** Computer and telephone technology in the sixties was antiquated compared to today's. **9.** For instance when one of my teachers assigned an essay no computers were available so I had to use a manual typewriter. **10.** Also there was usually only one telephone per family and its use was strictly governed; for example in my house no one was allowed to use the phone during dinner. **11.** Of course cell phones had not been invented so there was no messaging texting or phone sounding off at inappropriate times. **12.** Courtship customs were also quite different. **13.** For the most part a "respectable young woman" would not accept an invitation for a date unless it was made a week in advance. **14.** Teens were not as sexually active or so it seemed to me. **15.** Contraceptive devices were hard to come by and the pill had just recently been developed. **16.** Information about sex was

continued

not readily available and the unlucky young woman who became pregnant was not allowed

to attend school a double penalty. **17.** The early sixties a difficult and problematic time for

teens came to an end as the Beatles a group of young men from Liverpool England recorded

their first album and as Betty Friedan a leading figure in the women's movement published

The Feminine Mystique.

Exercise 1C

In the following paragraph, add commas wherever they are needed.

1. Even though the United States and Mexico share a common border, the customs, activities, and traditions differ when they celebrate holidays. **2.** For example Independence Day is an important occasion for each country. **3.** On the Fourth of July in the United States people shoot off fireworks and they eat American food like hotdogs hamburgers potato salad potato chips and ice cream. **4.** Mexico on the other hand celebrates its independence over two days September 15 and 16. **5.** As students parade through the streets people blow horns throw confetti and wave flags. **6.** Ever since September 16 1810 the Mexican president has yelled "Viva Mexico!" from the Presidential Palace at exactly 12:00 a.m. **7.** Two other holidays Halloween in the United States and *Dia de los Muertos* in Mexico are also celebrated in differing ways. **8.** On the night of the American Halloween young children dress up in costumes and then they go door-to-door begging for candies. **9.** Similarly many American adults dress up in costumes and attend parties. **10.** In Mexico on *Dia de los Muertos* people take food to the dead clean tombstones and decorate the graves with flowers and candles. **11.** Instead of asking for candy Mexican children in some cities go around town asking for gifts of candles or money. **12.** Finally Easter celebrations in Mexico and the United States have both similarities and differences. **13.** People in the United States dress up quite formally to go to church and then the children hunt for decorated Easter eggs to put in their Easter baskets. **14.** Of course people in Mexico also dress up and go to church; in addition many of them reenact the crucifixion of Christ. **15.** Some things that will not be found in a Mexican Easter celebration however are Easter eggs and bunnies. **16.** Having spent several years in both cultures I can appreciate and enjoy the differences in these holiday celebrations.

Other Punctuation Marks

Punctuation would be simple if we could just include a page of punctuation marks at the end of a piece of writing and invite readers to sprinkle them about anywhere they choose. But if you want to be an effective writer, it helps a great deal to know how to use not only those troublesome commas but also all of the other marks of punctuation. In this section, we will take up end punctuation and the other punctuation marks.

The placement of punctuation marks can affect the meaning of a sentence profoundly. Here are a few examples.

In this sentence, the dog recognizes its owner.

EXAMPLE   A clever dog knows **its** master.

In this one, the dog is in charge.

EXAMPLE   A clever dog knows **it's** master.

In this sentence, we find a deliberately rude butler.

EXAMPLE   The butler stood by the door and called the **guests** names as they entered.

In this sentence, he is more mannerly.

EXAMPLE   The butler stood by the door and called the **guests'** names as they entered.

And in this sentence, we find a person who doesn't trust his friends.

EXAMPLE   Everyone **I know** has secret ambitions.

Add two commas, and you change the meaning.

EXAMPLE   Everyone, **I know,** has secret ambitions.

As you can see, punctuation marks are potent tools.

End Punctuation

The Period

1. <u>The period is used at the end of a sentence that makes a statement or gives a command.</u>

EXAMPLES   This rule is probably the easiest of all.

Circle the subject in the above sentence.

2. The period is used with most abbreviations.

EXAMPLES   Mr., Mrs., Dr., A.D., Ph.D., U.S., St., Rd., Blvd., Sgt., Lt.

The Question Mark

1. The question mark is used at the end of sentences that ask questions.

EXAMPLES   Where have all the flowers gone?

Is the water hot yet?

2. A question mark is not used at the end of an indirect question.

EXAMPLES   (direct question)   Why is Emile going to the dance?

(indirect question)   I wonder why Emile is going to the dance.

The Exclamation Point

1. The exclamation point is used after words, phrases, and short sentences that show strong emotion.

EXAMPLES   Rats!

Not on your life!

Watch it, Buster!

Ouch! That hurt!

2. The exclamation point is not often used in college writing. For the most part, the words themselves should express the excitement.

EXAMPLE   Chased by a ravenous pack of ocelots, Cedric raced through the forest to his condo, bolted up his stairs, swiftly locked the door, and threw himself, quivering and exhausted, onto his beanbag chair.

PRACTICE   Use periods, question marks, and exclamation points in the following sentences.

1. Robinson wondered whether he would ever leave the island **.**

2. Have you tasted the dessert

3. The whole Atlantic coast is under attack

4. The pitcher asked his catcher if he should throw a curve

5. Has Ceres been waiting long for her daughter

6. How do you know it is an atom

7. Stop being stubborn

8. Michael received his PhD from Arizona State University

9. Why did they leave the game so early

10. After five days the fish wondered if it had worn out its welcome

Internal Punctuation

The Semicolon

1. A semicolon is used to join two main clauses that are not joined by a coordinating conjunction. Sometimes a transitional word or phrase follows the semicolon.

☯ EXAMPLES   Thirteen people saw the incident; each one described it differently.

All tragedies end in death; on the other hand, all comedies end in marriage.

2. A semicolon can be used to join elements in a series when the elements require further internal punctuation.

☯ EXAMPLE   Before making his decision, Elrod consulted his banker, who abused him; his lawyer, who ignored him; his minister, who consoled him; and his mother, who scolded him.

3. Do not use a semicolon to separate two phrases or two subordinate clauses.

☯ EXAMPLE   (incorrect)   I will pay you for the work when you return the tape deck that was stolen from our car; and when you repair the dented left fender.

The Colon

1. A colon is used to join two main clauses when the second clause is an example, an explanation, or a restatement of the first clause.

☯ EXAMPLES   The past fifty years had been a time of turmoil: war, drought, and famine had plagued the small country.

The garden was a delight to all insects: aphids abounded in it, ladybugs exulted in it, and praying mantises cavorted in it.

2. A colon is used when a complete sentence introduces an example, a series, a list, or a direct quotation. Often a colon will come after the words *follows* or *following*.

EXAMPLES

The paper explored the comic elements of three Melville novels: *Moby Dick, Mardi,* and *Pierre.*

The list of complaints included the following items: leaky faucets, peeling wallpaper, and a nauseating green love seat.

3. A colon is generally not used after a verb.

EXAMPLES

(incorrect) At the store I bought: bread, eggs, and bacon.

(correct)   At the store I bought bread, eggs, and bacon.

PRACTICE In the following sentences, add semicolons and colons where necessary.

1. You crack three eggs into the pan;then you stir them slowly.

2. The aspiring star did the following to prepare for his audition got disturbing tattoos all over his body, dyed his hair extravagant colors, and learned two chords on the guitar.

3. The child touched the burner on the stove however, she did not react.

4. At the private boys' school, students wore tan slacks, brown leather shoes, and white shirts.

5. There was one thing I really looked forward to when I visited my grandparents exploring the creek that ran by their house.

Quotation Marks

1. Quotation marks are used to enclose direct quotations and dialogue.

EXAMPLES

"When a stupid man is doing something he is ashamed of, he always declares that it is his duty."
—George Bernard Shaw

Woody Allen said, "If my film makes one more person miserable, I've done my job."

2. <u>Quotation marks are not used with indirect quotations.</u>

(direct quotation)   Fernando said, "I will be at the airfield before dawn."

(indirect quotation)   Fernando said that he would be at the airfield before dawn.

3. <u>Place periods and commas inside quotation marks.</u>

Flannery O'Connor wrote the short story "A Good Man Is Hard to Find."

"Always forgive your enemies—nothing annoys them so much," quipped Oscar Wilde.

4. <u>Place colons and semicolons outside quotation marks.</u>

Priscilla was disgusted by the story "The Great Toad Massacre": it was grossly unfair to toads and contained too much gratuitous violence.

Abner felt everyone should read the essay "The Shocking State of Okra Cookery"; he had even had several copies made just in case he found someone who was interested.

5. <u>Place the question mark inside the quotation marks if the quotation is a question. Place the question mark outside the quotation marks if the quotation is not a question but the whole sentence is.</u>

The poem asks, "What are patterns for?"

Did Mark Twain say, "Never put off until tomorrow what you can do the day after tomorrow"?

6. <u>Place the exclamation point inside the quotation marks if the quotation is an exclamation. Place it outside the quotation marks if the quotation is not an exclamation but the whole sentence is.</u>

"An earwig in my ointment!" the disgusted pharmacist proclaimed.

Please stop saying "It's time to leave"!

Add semicolons, colons, and quotation marks to the following sentences.

1. Dante said, "I like this place, but I would like to leave now"; however, Virgil told him that no one was allowed to leave.

2. Batman was afraid of losing his significant other to the district attorney moreover, he had lately developed a fear of heights.

3. Who was it who said, The truth is rarely pure and never simple?

4. My favorite Mae West quotation is this one When I'm good, I'm very good, but when I'm bad, I'm better.

5. Coltrane looked at Davis and said, Tell me a few of my favorite things.

6. For whom does the bell toll? asked the tourist.

7. Was it Mark Twain who said, I believe that our Heavenly Father invented man because he was disappointed in the monkey?

8. Daedalus screamed, Deploy your parachute!

9. Humpty fell off the wall and broke one of the King's men called for Super Glue.

10. Bill Clinton once said, It's the economy, stupid.

The Apostrophe

1. <u>Apostrophes are used to form contractions.</u> The apostrophe replaces the omitted letter or letters.

I am	I'm	did not	didn't
you are	you're	is not	isn't
it is	it's	were not	weren't
they are	they're	will not	won't
does not	doesn't	cannot	can't

2. <u>Apostrophes are used to form the possessives of nouns and indefinite pronouns.</u>

   a. Add *'s* to form the possessive of all singular nouns and all indefinite pronouns.

EXAMPLES

(singular nouns)	The **girl's** hair was shiny.
	Charles's car is rolling down the hill.
(indefinite pronouns)	**Everyone's** watch was affected by the giant magnet.
(compound words)	Mr. Giuliano left on Monday to attend his **son-in-law's** graduation.
(joint possession)	**Vladimir and Natasha's** wedding was long and elaborate.

   b. Add only an apostrophe to form the possessive of plural nouns that end in *s*. However, add *'s* to form the possessive of plural nouns that do not end in *s*.

⊚⊚ **EXAMPLES**	(plural nouns that end in *s*)	The **Joneses'** cabin had been visited by an untidy bear.
		We could hear the three **friends'** conversation all the way down the hall.
	(plural nouns that do not end in *s*)	During the storm the parents were concerned about their **children's** safety.

c. Expressions referring to time or money often require an apostrophe.

⊚⊚ **EXAMPLES**   Please give me one **dollar's** worth.

Two **weeks'** vacation is simply not enough.

3. <u>Do not use apostrophes with the possessive forms of personal pronouns.</u>

Incorrect	*Correct*
her's	hers
our's	ours
their's	theirs

NOTE: *It's* means "it is." The possessive form of *it* is *its*.

⊚⊚ **PRACTICE**   Add apostrophes (or *'s*) to the following sentences where necessary.

1. Everyone was looking for Alices rabbit; he wouldnt come when we called him.

2. Mr. Lewis sense of propriety was bothered by Mr. Clarks rude remarks.

3. Have you seen Rumpelstiltskins scissors?

4. Constance was given three months wages when she was terminated.

5. Popeyes can opener wasnt working, so he went to Walmart.

6. Its strange that Natasha wont write in anything but short, simple sentences.

7. Well applaud when we hear something thats worthwhile.

8. He had one weeks free stay at his father-in-laws hotel.

9. Staring over the rim of Sylvias soup bowl was a cockroach.

10. The childrens favorite bedtime story was the one about the man with the hatchet.

PRACTICE   Write sentences of your own according to the instructions.

1. Write a complete sentence in which you use the possessive form of *women*.

The women's basketball team is now playing in

the semifinals.

2. Write a complete sentence in which you use the possessive form of Thomas.

_____

_____

3. Write a complete sentence in which you use the possessive form of *brother-in-law*.

_____

_____

4. Write a complete sentence in which you use the possessive form of a plural word.

_____

_____

5. Write a complete sentence in which you use the possessive form of *Ms. Lewis* and the contraction for *did not*.

_____

_____

Section Two Review

1. Use a **period** at the end of sentences that make statements or commands.

2. Use a **period** to indicate most abbreviations.

3. Use a **question mark** at the end of sentences that ask questions.

4. Do not use a **question mark** at the end of an indirect question.

5. Use an **exclamation point** after exclamatory words, phrases, and short sentences.

6. Use the **exclamation point** sparingly in college writing.

7. Use a **semicolon** to join two main clauses that are not joined by a coordinating conjunction.

8. Use a **semicolon** to separate elements in a series when the elements require further internal punctuation.

9. Do not use a **semicolon** to separate two phrases or two subordinate clauses.

10. Use a **colon** to join two main clauses when the second main clause is an example, an explanation, or a restatement.

11. Use a **colon** to introduce an example, a series, a list, or a direct quotation.

12. Do not use a **colon** to introduce a series of items that follows a verb.

13. Use **quotation marks** to enclose direct quotations and dialogue.

14. Do not use **quotation marks** with indirect quotations.

15. Place periods and commas inside **quotation marks.**

16. Place colons and semicolons outside **quotation marks.**

17. If a quotation is a question, place the question mark <u>inside</u> the **quotation marks.** If the quotation is not a question, but the whole sentence is, place the question mark <u>outside</u> the quotation marks.

18. If the quotation is an exclamation, place the exclamation point <u>inside</u> the **quotation marks.** If the quotation is not an exclamation, but the whole sentence is, place the exclamation point <u>outside</u> the quotation marks.

19. Use **apostrophes** to form contractions.

20. Use **apostrophes** to form the possessives of nouns and indefinite pronouns.

Exercise 2A

Add periods, question marks, exclamation points, semicolons, colons, quotation marks, and apostrophes (or 's) to the following sentences as necessary.

1. The firefighter shouted, "Watch out!"

2. Picassos girlfriends wondered why his depictions of women were so weird

3. Wouldnt you prefer the Bordeaux asked the snob

4. Tony Sopranos request included these items some antipasto, a loaf of Sicilian bread, a big plate of ravioli with pesto sauce, and some candied olives

5. The poker players girlfriend asked if she could go to her brother-in laws home

6. Gills favorite Ralph Waldo Emerson quotation is Don't waste yourself in rejection nor bark against the bad, but chant the beauty of the good.

7. Where is the salt asked Mark as he opened the bag of tortilla chips

8. The Yankees let the Confederates escape from Gettysburg therefore, Lincoln was very angry

9. Did Thomas Jefferson write, Difference of opinion is helpful in religion

10. Igor Timidsky, PhD, wont board the airplane without his lucky rabbits foot

11. Lincolns wife battled depression however, she was a charming, witty, and intelligent first lady

12. When Leonard Cohens son heard his fathers song, he asked his father who his mother really was

13. Wont Italys trains ever run on time

14. The tail gunners last words were, Here come the Messerschmitts

15. Lawrence Putnam, MD, went to Afghanistan with these items goggles, water purifying tablets, a Swiss Army knife, and a dozen boxes of chocolate

Exercise 2B

Add periods, question marks, exclamation points, semicolons, colons, quotation marks, apostrophes (or 's), and commas to the following sentences where necessary.

1. The lobsters were bound for Rudy's Fish House, 591 Triton Street, Kansas City, Kansas.

2. Abandon ship shouted Ishmael as he leapt into the sea

3. Did Yogi Berra really say that or are you just joking

4. The students did not respond to Fergals knock-knock jokes however they woke up when he started imitating Queen Elizabeth

5. Jean Girardeaux said, Only the mediocre are always at their best

6. There aint no way to find out why a snorer cant hear himself snore said Tom Sawyer

7. The Queen placed her arm on Michelle Obamas back therefore it was not improper for Ms Obama to place her arm on the Queens back

8. Dont you think the custom of spitting after tasting some wine is gross

9. The bouncer at the door asked Do you think youre cool enough for this club

10. Shoot them now shouted Doc Holliday

11. The groups agent said Youll need the following to succeed in this business tattoos on both forearms a scar on one cheek tight leather pants earplugs and little sensitivity to music

12. Lady Macbeth asked her friends valet where the soap and water were

13. My daughter asked Lance Armstrong Arent you tired of the committees questions

14. The childrens babysitter arrived with these items a gallon of ice cream two bugles a jump rope and one set of earplugs

15. Bruce Springsteens band was ready to leave the stage after its performance at the Super Bowl however the enthusiastic crowd wouldnt let it leave

Exercise 2C

In the following paragraph, correct any errors in the use of periods, exclamation points, question marks, semicolons, colons, quotation marks, or apostrophes.

1. King Lear, the central character in Shakespeare's *The Tragedy of King Lear,* and Willy Loman, the protagonist in Arthur Miller's *Death of a Salesman,* are similar characters in some ways. **2.** For instance, both character's mistakenly believe that their favorite child no longer loves them, therefore, they respond with anger and resentment. **3.** Lears three daughters are: Goneril, Regan, and Cordelia. **4.** Goneril and Regan insincerely flatter Lear, Cordelia refuses to do so. **5.** When Lear asks her what she will say to show her love, she replies: Nothing, my lord as a result, Lear disinherits her. **6.** Willy Loman also think's he has lost the love of his son Biff. **7.** In one scene he addresses Biff this way You vengeful, spiteful mutt! **8.** Then, just a few lines later, he realizes that Biff actually love's him. **9.** Lear and Loman are also similar: in that both seem to be losing their minds. **10.** From the very start of the play, there is evidence that Lears' thoughts are not rational. **11.** Even his closest counselor tells Lear he is acting foolishly, however, the king will not listen. **12.** By the middle of the play: Lear seems completely mad! **13.** Similarly, Willy Loman is having trouble distinguishing between: reality and fantasy. **14.** Willy constantly drifts into scene's from his past; or talks to his dead brother. **15.** Finally, both main characters are abandoned by children they thought were loyal to them. **16.** Lear is stripped of all his dignity by Goneril and Regan therefore, he ends up wandering through a raging storm with the court fool. **17.** Willy Loman is abandoned by his son Happy; who leaves him in the bathroom of a restaurant. **18.** When a woman remind's Happy about Willy, Happy makes this unsettling statement No, that's not my father. He's just a guy. **19.** In many ways these two plays are quite different, however, the two main characters' have some remarkable similarities.

Titles, Capitalization, and Numbers

The rules regarding titles, capitalization, and numbers are not, perhaps, as critical to clear writing as the ones for the punctuation marks discussed in the previous two sections. In fact, you can forget to capitalize at all without losing the meaning of what you are writing. So why should you learn to apply these rules correctly? The answer is simple. You should know how to apply them for the same reason you should know whether it is appropriate to slap a person on the back or to kiss him or her on both cheeks when you are first introduced. **How people write** says as much about them as **how they act.** Your ability to apply the rules presented in this section, as well as in other sections, identifies you as an educated person.

Titles

1. <u>Place in italics the titles of works that are published separately, such as books, magazines, newspapers, websites, and plays.</u>

    - Books: *Huckleberry Finn, Webster's Dictionary*

    - Plays: *Hamlet, Death of a Salesman*

    - Pamphlets: *How to Paint Your House, Worms for Profit*

    - Websites: *CNN.com, Poetry Daily*

    - Long musical works: Beethoven's *Egmont Overture,* Miles Davis's *Kind of Blue*

    - Long poems: *Paradise Lost, Beowulf*

    - Newspapers and magazines: *The New York Times, Time*

    - Films: *The Artist, The King's Speech*

    - Television and radio programs: *Morning Edition, American Idol*

    - Works of art: Rembrandt's *Night Watch, Venus de Milo*

EXAMPLES

Hortencia has subscriptions to *Time* and *The New Yorker.*

The Los Angeles Chamber Orchestra played Bach's *Brandenburg Concerto Number Five.*

2. <u>Use quotation marks to enclose the titles of works that are parts of other works, such as articles, songs, poems, and short stories.</u>

    - Songs: "Honeysuckle Rose," "Yesterday"

    - Poems: "Stopping by Woods on a Snowy Evening," "The Waste Land"

- Articles in periodicals or websites: "Texas Air's New Flak Attack," "Of Planets and the Presidency"

- Short stories: "Paul's Case," "Barn Burning"

- Essays: "A Modest Proposal," "Once More to the Lake"

- Episodes of radio and television programs: "Tolstoy: From Rags to Riches," "Lord Mountbatten: The Last Viceroy"

- Subdivisions of books: "The Pulpit" (Chapter Eight of *Moby Dick*)

EXAMPLES

The professor played a recording of Dylan Thomas reading his poem "After the Funeral."

Many writing textbooks include Jonathan Swift's essay "A Modest Proposal."

PRACTICE

In the following sentences, correct any errors in the use of titles. Indicate the need for italics in a title by underlining it.

1. In New York's Central Park, a man was reciting the poem "When Lilacs Last in the Dooryard Bloom'd."

2. In Langston Hughes's short story Salvation, a boy ironically loses his faith while participating in church services.

3. Robert Frost's poem The Road Not Taken is one of his most well-known works.

4. After Hester put down the magazine Popular Sewing, she mended Pearl's stockings.

5. The movie Battleship earned only a quarter of what it cost to film it.

Capitalization

1. Capitalize the personal pronoun *I*.

EXAMPLE

In fact, I am not sure I like the way you said that.

2. Capitalize the first letter of every sentence.

EXAMPLE

The road through the desert was endlessly straight and boring.

3. <u>Capitalize the first letter of each word in a title except for *a, an,* and *the,* coordinating conjunctions, and prepositions.</u>

NOTE: The first letter of the first word and the first letter of the last word of a title are always capitalized.

- Titles of books: *Moby Dick, Encyclopaedia Britannica*

- Titles of newspapers and magazines: *People, Cosmopolitan, Los Angeles Times*

- Titles of stories, poems, plays, and films: "The Lady with the Dog," "The Road Not Taken," *Othello, Gone with the Wind*

4. <u>Capitalize the first letter of all proper nouns and adjectives derived from proper nouns.</u>

- Names and titles of people: Coretta Scott King, Mr. Birch, Mayor Golding, President Roosevelt, Cousin Alice, Aunt Bea

- Names of specific places: Yosemite National Park, Albuquerque, New Mexico, London, England, Saudi Arabia, Rockefeller Center, London Bridge, Elm Street, Venus, the Rio Grande, the Rocky Mountains, the Midwest

NOTE: Do not capitalize the first letter of words that refer to a direction (such as "north," "south," "east," or "west"). Do capitalize these words when they refer to a specific region.

EXAMPLES

Texas and Arizona are in the **Southwest.**

The police officer told us to drive **east** along the gravel road and turn **north** at the big pine tree.

- Names of national, ethnic, or racial groups: Indian, Native American, Spanish, Irish, Italian, African American

- Names of groups or organizations: Baptists, Mormons, Democrats, Republicans, American Indian Movement, Boy Scouts of America, Indianapolis Colts, U.S. Post Office

- Names of companies: Ford Motor Company, Montgomery Ward, Coca-Cola Bottling Company

- Names of the days of the week and months of the year but not the seasons: Thursday, August, spring

- Names of holidays and historical events: Memorial Day, the Fourth of July, the French Revolution, the Chicago Fire

- Names of <u>specific</u> gods and religious writings: God, Mohammed, Talmud, Bible

5. The names of academic subjects are not capitalized unless they refer to an ethnic or national origin or are the names of specific courses. Examples include mathematics, political science, English, History 105.

PRACTICE   Correct any errors in the use of titles or capitalization. Indicate the need for italics in a title by underlining it.

1. In february, the San Diego Symphony will present a series of concerts of Mozart's works.

2. mitt romney received a signed copy of john banville's latest novel the sea.

3. born in lorain, ohio, toni morrison has been on the cover of many magazines, including time.

4. uncle elvis was playing bruce springsteen's song born in the u.s.a. when I told him john updike had died.

5. a number of men and women from carlsbad, new mexico, participated in the iraq war and are now continuing to fight in the war in afghanistan.

6. during the christmas holidays, one can see beautiful decorations in santa fe and albuquerque.

7. The online newspaper the huffington post recently published an article titled colorado wildfires.

8. on my ipad, I bought the play waiting for godot by samuel beckett.

9. charlie showed marisa his collection of t.v. guide magazines.

10. the barnes and noble on grand avenue is closing by the end of winter.

Numbers

The following rules about numbers apply to general writing rather than to technical or scientific writing.

1. <u>Spell out numbers that require no more than two words. Use numerals for numbers that require more than two words.</u>

EXAMPLES   Last year it rained on only **eighty-four** days.

In 1986 it rained on more than **120** days.

2. <u>Always spell out a number at the beginning of a sentence.</u>

EXAMPLE   **Six hundred ninety** miles in one day is a long way to drive.

3. <u>In general, use numerals in the following situations:</u>

- Dates: August 9, 2014   30 CE   110 AD

- Sections of books and plays: Chapter 5, page 22
                                       Act 1, scene 3, lines 30–41

- Addresses: 1756 Grand Avenue
                    Hemostat, Idaho 60047

- Decimals, percents, and fractions: 75.8   30%, 30 percent   1/5

- Exact amounts of money: $7.95 $1,300,000

- Scores and statistics: Padres 8 Dodgers 5   a ratio of 6 to 1

- Time of day: 3:05   8:15

NOTE: Round amounts of money that can be expressed in a few words can be written out: *twenty cents, fifty dollars, one hundred dollars.* Also, when the word *o'clock* is used with the time of day, the time of day can be written out: *seven o'clock.*

4. <u>When numbers are compared, are joined by conjunctions, or occur in a series, either consistently use numerals or consistently spell them out.</u> Although either method is acceptable, using numerals is often clearer—and certainly easier.

EXAMPLE   For the company picnic we need **twenty-five** pounds of fried chicken, **fifteen** pounds of potato salad, **one hundred twenty-five** cans of soda, **eighty-five** paper plates, **two hundred thirty** napkins, and **eighty-five** sets of plastic utensils.

OR

For the company picnic we need **25** pounds of fried chicken, **15** pounds of potato salad, **125** cans of soda, **85** paper plates, **230** napkins, and **85** sets of plastic utensils.

PRACTICE   Correct any errors in the use of numbers in the following sentences.

1. *Five hundred* 500 fans attended the Patti Smith concert at the amphitheater, and *two* 2 of them were ejected for various offenses.

2. One never knows when all 5 members of Jim's jazz band will show up; it could be at nine fifteen or at twelve forty-five.

3. For the retirement party, Charlie brought 15 pastries, Blair brought 1 Clark Bar, Barbara brought one hundred fifteen pounds of fresh tuna, and Deborah brought 3 chocolate cheesecakes.

4. The inauguration ceremony on January twenty-first, two thousand thirteen, featured Barack Obama, who had defeated Mitt Romney.

5. On the first day of the 2011 baseball season, sixty thousand people in Petco Park watched San Diego defeat San Francisco by a score of 3 to 1.

Section Three Review

1. Underline or place in italics the **titles** of works that are published separately, such as books, plays, and films.

2. Use quotation marks to enclose the **titles** of works that are parts of other works, such as songs, poems, and short stories.

3. **Capitalize** the personal pronoun *I*.

4. **Capitalize** the first letter of every sentence.

5. **Capitalize** the first letter of each word in a title except *a, an, the,* coordinating conjunctions, and prepositions.

6. **Capitalize** all proper nouns and adjectives derived from proper nouns.

7. **Do not capitalize** names of academic subjects unless they refer to an ethnic or national origin or are the names of specific courses.

8. Spell out **numbers** that require no more than two words. Use numerals for numbers that require more than two words.

9. Always spell out a **number** at the beginning of a sentence.

10. In general, use **numerals** for dates, sections of books and plays, addresses, decimals, percentages, fractions, exact amounts of money, scores, statistics, and time of day.

11. When **numbers** are compared, are joined by conjunctions, or occur in a series, either consistently use numerals or consistently spell them out.

Exercise 3A

The following sentences contain errors in the use of titles, capitalization, and numbers. Correct any errors you find. (Indicate the need for italics in a title by underlining it.)

1. The movie <u>K̸ill B̸ill</u> caused a discussion about how much bloody violence is needed to make the filmmaker's point.

2. The television series homeland is about an american prisoner from the afghanistan war who may or may not be a spy.

3. president obama decided to leave afghanistan not long after the christmas season in two hundred thirteen.

4. 30 people from st. barnaby's church gathered at 5 o'clock on the top of mount harrison to observe easter sunday.

5. When tony said "sex" instead of "6," his teacher said he had made a freudian slip.

6. The marxist strategy used by yale university helped its philosophy department defeat the english department of harvard university by a score of 15 to twelve.

7. On his way to rome on march fifteenth, forty-four BCE, brutus bought a cheap dagger for the equivalent of five dollars and ninety-five cents.

8. After he typed the memorandum on his macbook pro, the secretary ordered three reams of copy paper, 250 file folders, four boxes of pencils, and 150 filters for the coffee machine.

9. The prudence software company donated five million three thousand dollars to washington and lee college for computer programs to study the effect of tattoos and body piercings on sophomores and juniors.

10. lady gaga recently appeared in cuernavaca and sang 1 of my favorite songs, bad romance.

11. when the late show with david letterman ended, a commercial for wit magazine followed.

12. One student in our shakespeare class told of an article in people magazine titled the bard, his mother, and freud.

Exercise 3A

continued

13. bruce smiled as he told the class the significance of willy loman's 2 heavy valises in the play death of a salesman.

14. Every day at the chicago art institute, over 150 people ask guards about the secret meaning of the pitchfork in grant wood's painting american gothic.

15. after professor landon explained the poem the road not taken to his literature 202 class, he bought 2 bottles of cutty sark scotch and got lost on the way home.

Exercise 3B

Compose sentences of your own according to the instructions. (Indicate the need for italics in a title by underlining it.)

1. Write a sentence that includes the author and title of a book.

   During his vacation, Rafael read Jane Smiley's novel <u>A Thousand Acres</u>.

   _____

2. Write a sentence that describes a song you like and the musician who wrote it or performs it.

   _____

   _____

3. Tell what movie you last saw in a theater and how much you paid to see it.

   _____

   _____

4. Write a sentence that tells what school you attend and what classes you are taking.

   _____

   _____

5. Write a sentence that tells the number of people in your family, the number of years you have gone to school, the number of classes you are taking, and the approximate number of students at your school.

   _____

   _____

6. Write a sentence that mentions a website you have looked at lately. If possible, include the title of an article from that website.

   _____

   _____

7. In a sentence, describe your favorite television program.

   _____

   _____

Exercise 3B

continued

8. Tell where you would go on your ideal vacation. Be specific about the name of the place and its geographical location.

   _____

   _____

9. Write a sentence that includes your age and address. (Feel free to lie about either one.)

   _____

   _____

10. Write a sentence that names a musician, musical group, or CD that you like.

    _____

    _____

11. Write a sentence that includes the name of a local newspaper, its approximate circulation, and the average number of pages during the week.

    _____

    _____

12. Write a sentence that includes a work of art that you know about and the name of the artist. If you need to, make up the name of a work of art and its artist.

    _____

    _____

13. Write a sentence that includes the score of the last baseball, football, or basketball game you were aware of. If you are not a sports fan, make up a score.

    _____

    _____

continued

14. Write a sentence that tells what time you get up on Mondays, what time your first class starts, what time you have lunch, and what time you usually have dinner.

_____

_____

Exercise 3C

In the following paragraph, correct any errors in the use of capitalization, numbers, or titles. (Indicate the need for italics in a title by underlining it.)

1. Computer technology has transformed the *Movie Industry* [*movie industry*], creating visual effects that are often stunning in their realism, but the story lines in the last *20* [*twenty*] years are not much different from those of *60* [*sixty*] years ago. **2.** Consider, for example, "Jurassic Park" of the 1990s and "Mysterious Island" of the 1950s. **3.** Both movies involve a group of about 5 people who are trapped on an Island inhabited by huge, dangerous animals that do not exist anywhere else. **4.** The animals in Jurassic Park, of course, are Dinosaurs; in Mysterious Island they are a gigantic bee, crab, and bird. **5.** As the magazine article <u>Monsters And Madness</u> points out, the plots in both movies are about the same. **6.** Two other movies that are not so different from each other are Mimic of nineteen ninety-seven and Them of the late nineteen fifties. **7.** Mimic involves cockroaches that have been genetically altered by a Scientist working in the Eastern part of <u>New York</u>. **8.** They live in old subway tunnels of new york city and have mutated until they are able to mimic the size and appearance of Humans. **9.** 100s of them are feasting on captured humans and are threatening to establish new colonies in the Spring, but luckily they are destroyed by fire and explosives. **10.** According to a review in time, the plot of "Them" from the 1950s is very similar. **11.** In it ants have been mutated by radiation from Atomic testing. **12.** The giant Queen Ant and a consort of over 25 males have flown into the sewer tunnels under "Los Angeles" and have started a colony that threatens Civilization. **13.** They are destroyed the same way the cockroaches in <u>Mimic</u> are, with fire and explosives. **14.** Finally, the movie Independence Day, which came out on the fourth of july a few years ago, is similar in many ways to Invaders From Mars from the 1950s. **15.** As the los angeles times newspaper points out in an article titled save us from the aliens, both movies involve Aliens from Outer Space intent upon taking over the Planet. **16.** In addition, the 2 movies feature similar bug-headed enemies with no apparent sympathy or concern for Humanity. **17.** And in both movies representatives of the <u>Military</u> are called upon to save the day. **18.** Obviously, computer technology has made the movies of the past twenty years exciting, but plots themselves have not changed much in the past 60 years.

Sentence Practice: Sentence Variety

Writing is challenging. As we have pointed out a number of times already, writing is a process that requires constant and countless choices. Much head scratching and crossing out go on between the beginning and the end of composing a paragraph. Each sentence can be framed in numerous ways, each version changing—subtly or dramatically—the relationships among the ideas.

Sometimes a short sentence is best. Look at the one that begins this paragraph and the one that begins the paragraph above. At other times you will need longer sentences to get just the right meaning and feeling. Sentence combining exercises give you an opportunity to practice how to express ideas in various ways by encouraging you to move around words, phrases, and clauses to achieve different effects.

When you construct a sentence, you should be aware not only of how it expresses your ideas but also of how it affects the other sentences in the paragraph. Consider the following paragraph as an example. It is the opening paragraph of Rachel Carson's book *The Edge of the Sea*.

> The edge of the sea is a strange and beautiful place. All through the long history of the earth it has been an area of unrest where waves have broken heavily against the land, where the tides have pressed forward over the continents, receded, and then returned. For no two successive days is the shoreline precisely the same. Not only do the tides advance and retreat in their eternal rhythms, but the level of the sea itself is never at rest. It rises or falls as the glaciers melt or grow, as the floor of the deep ocean basins shifts under its increasing load of sediments, or as the earth's crust along the continental margins warps up or down in adjustment to strain and tension. Today a little more land may belong to the sea, tomorrow a little less. Always the edge of the sea remains an elusive and indefinable boundary.

As you can see, Rachel Carson opens her paragraph with a short, simple sentence. Then she writes a sentence that is much longer and more complicated because it begins to explain the general ideas in the first one. It even seems to capture the rhythm of the sea against the land. She follows that one with another short, simple sentence. As the paragraph continues, she varies the length and complexity of her sentences according to what she needs to say. Notice how she ends the paragraph with another simple statement that matches her opening sentence.

Sentence Combining Exercises

In the following sentence combining exercises, you will practice writing sentences so that some are short and concise and others are lengthier and more complex.

EXAMPLE   Combine the following sentences into either two or three sentences. Experiment with which sounds best.

a. There was a feud.
b. It began simply enough.
c. The Smiths' youngest son refused to marry the Millers' favorite daughter.
d. Mrs. Miller fed Grandfather Smith some potato salad.
e. The potato salad was tainted.
f. They were at the annual Presidents' Day picnic.
g. Nothing was the same after that.

The feud began simply enough. When the Smiths' youngest son refused to marry the Millers' favorite daughter, Mrs. Miller fed Grandfather Smith some tainted potato salad at the annual Presidents' Day picnic. Nothing was the same after that.

1. Combine the following sentences into three or four sentences.

a. I visited the South Pacific in my twenties.
b. I had the chance to go snorkeling at several beautiful atolls.
c. Atolls are formed when coral grows around the edge of a small volcanic island.
d. The island slowly sinks back into the sea.
e. The coral continues to grow.
f. A lagoon is formed.
g. The volcanic island completely disappears.
h. The coral forms a barrier reef around the lagoon.
i. It becomes the home of a variety of sea life, like multicolored fish, sea anemones, and starfish.

_____

_____

_____

_____

_____

_____

Sentence Combining Exercises

continued

2. Combine the following sentences into three to four sentences.

   a. Chop suey was developed under unusual circumstances in 1896.
   b. The cook for the Chinese ambassador to the United States was ordered to create a new dish.
   c. It was to honor the ambassador.
   d. The cook called his new dish *tsa sui*.
   e. It means "odds and ends."
   f. It was translated from Chinese as "chop suey."
   g. After the dinner, the recipe was published in a New York newspaper.
   h. Soon it became a popular American dish.

   _____

   _____

   _____

   _____

3. Combine the following sentences into three or four sentences.

   a. Virginia Military Institute is a well-respected university.
   b. It is located in Lexington, Virginia.
   c. Its students have fought in all of America's wars since the Civil War.
   d. During the Civil War, they participated in the Battle of New Market.
   e. A large Union force was near the small town of New Market.
   f. It was approaching Lexington.
   g. All of the cadets of VMI went out to meet the Yankees.
   h. Some of the cadets were only sixteen years old.

   _____

   _____

   _____

   _____

Sentence Combining Exercises

continued

4. Combine the following sentences into two or three sentences.

    a. Some dictators are called benevolent.
    b. They do good things for the people.
    c. Napoleon Bonaparte was considered benevolent.
    d. Under Napoleon, industry expanded.
    e. Universities flourished.
    f. The civil law system was improved.
    g. The judicial system was reorganized.
    h. The Bank of France was established.
    i. Most dictators, however, are not benevolent.

_____

_____

_____

_____

_____

5. Combine the following sentences into four sentences.

    a. An astounding number of Americans died in the Civil War.
    b. More died than in all other wars combined.
    c. At first the northerners thought the war would be short.
    d. They called it the "Ninety Day War."
    e. No one believed it could last four bloody years.
    f. As many as 700,000 died in the war.
    g. That was more than double the number killed in World War II.

_____

_____

_____

_____

_____

Sentence Combining Exercises

continued

6. Combine the following sentences into three or four sentences.

   a. Forms of pizza have been around for hundreds of years.
   b. The pizza as we know it today did not come about until 1889.
   c. A tavern owner in Naples, Italy, was asked to concoct a dish to honor the visit of the queen of Italy.
   d. His dish represented the colors of the Italian flag.
   e. Those colors are red, white, and green.
   f. The ingredients were tomatoes, mozzarella cheese, and basil.

_____

_____

_____

_____

_____

7. Combine the following sentences into three sentences.

   a. In 1946 the United States conducted several atomic bomb tests.
   b. The tests took place on Bikini Atoll in the Marshall Islands.
   c. At the same time, the French introduced a new bathing suit.
   d. The bathing suit was skimpy.
   e. The bathing suit suggested an uninhibited state of nature.
   f. The bathing suit seemed to have the impact of an atomic bomb.
   g. It was quickly named the "bikini."

_____

_____

_____

_____

Sentence Combining Exercises

continued

8. Combine the following sentences into three sentences.

   a. The house was almost silent.
   b. A couple sat at a table.
   c. The table was in the kitchen.
   d. They were talking softly.
   e. They were talking about their children.
   f. The children were sleeping.
   g. The children were in their rooms upstairs.
   h. A clock was on a wall.
   i. The wall was filled with brightly colored crayon drawings.
   j. The clock had looked down on almost twenty years of family meals.
   k. The clock ticked quietly.

   _____

   _____

   _____

   _____

9. Combine the following sentences into three sentences.

   a. The first piece of Tupperware was a bathroom tumbler.
   b. It was made of polyethylene.
   c. It was made by Earl Tupper.
   d. Earl Tupper was a Du Pont chemist.
   e. He made it in 1945.
   f. The tumblers were popular.
   g. Next he made bowls.
   h. The bowls were in a variety of sizes.
   i. They had a revolutionary new seal.
   j. Flexing of the bowl's tight-fitting lid caused air to be expelled.
   k. The expelling of the air formed a vacuum.
   l. The vacuum caused outside air pressure to reinforce the seal.

   _____

   _____

   _____

   _____

Sentence Combining Exercises

continued

10. Combine the following sentences into three or four sentences.

    a. Today's "hot dog" really is named after a dog.
    b. The popular sausage was first developed in the 1850s.
    c. It was developed in Frankfurt, Germany.
    d. Some people called it a "frankfurter," after the city.
    e. Others called it a "dachshund sausage."
    f. It had a dachshund-like shape.
    g. In 1906 a New York cartoonist was drawing a vendor.
    h. The vendor was selling "hot dachshund sausages."
    i. The vendor was at a baseball game.
    j. The cartoonist abbreviated the term to "hot dog."
    k. The name stuck.

Essay and Paragraph Practice: Comparing and Contrasting

Assignment

Comparing or contrasting two topics is an activity that you participate in nearly every day. When you recognize that two people have much in common, you have observed similarities between them. When you decide to take one route rather than another, you have noticed differences between the two routes. Even something as simple as buying one toothpaste rather than another involves some sort of comparison and contrast. In fact, recognizing similarities and differences affects every part of our lives. How could you know if you were looking at a tree or a bush if you were not able to see their differences as well as their similarities?

Much college writing involves comparing or contrasting two topics. You may be asked to compare (show similarities between) the results of two lab experiments in a biology class or to contrast (show differences between) the religious beliefs of two cultures in an anthropology class. In addition, in many classes you may be asked to write papers or reports or to take essay exams in which you show both the similarities and the differences between two related topics.

Exercises 1B (pages 295–296), 1C (page 297), 2C (page 309), and 3C (page 332) in this chapter are comparison/contrast paragraphs. Exercise 1B compares high school life in the 1960s to high school life today; Exercise 1C compares holidays in the United States to holidays in Mexico; Exercise 2C compares King Lear in *The Tragedy of King Lear* to Willy Loman in *Death of a Salesman*; and Exercise 3C compares several movies of the 1990s to those of the 1950s. Note that each of these paragraphs opens with a topic sentence that makes a statement about similarities or differences.

Your assignment is to write an essay or a paragraph (whichever your instructor assigns) that compares and/or contrasts two related topics. Develop your paper from the ideas that follow.

Prewriting to Generate Ideas

Prewriting Application: Finding Your Topic

As you read the following topics, remember that the one that looks the easiest may not result in the best paper for you. Use the techniques of freewriting, brainstorming, and/or clustering to develop your reactions to several of these ideas before you choose one of them. Look for the topic idea that interests you the most, the one to which you have an emotional or personal reaction.

1. Compare and/or contrast your city or neighborhood with one you used to live in.

2. Compare and/or contrast a place as it is today with the way it was when you were a child.

3. Compare and/or contrast what you expected college to be like before you enrolled in your first class with what you found it to be like later on.

4. If you are returning to school after several years' absence, compare and/or contrast your last school experience with your current one.

5. Compare and/or contrast the characteristics of someone you know with a stereotype. For example, if you know an athlete or a police officer, compare and/or contrast that person's actual personality with the stereotype people have of athletes or police officers.

6. Compare and/or contrast your latest vacation or trip with your vision of the ideal vacation or trip.

7. Compare and/or contrast two sports, two athletes, or two teams.

8. Compare and/or contrast the person you are today with the person you were several years ago.

9. Compare and/or contrast any two places, persons, or events that you remember well.

10. If you have a background in two cultures, compare and/or contrast a few specific characteristics of both cultures.

Choosing and Narrowing the Topic

Once you have settled on several possible topics, consider these points as you make your final selection.

- Choose the more limited topic rather than the more general one.
- Choose the topic about which you could discuss several, not just one or two, similarities or differences.
- Choose the topic about which you have the most experience or knowledge.
- Choose the topic in which you have the most personal interest. Avoid topics about which you do not really care.

Writing a Thesis Statement or Topic Sentence

If your assignment is to write a single paragraph, you will open it with a topic sentence. If you are writing a complete essay, you will need a thesis statement at the end of your introductory paragraph. In either case, you will need a clear statement of the topic and central idea of your paper.

Prewriting Application: Working with Topic Sentences

Identify the topic sentences in Exercises 1B (pages 295–296), 1C (page 297), 2C (page 309), and 3C (page 322). Then identify the topic and the central point in each topic sentence. Finally, state whether the topic sentence is introducing a paragraph that will examine similarities or differences.

Prewriting Application: Evaluating Thesis Statements and Topic Sentences

Write "No" before each sentence that would not make an effective thesis statement or topic sentence for a comparison or contrast paper. Write "Yes" before each sentence that *would* make an effective one. Determine whether each effective sentence is introducing a comparison paper or a contrast paper. Using ideas of your own, rewrite each ineffective sentence into one that might work.

_____ **1.** I had not seen my hometown of Monroe, South Dakota, for over fifteen years, so when I visited it last summer I was amazed at how little it had changed.

_____

_____

_____ **2.** I have studied many different types of horse races in the past few years.

_____

_____

_____ **3.** Many holidays that are common to both Mexico and the United States are celebrated in very different ways.

_____

_____

_____ **4.** The 1990s were really great.

_____

_____

_____ **5.** The sitcoms of the 1950s were much less risqué than those we
see now.

_____

_____

_____ **6.** *Roxanne*, a 1980s movie starring Steve Martin, contains many
similarities to the play *Cyrano de Bergerac*.

_____

_____

_____ **7.** About the only thing that snowboarders and skiers have in
common is that they share the same mountain.

_____

_____

_____ **8.** I really like to watch poker like "Texas Hold'em" on TV.

_____

_____

_____ **9.** Although both the San Diego Zoo and the Wild Animal Park
feature exotic animals, the two places are not at all similar.

_____

_____

_____ **10.** The school from which I graduated, Arizona State University,
has drastically changed since I attended it in the 1960s and
1970s.

_____

_____

Prewriting Application: Talking to Others

Form a group of three or four people and discuss the topics you have chosen. Your goal here is to help each other clarify the differences or similarities that you are writing about. Explain your points as clearly as you can. As you listen to the others in your group, use the following questions to help them clarify their ideas.

1. Is the paper focusing on similarities or on differences?

2. Exactly what similarities or differences will be examined in the paper? Can you list them?

3. Which similarities or differences need to be explained more clearly or fully?

4. Which points are the most significant or most interesting? Why?

5. Which similarity or difference should the paper open with? Which should it close with?

Organizing Similarities and Differences

Point-by-Point Order

One of the most effective ways to present your ideas when you compare or contrast two topics is called a **point-by-point** organization. Using this method, you cover one similarity or difference at a time. For example, if you were contrasting snowboarders and skiers, one of the differences might be the general age level of each group. The first part of your paper would then contrast the ages of most snowboarders with the ages of most skiers. Another difference might be the clothing worn by the two groups. So you would next contrast the clothing of snowboarders with the clothing of skiers. You might then contrast the physical activity itself, explaining what snowboarders do on the snow that is different from what skiers do. Whatever points you cover, you take them one at a time, point by point. An outline of this method for a single paragraph would look like this:

Point by Point—Single Paragraph

Topic Sentence:	About the only thing that snowboarders and skiers have in common is that they share the same mountain.

I. Ages

    A.   Snowboarders

    B.   Skiers

II. Clothing

    A.   Snowboarders

    B.   Skiers

III. Physical Activity

    A.   Snowboarders

    B.   Skiers

Concluding Sentence

Point by Point—Essay

If you are writing a complete essay, the point-by-point pattern changes only in that you devote a separate paragraph to each point. Develop each paragraph with details and examples to illustrate the differences or similarities you are discussing.

Introductory Paragraph

Introductory sentences
ending with a
thesis statement
Thesis Statement: About the only thing that snowboarders and skiers have in common is that they share the same mountain.

1st Body Paragraph

I. *Topic sentence* about the difference in ages

    A.   Snowboarders

                Examples

    B.   Skiers

                Examples

2nd Body Paragraph

II. *Topic sentence* about the difference in clothing

    A.   Snowboarders

                Examples

    B.   Skiers

                Examples

3rd Body Paragraph

III. *Topic sentence* about the difference in technique

    A.   Snowboarders

                Examples

    B.   Skiers

                Examples

Concluding Paragraph

> Concluding sentences
>
> bringing the essay
>
> to a close

Subject-by-Subject Order

Another method of organization presents the topics **subject by subject.** Using this method, you cover each point of one topic first and then each point of the second topic. Be careful with this organization. Because the points are presented separately rather than together, your paper might end up reading like two separate descriptions rather than like a comparison or contrast of the two topics. To make the comparison or contrast clear, cover the same points in the same order, like this:

Subject by Subject—Single Paragraph

> *Topic Sentence:* About the only thing that snowboarders and skiers have in common is that they share the same mountain.
>
> I. Snowboarders
>
>   A.   Ages
>
>   B.   Clothing
>
>   C.   Technique
>
> II. Skiers
>
>   A.   Ages
>
>   B.   Clothing
>
>   C.   Technique
>
> *Concluding Sentence*

Subject by Subject—Essay

The following example illustrates a paper with two body paragraphs—one for each subject. Depending on the complexity of your topic or assigned length of your paper, you may need to write more than one body paragraph per subject.

Introductory Paragraph

> Introductory sentences
>
> ending with a
>
> **thesis statement**
>
> *Thesis Statement:* About the only thing that snowboarders and skiers have in common is that they share the same mountain.

1st Body Paragraph

> I. *Topic sentence* about characteristics of snowboarders
>
> A.   Ages
>
>   Examples
>
> B.   Clothing
>
>   Examples
>
> C.   Technique
>
>   Examples

2nd Body Paragraph

> II. *Topic sentence* about characteristics of skiers
>
> A.   Ages
>
>   Examples
>
> B.   Clothing
>
>   Examples
>
> C.   Technique
>
>   Examples

Concluding Paragraph

> Concluding sentences
>
> bringing the essay
>
> to a close

Prewriting Application: Organization of the Comparison/Contrast Paragraph

Examine Exercise 1B (pages 295–296), Exercise 1C (page 297), Exercise 2C (page 309), and Exercise 3C (page 322). Outline the paragraph in each exercise to determine its point-by-point or subject-by-subject organization.

Writing the Paper

Now write the rough draft of your paper. Pay particular attention to transitions as you write. If you are using a point-by-point organization, use a clear transition to introduce each point of comparison or contrast. For subject-by-subject organizations, write a clear transition as you move from the first subject of your paper to the second. In addition, as you write the second half of a subject-by-subject paper, use transitional words and phrases that refer to the first half of the paper in order to emphasize the similarities or differences.

Writing Application: Identifying Transitional Words, Phrases, and Sentences

Examine Exercises 1B (pages 295–296), 1C (page 297), 2C (page 309), and 3C (page 322).

1. Identify the organizational pattern of each as point by point or subject by subject.

2. Identify transitions that introduce each point of comparison or contrast in a point-by-point paper or that move from one subject to another in a subject-by-subject paper.

3. In the subject-by-subject paper, identify transitions in the second half of the paper that emphasize the comparison or contrast by referring to the subject of the first half.

4. Identify any other transitions that serve to connect ideas between sentences.

Rewriting and Improving the Paper

1. Revise your sentences so they include specific and concrete details. As much as possible, use actual names of people and places, and refer to specific details whenever possible.

2. Add or revise transitions wherever doing so would help clarify movement from one idea to another.

3. Improve your preliminary thesis statement (if you are writing an essay) or your preliminary topic sentence (if you are writing a single paragraph) so that it more accurately states the central point of your paper.

4. Examine your draft for sentence variety. If many of your sentences tend to be of the same length, try varying their length and their structure by combining sentences using the techniques you have studied in the Sentence Practice sections of this text.

Rewriting Application: Responding to Paragraph Writing

Read the following paragraph. Then respond to the questions following it.

Romeo and Juliet—Then and Now

The 1968 movie version of William Shakespeare's play *Romeo and Juliet* contrasts with the updated version of 1996 in a number of ways. First, the 1968 director had the characters battle each other with swords. That is the way they fought back then, but today's youth couldn't really relate to that kind of situation. In the 1996 version the director wanted to

---

show a weapon that the audience had seen on TV shows and in other movies. Swords were replaced with shiny, artistic-looking handguns. Another contrast between the '68 version and the '96 one is the style of costumes. The '68 designers kept the clothing as it would have looked during Shakespeare's time, making the male actors wear puffy-sleeved shirts, tights, and little beanie hats. The women had to endure much worse attire, such as long, heavy dresses. The designers in the updated version knew that today's youth wouldn't sit through a movie about guys wearing tights or women wearing clothes that hid everything. Instead, they had the men wear shirts that were colorful, comfortable, and modern. They also wore basic black and dark blue pants. I felt I could take the characters more seriously in normal clothes than in the old English attire. Although both versions did keep the original words of the play, I am glad that the new version changed the music of the earlier one. For instance, the boring love song "A Time for Us" was replaced by a touching, romantic tune called "Kissing You." The new music helped me follow the plot a little better. When I watched the old version, there wasn't very much background music at all. I really had to follow what was going on by watching the actors, and even then the movie was hard to follow. In conclusion, I think the director of the '96 version did a wonderful job making *Romeo and Juliet* into a movie that appeals to the young people of today.

1. Identify the topic sentence. State its topic and central idea. Is it an effective topic sentence? Can you tell whether the paper will focus on similarities or differences?

2. Is this a point-by-point or subject-by-subject organization? How many points of contrast are covered in this paper? Identify them.

3. Identify the transitional sentences that introduce each major section of the paragraph. What other transitions are used between sentences?

4. Consider the organization of the paragraph. Would you change the order of the contrasts? Explain why or why not.

5. Consider the sentence variety. What sentences would you combine to improve the paragraph?

Rewriting Application: Responding to Essay Writing

Read the following essay. Then respond to the questions at the end of it.

Guamuchil

I was born in Guamuchil, Mexico, which is a small town near the Gulf of California. It is about six hundred miles south of the border in the state of Sinaloa. I have wonderful memories of growing up there, and I have wanted to visit it for many years. Therefore, I was really excited when my husband and I decided to return to my hometown in 1994. Unfortunately, I found many changes there.

The very first difference I saw was the bridge that we crossed to enter the city from north to south. It used to be an attractive green bridge that crossed a wide, flowing river. It had brightly painted rails that protected sidewalks on each side of it. In contrast to what I had described to my husband, the bridge now looked old and rundown. The paint on the rails was peeling off, and in some places the rails were crushed into the sidewalk because they had been hit by cars and never fixed. Even the river that I used to see every time I went across the bridge was almost gone. A very small stream was all that we could see.

Another thing that I had told my husband was that, even though the city was small, it had good streets and was well kept. I had even mentioned that many new stores with large, clean parking lots were being built when I had left. Unfortunately, the streets and stores now were very different. From the entrance of the city to the middle of it, we kept finding streets where the pavement was cracked and broken. In some streets as well as in parking lots, there were many big holes. And the stores were even worse. They looked run-down, and many of them were out of business. I was very unhappy at the sight.

Finally, when I lived in Guamuchil, it was a lively place, but now all that had changed. When I was young, I knew that we were not the richest town in the state, but the houses, shops, and cars remained well painted at all times, so the overall appearance of the city was presentable. However, when I visited it in 1994, everybody seemed to have lost hope for a better future, and they did not have the will or perhaps the money to fix the things they owned or to maintain a lively city instead of an old, run-down town.

I have not been back to Guamuchil since 1994, but I think I will visit it again soon. I know it will not be the way it was when I was young, but it is still my hometown, and I will never forget that.

1. Identify the thesis statement. State its topic and central idea. Is it an effective thesis statement? Can you tell whether the paper will focus on similarities or differences?

2. Identify each topic sentence. State its topic and central idea. Does each topic sentence clearly introduce one specific similarity or difference?

3. What transitional words introduce each new body paragraph?

4. Does the essay use a point-by-point or a subject-by-subject organization? Would you change the order of the paragraphs? Why or why not?

5. Is each similarity or difference explained clearly and fully? If you would improve any, explain how you would do so.

Proofreading

When proofreading your paper, watch for the following errors:

Sentence fragments, comma splices, and fused sentences

Misplaced modifiers and dangling modifiers

Errors in subject–verb agreement

Errors in pronoun case, pronoun–antecedent agreement, and pronoun reference

Errors in comma use

Errors in the use of periods, question marks, exclamation points, colons, semicolons, and quotation marks

Errors in capitalization, titles, and numbers

Misspelled words

Prepare a clean final draft, following the format your instructor has requested.

Chapter 5 Practice Test

I. Review of Chapters Two, Three, and Four

A. Correct any fragments, fused sentences, or comma splices in the following sentences. Do nothing if the sentence is correct.

1. Zoe, thinking about whom to vote for in the next election.

2. The Somali bandits would not surrender the ship, therefore, the negotiators decided to sink it.

3. When William Tell's son saw his father aiming the arrow at him.

4. Leaving the harbor, Aeneas looked for Dido she was standing on the cliff.

5. The Xerox salesperson had the new machines ready to be demonstrated, she wondered why no one had entered the auditorium.

B. Correct any dangling or misplaced modifiers in the following sentences. Do nothing if the sentence is correct.

6. After going off the vitamin supplements, the baseball player's uniform was too large for him to wear.

continued

7. Beginning to feel fatigued, the twenty-four pack of beer was removed from her backpack by Hillary.

_____

_____

8. The vagabond walking past the farmhouse clothed in a tattered black jacket looked longingly at the empty barn.

_____

_____

9. The fire was at his back door, so Ulrich was only able to grab the family pictures.

_____

_____

10. Worried about the next day's climb, a long nap seemed to be a good idea.

_____

_____

C. Correct any subject–verb agreement errors in the following sentences. Do nothing if the sentence is correct.

11. Everyone in the arena want the Canadian woman to win the gold medal.

12. Do the grocery bagger or the cashier remember the customer who forgot to pay?

13. A pack of timber wolves have been seen running through Yellowstone this year.

14. In the back seat of Vincent's 1978 Saab was an unusable printer, a 1989 Macintosh computer, and a copy of Steve Jobs's biography.

15. Twenty years of fighting and wandering were a long time for Odysseus to be away from Penelope.

continued

D. Correct any pronoun use errors in the following sentences. Do nothing if the sentence is correct.

16. Someone on one of the upper floors was playing a song by the Rolling Stones on his or her saxophone.

17. Umberto stared at the Amazon Fire and at the Barnes and Noble Nook, but he decided not to buy it.

18. In Barcelona, people kept staring at Penelope Cruz and I.

19. Tovar knew it was him who knew about his secret.

20. Tsali told me that among the Cherokee people your name was quite important.

Chapter 5 Practice Test

II. Chapter Five

A. Add commas to the following sentences where necessary. Do nothing if the sentence is correct.

1. The fierce loyal Cerberus knew that the place he guarded was of significant cultural importance.

2. After visiting Disneyland in Anaheim California President Obama and his daughters headed for Disney World in Orlando Florida.

3. Zeus do you prefer life on Mount Olympus or would you rather live with the mortals?

4. At the annual neighborhood garage sale Jon bought a rusty wheelbarrow a velvet portrait of Elvis Presley a tub of wallpaper paste and a pair of wooden snow skis.

5. Even though they were devastated the people of New Orleans Louisiana did not let the hurricane of August 29 2005 break their spirits.

6. Before the play began Tennessee found some glass figurines and placed them on the stage.

7. Willy Loman loved his oldest son Biff; however he did not know how to advise him to be happy.

8. Ebenezer Scrooge who was a miserly old man was surprised to see Jacob Marley his dead partner.

9. Cyrano said "Although the average human nose can detect more than 10,000 different odors mine can detect even more."

10. Carlton wanted to put the candidate's sticker on the side of his sailboat but Deb's smile turned to a grimace which meant that she did not agree.

B. Add periods, exclamation points, question marks, quotation marks, semicolons, colons, and apostrophes (or 's) where necessary. Do not add or delete any commas.

11. Ptolemy wondered if the earth really was at the center of the universe

12. As the Confederates formed a line twenty-five feet from the Yankees, Jed asked Ebenezer, Aint this rather crazy

continued

13. Hurley amassed the following supplies for Super Bowl Sunday eight pounds of popcorn, twenty kegs of beer, five widescreen televisions, the cheerleaders from his local high school, and ten cases of M&M's

14. Never again yelled Batman as he leapt from the skyscraper

15. Bonnie and Clyde received invitations to the bank presidents barbeque however, they decided it wouldnt be a good idea to go

16. The dam had a small hole in it the little Dutch boy put his finger in it

17. The idea that our behavior is determined only by environment has been largely disproved, stated psychologist Steven Pinker

18. Abraham Lincolns children tried to improve their mothers attitude

19. Beatrice asked Are you sure he knows how to get out of here

20. Jackson Pollock was unable to paint between the lines fortunately, no one seemed to mind

C. In the following sentences correct any errors in the use of titles, capitalization, and numbers. (Indicate the need for italics in a title by underlining it.) Do not add or delete any commas. Do nothing if the sentence is correct.

21. Many people walked out on the film the master, starring joaquin phoenix, phillip seymour hoffman, and amy adams because they did not understand it.

22. sir lawrence olivier starred in and directed shakespeare's play henry v to raise the morale of the british people during world war ii.

23. Nearly 6,000 protesters lined the street in Peabody, Illinois, on january twenty-first, two thousand nine, when the last carton of twinkies was removed.

24. 912 fans enjoyed a concert by the jazz singer diana krall at the hollywood bowl on thursday night.

continued

25. Peter Sprague, who performs on the CD titled blurring the edges, is a member of the san diego jazz society.

26. When my daughter michelle took me to see the play inherit the wind at the old globe theater, she sneaked in 5 bags of reese's pieces.

27. By the end of the revolutionary war, only his mother still loved benedict arnold.

28. many math and engineering majors are puzzled when they discuss t.s. eliot's poem the love song of j. alfred prufock in their english classes.

29. When he arrived in los angeles from the war in afghanistan, musef was admitted as a junior to ucla.

30. It was two twenty-five p.m. when Arlo entered the sweet tooth candy company and stole thirty-three pieces of saltwater taffy, three hundred ten jelly beans, and 6 large chunks of dark chocolate.

I. Chapter One

A. Underline all subjects once and all verbs twice.

  1. Has the president written his acceptance speech yet?

  2. Hera and Zeus remarried for the thousandth time.

  3. Kate Chopin wrote in the nineteenth century, yet she was not recognized as a great

  artist until the twentieth century.

  4. Steve anxiously opened the envelope from *The New Yorker* magazine.

  5. Above Isaac stood his father with a knife.

B. In the space provided, indicate whether the underlined word is a noun (N), pronoun (Pro), verb (V), adjective (Adj), adverb (Adv), preposition (Prep), or conjunction (Conj).

  _____ **6.** London Bridge <u>eventually</u> deteriorated and fell into the river.

  _____ **7.** Clint Eastwood must have appeared in over one hundred <u>films</u>.

  _____ **8.** Ophelia was feeling mentally ill, <u>so</u> she headed for the river.

  _____ **9.** Persephone <u>arrived</u> in the spring.

  _____ **10.** <u>Everyone</u> knew that Lord Byron was born with clubfoot.

C. In the following sentences, place all prepositional phrases in parentheses.

  11. Some of the people sneered at Elvis's haircut.

  12. Staring at the two roads converging in the woods, she had to decide which to take.

  13. Driving down Highway 51, Bobby Zimmerman felt like a rolling stone.

  14. Michelle Obama sat in the plane with her daughters and played Scrabble.

  15. Worried about his image, the candidate selected his ties with care.

continued

D. In the following sentences, correct any errors in the use of adjectives or adverbs (or the use of *then* and *than*) by crossing out any incorrect words and writing the correct words above them.

16. I was more angrier than Adam when the coach yelled real hard at us.

17. Travis was happier then his girlfriend, but she was the richest of the two.

18. Claude prepared dinner careful, and then we all ate it quick.

19. Maria's fever made her feel badly, much worst than she had expected.

20. Who would you say is the wiser and most humane philosopher: Aristotle, Mark

    Twain, or Simone Weil?

Practice Final Examination

II. Chapter Two

A. Correct all fragments, comma splices, and fused sentences. If the sentence is correct, do nothing to it.

21. The student, worried about being late for class.

_____

_____

22. Dimmesdale saw Hester in town, then he was unable to sleep.

_____

_____

23. Wondering where he was going, Faith watched as her husband walked into the forest.

_____

_____

24. The new mechanic kept asking for a left-handed screwdriver nobody had one.

_____

_____

25. Hawthorne was having a writing crisis, he did not know if seven gables were enough.

_____

_____

26. As van Gogh was looking up at the night sky.

_____

_____

27. The young girl idolized Spiderman, however, she wondered if he ate flies.

_____

_____

continued

28. Helen enjoyed her time in Troy she had an ominous feeling, though.

_____

_____

29. Show me your new iPhone.

_____

_____

30. Holding the microphone as he sang "Satisfaction."

_____

_____

B. In the spaces provided, identify the following sentences as simple, compound, complex, or compound-complex.

31. As the battle unfolded, Admiral Halsey became more pleased.   _____

32. The stock market rose rapidly last week; moreover, the unemployment rate went down.   _____

33. The dentist approached with his new drill, a strange smile on his face.   _____

34. As the election drew near, one side started to show smear ads of its opponent, but the other sided refrained from dirty advertising.   _____

35. The police officer refused to let them go until they had apologized.   _____

C. Compose simple, compound, complex, and compound-complex sentences according to the instructions.

36. Write a simple sentence that contains at least one prepositional phrase.

_____

_____

continued

37. Write a compound sentence. Use a coordinating conjunction and appropriate punctuation to join the clauses.

_____

_____

38. Write a compound sentence. Use a transitional word or phrase and appropriate punctuation to join the clauses.

_____

_____

39. Write a complex sentence. Use *if* as the subordinator.

_____

_____

40. Write a compound-complex sentence. Use the subordinator *after*.

_____

_____

III. Chapter Three

A. Correct any misplaced or dangling modifiers in the following sentences. If the sentence is correct, do nothing to it.

41. Determined to liberate India, Gandhi's success came through his philosophy of nonviolent resistance.

_____

_____

42. A huge brown bear approached the boy with angry yellow eyes and then suddenly turned away.

_____

_____

43. Concerned about the rising waters, the freeway was closed.

_____

_____

44. Giselle only cared for black licorice.

_____

_____

45. Avoiding the heavy traffic on the main street, James Bond's route took him into a dark alley.

_____

_____

46. The terrified pilot tried desperately to calm the passengers, who had lost control of the plane.

_____

_____

continued

47. A woman speaking to the minister quietly began to weep.

_____

_____

48. Stopping to pick up the trash by the trail, the hiker continued up the mountain.

_____

_____

49. A black spider crawled onto the dog with a red hour-glass on its belly when it sat next to the woodpile.

_____

_____

50. Seeing the man who had been stalking her, her heart began to pound.

_____

_____

B. In the following sentences, underline any infinitive phrases, participial phrases, adjective clauses, or appositive phrases and circle the words that they modify.

51. Marcia had only a few dollars to donate to the food drive.

52. Handling the baby condor carefully, Michelle placed it into its mother's nest.

53. The American women who won the gold medals in the 2012 Olympics were smiling broadly.

54. Our dates, Shalma and Devanne, kept laughing during the concert.

55. The skunk cornered by the angry dog raised its black and white tail.

C. Add phrases or clauses to the following sentences according to the instructions. Be sure to punctuate carefully.

56. Add a verbal phrase. Use the verb *hurry*.

Jacqueline caught the early shuttle.

_____

_____

57. Add an adjective clause.

The woman ran into the old house.

_____

_____

58. Add a present participial phrase to the beginning of this sentence. Use the verb *anticipate*.

Sonia and Mireya stayed up all night studying.

_____

_____

59. Add an appositive phrase.

The delivery reached its destination ahead of time.

_____

_____

60. Add an infinitive verbal phrase to this sentence. Use the verb *hang*.

After searching all day, Rosario found the perfect picture.

_____

_____

IV. Chapter Four

A. Correct any subject–verb agreement errors in the following sentences by crossing out the incorrect verb form and writing in the correct form above it. If the sentence is correct, do nothing to it.

61. Each passenger going through the check-in lines receive a full-body search.

62. A heavily armed team with rifles, pistols, machine guns, and other weapons are watching the house where the suspect lives.

63. Does the soldiers or their sergeant know why the theater is closed?

64. Every Friday at 3:00, a teacher with fifteen students arrive at my sugar-free ice cream store.

65. Someone who seems to like you have left a bouquet of flowers outside your door.

66. Yesterday, fifty pounds of fresh fish were delivered to the homeless shelter.

67. Rice or baked potatoes serve as a good side dish for many meals.

68. Anyone who brings a bag of groceries receive free admission to the concert.

69. There is the spool of thread and the needle that Betsy Ross used to sew the first American flag.

70. Every candidate for the three available positions hope to be chosen for an interview.

B. Correct any pronoun use errors in the following sentences by crossing out the incorrect pronoun and writing in the correct one above it. In some cases you may have to rewrite part of the sentence. If the sentence is correct, do nothing to it.

71. Whenever a voter enters the polling place, you are given a ballot.

72. As we neared the football stadium, Jacob and myself bet on our favorite team.

73. Chad left his messenger bag on his motorcycle, but when he returned, he could not find it.

74. Both Deborah and Carlton have lovely voices, but Deborah practices her singing more often than him.

75. Fern said that she hated Montana and was scared of flying; this changed our plans for the trip.

continued

76. The jazz orchestra from Memphis got on their bus and headed for Louisiana.

77. My daughters wanted to plan the wedding by theirselfs.

78. Bruce proudly announced that the best bowlers in the league were Brent and him.

79. My father told me to study two hours and clean my room, which I resented.

80. After the game, one of the fraternity boys left their wallet on the kitchen table.

Practice Final Examination

V. Chapter Five

A. Add commas to the following sentences where necessary. If the sentence is correct, do nothing to it.

81. Of course I prefer tartar sauce on my trout but I don't like it on red meat.

82. The server brought the soup lit the candles picked up the salad plates and tried to remain dignified as he spilled the wine into the diner's lap.

83. I was married on July 19 1969 and on July 20 1969 a man walked on the moon.

84. Bring your bottle of antiacid however when you go to Olaf's for dinner.

85. After writing a series of short choppy sentences Ernest decided to try to write some longer ones.

86. Once upon a time for example children dressed in costumes on Halloween night and then trusted that the treats they received were perfectly safe.

87. The African gray a soft-spoken friendly parrot can imitate hundreds of words and other sounds.

88. As I was touring Death Valley California someone was burglarizing my apartment.

89. Arlene stood before the volunteers and announced "We need help cooking food cleaning walls washing clothes and babysitting the children."

90. Albert Einstein on the other hand was sometimes unable to add up his dinner bill.

B. Add periods, exclamation points, question marks, semicolons, colons, quotation marks, or apostrophes (or 's) where necessary in the following sentences. If the sentence is correct, do nothing to it. Do not add or delete any commas.

91. Could the saxophonist Rahsaan Roland Kirk really hold a note for more than five minutes

92. Helen Keller said, Hope sees the invisible, feels the intangible, and achieves the impossible.

359

continued

93. Maxwells list included the following items a telephone in his shoe, a pen with invisible ink, and a secret agent trench coat

94. Havent the artichokes arrived asked the worried chef

95. The sheriff asked Bonnies boyfriend if he had seen any bank robbers.

C. Correct any errors in the use of capitalization, titles, or numbers in the following sentences. If the sentence is correct, do nothing to it. (Indicate the need for italics in a title by underlining it.)

96. harper lee's book to kill a mockingbird, which is set in the south, is her only novel.

97. randy attended arizona state university, which is about 10 miles away from a popular community college in phoenix.

98. professor alabaster brought 55 gold coins from his civil war collection to his class called introduction to american history.

99. In our literature class we read the poem fern hill, which is one of dylan thomas's most popular poems.

100. A full dinner at pollos maria's in carlsbad costs only one dollar and fifty cents.

Appendix: Working with ESL Issues

If English is your second language, you know the confusion and frustration that can sometimes result when you try to apply the many different grammar rules and usage patterns of English. Of course, you are not alone. Anyone who has ever tried to speak or write a second language has encountered the same problem. This appendix is meant to review some of the more common issues that ESL writers face. Just remember that you were able to learn all the different grammar rules of your own language, so there is no reason why you should not be able to learn them for the English language as well.

Count and Noncount Nouns

- **Count nouns** are nouns that exist as separate items that can be counted. They usually have singular and plural forms: *one bottle, two bottles; one thought, two thoughts; one teacher, two teachers.*

- **Noncount nouns** are nouns that cannot be counted and usually do not take plural forms. Here are some common noncount nouns:

EXAMPLES

Food and drink:	*meat, bacon, spinach, celery, water, milk, wine*
Nonfood material:	*equipment, furniture, luggage, rain, silver, gasoline*
Abstractions:	*anger, beauty, happiness, honesty, courage*

Note that **noncount nouns** stay in their singular form. It would be incorrect to say *bacons, furnitures, or courages.*

- Some nouns can be either **count** or **noncount,** depending on whether you use them as specific, countable items or as a substance or general concept.

EXAMPLES

Noncount:	The *fruit* on the table looks delicious.
Count:	Eat as many *fruits* and vegetables as you can each day.
Noncount:	Supposedly, nothing can travel faster than the speed of *light.*
Count:	The *lights* in the house were all on when we arrived home.

PRACTICE   If the underlined word is a count noun, write its plural form in the blank. If it is a noncount noun, write *noncount* in the blank.

1. Alyssa's <u>happiness</u> was apparent as she drove into the driveway.   *noncount*

2. Daniela stood before her <u>bookshelf</u> and added another book.   _____

3. Carlos and Hakim discussed the <u>outcome</u> of the soccer game.   _____

4. Takanori wondered whether <u>anger</u> was the right reaction to

   the stupid joke.   _____

5. The emperor was angry when he realized the <u>laughter</u> was

   directed at his new suit of clothes.   _____

6. Chenxi knew that the next solar <u>system</u> was too far away to

   be reached in this century.   _____

7. Quarters used to be made out of <u>silver</u>, but today copper

   makes up more than 90 percent of each quarter.   _____

8. Should the state <u>government</u> protect corporations or citizens?   _____

9. Jacob's teacher was unimpressed when he identified the

   Dust Bowl as a popular football game held every <u>year</u> in January.   _____

10. Yesenia's <u>claustrophobia</u> prevented her from boarding

    the airplane.   _____

Articles with Count and Noncount Nouns

Indefinite Articles

- The **indefinite articles** are *a* and *an*. They are used with *singular count nouns* that are *general* or *nonspecific*. Usually, the noun is being introduced for the first time.

◎◎ EXAMPLES   Yesterday I saw **a car** with two teenagers in it.

An apple fell from the tree and rolled into the pool.

In these sentences, *car* and *apple* are general count nouns that could refer to any car or any apple at all, so the articles *a* and *an* are used with them.

- Do not use indefinite articles with noncount nouns.

◎◎ EXAMPLES

(incorrect)	She suffers from an insomnia.
(correct)	She suffers from insomnia.
(incorrect)	Americans value a freedom and an independence.
(correct)	Americans value freedom and independence.

◎◎ PRACTICE   Correct the following sentences by crossing out any unnecessary use of *a* or *an* or by adding *a* or *an* where needed. If a sentence is correct, do nothing to it.

1. My sister gave me ̭*a* radio to take to the beach.

2. Aisha experienced a nervousness because she was going to a job interview.

3. He is a vegetarian, so he doesn't eat a meat.

4. Ahmed and Brigitte were planning on attending concert.

5. As long as there is a hope, there still is chance.

Definite Articles

The word *the* is a **definite article**. It is used with *specific nouns,* both *count* and *noncount.* That means that when there is *the* before a noun, as in "the tree," the sentence refers to a specific tree, not just any tree. You can usually tell if a noun is specific by its context. In some cases, other words in a sentence make it clear that the noun refers to a specific thing or things. In other instances, the noun has been mentioned in a previous sentence, so the second reference to it is specific.

EXAMPLES

I bumped into *the table* in the hallway.	(This singular count noun refers to a *specific* table, the one in the hallway.)
A car and a motorcycle roared down the street. The car sounded as if it had no muffler.	(This singular count noun refers to a specific car, the one in the previous sentence.)
The men who robbed the bank looked young.	(This plural count noun refers to specific men, the ones who robbed the bank.)
The courage that he demonstrated impressed me.	(This noncount noun refers to the specific courage of one man.)

PRACTICE

Correct the following sentences by crossing out any unnecessary use of *the* or by adding *the* where needed. If a sentence is correct, do nothing to it.

1. I do not like ^*the* man who lives next door.

2. The generosity is a quality that many of us could use more of.

3. The generosity she exhibited during the crisis was admirable.

4. The psychiatrist in the next office specializes in treating the insomnia.

5. My car does not use the gasoline in its diesel engine.

Articles with Proper Nouns

- Use *the* with plural proper nouns (*the United States, the Smiths*).

- Do not use *the* with most singular proper nouns (*John, San Diego, Germany*). There are, however, many exceptions.

- Use *the* with some singular proper nouns, including names of oceans, seas, and rivers (*the Mississippi River, the Atlantic Ocean*), names using *of* (*the Republic of China, the University of Colorado*), and names of large regions, deserts, and peninsulas (*the Mideast, the Sahara Desert, the Iberian Peninsula*).

No Articles

Noncount nouns and plural nouns are often used without an article to make general statements. (Remember that *all* singular count nouns require an article, whether they are specific or general.)

◎◎ EXAMPLE

Racism and *prejudice* should worry *parents* and *teachers.*

In this sentence, the noncount nouns *racism* and *prejudice* as well as the plural count nouns *parents* and *teachers* do not use articles because they are general, referring to *any* racism or prejudice and *any* parent or teacher.

◎◎ PRACTICE

In the spaces provided, write the appropriate article (*a*, *an*, or *the*) wherever one is needed. If no article is needed, leave the space blank.

1. Jerry had never seen __*a*__ giraffe before he traveled to _____ Tanzania.

2. Cerberus is the name of _____ dog that won _____ Most Beautiful Pet contest.

3. To tell _____ truth about one's character flaws requires _____ courage

    or _____ recklessness.

4. When Bill sees _____ homeless person, he always offers to buy him _____ meal.

5. _____ traveler who went to Kuala Lumpur on _____ cruise ship told many

    tales of his wonderful experiences.

6. _____ resentment was _____ only personal characteristic that Marie would

    not give up.

7. When she was asked to pronounce her name for _____ third time, Suprava

    experienced a bout of _____ restlessness.

8. _____ surgeon was surprised by what she saw when she performed surgery

    on _____ baseball player's stomach.

9. Next year John will take _____ trip to _____ Manila, the capital of _____

    Philippines.

10. Marissa eats _____ doughnuts every day because they give her a sense

    of _____ happiness.

Subjects

- English, unlike some other languages, requires a *stated* subject in nearly every sentence. (Commands are an exception. See Chapter 1.) Subjects are required in all subordinate clauses as well as in all main clauses.

⊚⊚ EXAMPLES

(incorrect)	Is hot in Las Vegas in August.
(correct)	*It* is hot in Las Vegas in August.

(incorrect)	My brother yelled with delight when hit a home run.
(correct)	My brother yelled with delight when *he* hit a home run.

- Although some languages immediately follow a subject with a pronoun that refers to the subject, it is incorrect to do so in English.

⊚⊚ EXAMPLES

(incorrect)	The cashier *she* gave me the wrong amount of change.
(correct)	The cashier gave me the wrong amount of change.

- If a subject follows the verb, a "dummy" subject (a word that seems like a subject but is not one) is used before the verb.

⊚⊚ EXAMPLES

(incorrect)	Are some suspicious men at the door.
(correct)	*There* are some suspicious men at the door.

⊚⊚ PRACTICE

Correct any errors in the following sentences by crossing out subjects that are not needed or by adding subjects that are missing.

1. *There i*~~Is~~ no chance that we are going to catch the train.

2. Prometheus he was chained to a rock.

3. Sohini wanted to return to India because missed her family.

4. Although we were all hungry, the fish it was too spoiled to eat.

5. My friend called and said is playing soccer tomorrow.

6. When Moussa returned to Dakar, wanted to eat some Jollof rice immediately.

7. My wife's parents they were happy to see me last year.

8. Is too hot to wear a long-sleeved shirt today.

9. After the party it had ended, everyone left Ensenada and drove home.

10. Confucius taught that studying was very important and that should be
respectful to parents.

Helping Verbs and Main Verbs

Choosing the right combination of helping verbs and main verbs can be difficult
if English is your second language. To make the correct choices, you must first
understand a few things about main verbs and helping verbs. (See Chapter 1 for
a more thorough discussion of this topic.)

■ If the verb consists of one word, it is a main verb (MV).

EXAMPLE

         MV

The old server stared at the table.

■ If the verb consists of two or more words, the last word of the verb is the
main verb (MV). The earlier words are helping verbs (HV).

EXAMPLES

      HV   MV

The old server is staring at the table.

      HV   MV

The old server must leave soon.

Helping Verbs

There are only twenty-three helping verbs in English, so it is not difficult to
become familiar with them. Nine of the helping verbs are called *modals*. They
are always helping verbs. The other fourteen words sometimes function as
helping verbs and sometimes as main verbs. Here are the twenty-three helping
verbs:

Modals:	can	will	shall	may
	could	would	should	might
				must

Forms of *do:*	do, does, did
Forms of *have:*	have, has, had
Forms of *be:*	am, is, are, was, were, be, being, been

Main Verbs

To use helping verbs and main verbs correctly, you need to know the forms that main verbs can take. All main verbs use five forms (except for *be,* which uses eight).

Base Form	-S Form	Past Tense	Past Participle	Present Participle
walk	walks	walked	walked	walking
call	calls	called	called	calling
eat	eats	ate	eaten	eating
give	gives	gave	given	giving
ring	rings	rang	rung	ringing

Notice that the past tense and the past participle of *call* and *walk* are spelled the same way, by adding *-ed.* They are called regular verbs. However, the past tense and past participle of *eat* and *ring* change spelling dramatically. These are irregular verbs. If you are unsure how to spell any form of a verb, use your dictionary. The spelling of each form is listed there.

Combining Helping Verbs and Main Verbs

When combining helping verbs and main verbs, pay careful attention to the verb forms that you use.

- **Modal + base form.** After one of the nine modals (*can, could, will, would, shall, should, may, might, must*), use the base form of a verb.

EXAMPLES

(incorrect)	He will leaving soon.
(correct)	He will leave soon.

- ***Do, does, did* + base form.** When forms of *do* are used as helping verbs, use the base form after them.

EXAMPLES

(incorrect)	Did your daughter asked you for a present?
(correct)	Did your daughter ask you for a present?

- ***Have, has,* or *had* + past participle.** Use the past participle form after *have, has,* or *had.* Check a dictionary if you are not sure how to spell the past participle.

EXAMPLES

(incorrect)	The monkey has eating all of the fruit.
(correct)	The monkey has eaten all of the fruit.
(incorrect)	We had walk ten miles before noon.
(correct)	We had walked ten miles before noon.

- **Forms of *be* + present participle.** To show continuous action, use the present participle (the *-ing* form) after a form of *be* (*am, is, are, was, were, be, been*).

EXAMPLES (incorrect)   I reading the book.

(correct)   I **am reading** the book.

- **Forms of *be* + past participle.** To express passive voice (the subject receives the action rather than performs it), use a form of *be* followed by the past participle form.

EXAMPLES (incorrect)   The football **was threw** by the quarterback.

(correct)   The football **was thrown** by the quarterback.

PRACTICE   Correct any errors in the use of helping verbs and main verbs.

1. After the biryani, I will ~~eating~~ *eat* desert.

2. He had trained hard, but he did not ran fast enough to win the marathon.

3. Diego was waiting for the bus when he saw a man who had falling on the street.

4. The suspect said the bag of money was gave to him by someone else.

5. Did Maribel talked to her neighbor during class?

6. Benjamin's son does not wants any of his good advice.

7. When Maurice walked home alone after the horror movie, he was scare but did not want to admit it.

8. My neighbor Zaira has work hard all her life to support her children.

9. Please be quiet because I am concentrate on my homework.

10. If you are traveling to other countries, you must showing your passport.

Two-Word Verbs

Many verbs in English consist of a verb with a preposition. Together, the verb and its paired word create an *idiom,* which has a meaning you cannot know simply by learning the meaning of the verb or its paired word. For example, both *up* and *out* can be used with the verb *stay,* but they have very different meanings. *To stay up* means to remain awake. *To stay out* means to remain out of the house or out of a discussion.

When a verb is joined to a preposition introducing a prepositional phrase, the two words will not usually be separated.

◎◎ EXAMPLES

(incorrect)   Danny and Jenna *argued* the proposed law about.

(correct)   Danny and Jenna *argued* about the proposed law.

However, sometimes a verb is joined to a word *not* introducing a prepositional phrase, even though the word itself seems to be a preposition. (The words *off, on, up, down,* and *out* commonly do not introduce prepositional phrases after a verb.) In such cases, the verb and its paired word are sometimes separated.

◎◎ EXAMPLES

(correct)   Hector decided to *try on* the blue tuxedo before he left.

(correct)   Hector decided to *try* the blue tuxedo *on* before he left.

Here are some common two-word verbs:

approve of	Her mother did not *approve of* the gown she chose for her prom.
ask out	Fabiana hoped that Nick would not *ask* her *out*.
call off	When it started to rain, we *called off* the game.
call on	Because he was in the neighborhood, Farbod decided to *call on* his aunt.
come across	While shopping at Macy's, we *came across* my biology instructor.
drop by	Lester does not appreciate it when people *drop by* (or *in*) unexpectedly.
drop off	Will you *drop* me *off* at the dentist's office?
figure out	After much discussion, we finally *figured out* what to do.
find out	Did you ever *find out* where he lives?
interfere with	It is not wise to *interfere with* a police officer on duty.
look after	Will Rachel *look after* our cockatiel while we are gone?
look over	Irene wanted to *look* the place *over* before they rented it.
look up	Please *look up* his phone number in your address book.
make up	Waldo loves to *make up* stories about his childhood.
object to	Does anyone here *object to* the smell of cigarette smoke?
pick out	Shauna was unable to *pick out* the man who robbed her.
reason with	It is difficult to *reason with* an angry two-year-old.
show up	We were all surprised when the mayor *showed up* at the party.
think over	Give me a few minutes while I *think* it *over*.

try on	The shoes looked too small, but he *tried* them *on* anyway.
turn up	Cathy was certain the lost hamster would *turn up* somewhere.
wait for	Isabel listened to music while she *waited for* the train.
wait on	The server who *waited on* us asked if we had enjoyed the food.

⊚⊚ PRACTICE   Create sentences of your own using the following two-word verbs. Use the sentences above as models. If you are uncertain of the meaning of a verb, consult a dictionary.

1. turn up   *If my lost keys don't turn up soon, we'll have to call a cab.*

2. figure out

3. drop off

4. wait for

5. interfere with

6. approve of

7. think over

8. make up

_____

_____

9. try on

_____

_____

10. look up

_____

_____

Adjectives in the Correct Order

Adjectives usually precede the nouns that they modify. When one or more adjectives precede a noun, follow these guidelines.

- In a series of adjectives, place determiners first. (Determiners consist of articles, possessives, limiting and quantity words, and numerals.) Examples of determiners: _the_ old car, _Jim's_ empty wallet, _her_ sad face, _this_ heavy box, _some_ scattered coins, _three_ dead trees.

- If one of the modifiers is usually a noun, place it directly before the word it modifies: _the boring basketball game, the rusty trash can._

- Evaluative adjectives (_beautiful, interesting, courageous_) usually come before descriptive adjectives (_small, round, red, wooden_): _the beautiful red rose, an interesting wooden cabinet._

- Descriptive adjectives indicating size usually appear before other descriptive adjectives (but they appear after evaluative adjectives): _my huge leather sofa, a strange little old man._

In general, avoid long strings of adjectives. More than two or three adjectives in a row will usually sound awkward to the native English speaker.

◎◎ PRACTICE   Arrange the following groups of adjectives in the correct order.

1. (green, the, used) skateboard

the used green skateboard
_____

2. (leather, torn, his) jacket

_____

3. (gray, four, large) elephants

_____

4. (Chinese, an, expensive) restaurant

_____

5. (plastic, this, unimpressive) watch

_____

6. (favorite, father's, family, my) tradition

_____

7. (recent, a, art, modern) exhibit

_____

8. (famous, vinyl, old, this) record

_____

9. (well-known, tennis, championship, several) players

_____

10. (blue, five, beach, these, enormous) balls

_____

Answers to Practices

Chapter One

Page 3:

2. Harebrained, name, salon, city
3. Pandora, box, hand

4. Humpty, men, wall, problem
5. Barack Obama, speech, inauguration

Page 4:

2. Hades, Persephone, marriage
3. spring, Persephone, coast, Greece
4. husband, breezes, Aegean Sea
5. autumn, clothes, home, underworld
6. Alice, amazement, cat, grin
7. Love, tolerance, characteristics, racism, prejudice

8. success, experiment, shock, Benjamin Franklin
9. candle, light, condition, room
10. Hafiz, poet, century, wit, humor, eroticism, reverence, sacred

Pages 5–6:

2. nouns: entry, Facebook, rumor
   pronouns: Each, us, whose
3. nouns: winners, *Survivor,* taste, insects
   pronouns: all
4. nouns: Richard Nixon, China, 1972
   pronouns: Whom, he
5. nouns: account, Twitter, smartphone
   pronouns: My, your
6. nouns: term, bond
   pronouns: anyone, what
7. nouns: Black Eyed Peas, dozens, hits, brother, iPhone
   pronouns: my, all, them, his

8. nouns: veterans, Korea, Vietnam, Iraq, Afghanistan, injuries
   pronouns: Many, those, who
9. nouns: novel, *Beloved,* Toni Morrison, sister
   pronouns: I, myself, I, it, my, it, me
10. nouns: Kanye West, rapper, mother, Tupac Shakur
    pronouns: Some, that, my

Page 6:

Answers will vary. Here are some possible ones.

2. John will share his dinner with your sister.
3. Helga asked us to be quiet while Maria shot her free throw.

4. Josefina liked the puppy that she bought at the pound.
5. Oscar searched his backpack to find a bandage because his sister had cut her foot.

Page 7:

2. cut
3. wore

4. fought
5. invaded

Page 8:

2. was
3. felt

4. becomes
5. were

Page 9:

2. verb: wanted
   tense: past
3. verb: will obey
   tense: future

4. verb: made
   tense: past
5. verb: plays
   tense: present

Page 11:

2. MV
3. HV
4. HV
5. MV
6. MV

7. HV
8. HV
9. MV
10. HV

Pages 11–12:

A.

2. HV: has
   MV: foreseen
3. HV: was
   MV: swinging

4. HV: could
   MV: memorize
5. HV: should have
   MV: offered

B. Answers will vary. Here are some possible ones.

7. Wyatt Earp <u>grabbed</u> the revolver and <u>threw</u> it to Doc Holliday.
8. Penelope <u>had waited</u> patiently for Odysseus for twenty years.

9. <u>Has</u> Shakespeare <u>used</u> the tragedy that I <u>wrote</u> for him?
10. Georg Gershwin <u>had listened</u> to a lot of African American music before he <u>composed</u> *Porgy and Bess.*

Page 13:

2.
   MV: noticed
   Verbal: Texting
3. HV: will
   MV: describe
   Verbal: To illustrate

4. HV: had
   MV: taken
   Verbal: attending
5. HV: might
   MV: agree
   Verbal: stirring, to give

Page 13:

2. HV: were
   MV: discussing
   Verbal: to alleviate
3. HV: Does
   MV: want
   Verbal: to marry
4. MV: had
   Verbal: creating
5. HV: must have
   MV: seen
   Verbal: rising
6. HV: was
   MV: looking
   Verbal: to make

7.
   MV: decided
   Verbal: To impress, to do
8. HV: could
   MV: wondered, have
   Verbal: Becoming
9. HV: has been
   MV: trying
   Verbal: to find
10.
   MV: needed
   Verbal: writing

Page 14:

2. S: prison
   MV: sits
3. S: prisoners
   HV: would
   MV: drown

4. S: men
   HV: were
   MV: shot
5. S: Alcatraz
   HV: was
   MV: closed

Page 15:

2. S: sign
   HV: had been
   MV: rained, was

3. S: demonstrator
   HV: had
   MV: protested

4. S: Wendy
   HV: had
   MV: lost

5. S: Wendy
   HV: has been
   MV: living

Page 16:

2. S: African Americans
   MV: took, fought

3. S: Revolutionary War
   HV: had
   MV: ended
   S: British
   MV: transported

4. S: African Americans
   HV: were
   MV: brought
   S: they
   MV: settled

5. S: descendants
   HV: are
   MV: living

Page 17:

2. S: inventor
   MV: dreams

3. S: smartphone
   HV: does
   MV: have

4. S: Egyptians
   HV: were
   MV: helping
   S: he
   HV: had
   MV: ruled

5. S: You (understood)
   MV: Enter

Pages 17–18:

2. subject: Sonny
   verb: could have treated

3. subject: Neil Armstrong
   verb: might have hesitated

4. subject: glue
   verb: is certified

5. subject: person
   verb: Will close

6. subject: Godzilla
   verb: was looking

7. subject: You (understood)
   verb: Tell

8. subject: daughter
   verb: loves
   subject: I
   verb: would prefer

9. subject: people
   verb: must have been

10. subject: little mermaid
    verbs: looked, winked

Pages 18–19:

Answers will vary. Here are some possible ones.

2. The huge android jumped from its vehicle
   (S)   (MV)
   and shot at us.
   (MV)

3. My best friend is leaving for Afghanistan.
   (S)   (HV) (MV)

4. Have you seen my new car?
   (HV) (S) (MV)

5. Put the package on the floor.
   (MV)

6. Here is my resignation.
   (MV)   (S)

S   S   MV
7. Enrique and Eugenia sent flowers

to Maria.
S HV MV   S   MV
8. I will eat dinner after you leave.

S   HV MV
9. My computer has crashed, and my
S   HV MV
printer has run out of ink.
S   MV
10. Brent went to the party although
S   MV
Frances decided to stay home.

Page 27:

2. *Cold* and *salty* modify
pizza.

3. *Rarely* modifies *uses,* and *his* and
new modify *skateboard.*

4. *Expanded* modifies *version, extremely*
modifies *long,* and *long* modifies *song.*

5. *Corn* modifies *tortilla, fresh* modifies
cilantro, and *sliced* modifies *radishes.*

Page 28:

A.

2. The team's orange uniforms are unique.

3. Our two turtledoves keep fighting with that stupid partridge in the pear tree.

4. My fancy new espresso maker has many buttons with unknown uses.

5. Emily Dickinson wrote many excellent poems, yet she asked her sister to burn them.

B. Answers will vary. Here are some possible ones.

7. The ^*solitary* jogger felt uneasy when he was jogging alone in the ^*empty* desert.

8. The water in the ^*swimming* pool was colder than the ^*young* boy had expected.

9. The ^*tempting* dessert was displayed on the ^*dining* table.

10. ^*Many* Students who learn about recipes for ^*unusual* food begin to feel hungry.

Page 30:

A.

2. The bachelorette instinctively knew that she had a very small chance of finding love on a reality show.

3. The patient's pulse accelerated quickly when the doctor slowly approached.

4. The studio immediately scheduled a sequel to the awful movie even though it did not make a lot of money.

5. The quarterback was rather surprised when his team won decisively.

B. Answers will vary. Here are some possible ones.

7. Michael ^*vehemently* argued that soccer was a more interesting sport than baseball, but Jamie disagreed.

8. Surfers were ^*extremely* excited when they heard that winds were blowing.

9. Although she avoided the traffic, she ^*still* missed the show.

10. The doctor ^*carefully* performed the surgery, and she was satisfied with the outcome.

Page 32:

1. quieter, quietest
2. slower, slowest
3. prettier, prettiest
4. more deceitful, most deceitful
5. more rapidly, most rapidly
6. easier, easiest
7. more convenient, most convenient
8. farther, farthest
9. more slowly, most slowly
10. more effective, most effective

Pages 33–34:

1. The car looked **better** without rims **than** with them.
2. When gas prices reached the **highest** average ever, she thought that buying an SUV was the **worst** mistake she had ever made.
3. Under Cyrus the Great, the ancient Persian Empire reached its **greatest** expansion.
4. Once can dance **well** to techno music, but it can also be **really** repetitive.
5. Of the two, which is the **more** popular, Facebook or MySpace?
6. The pizza tasted **bad,** but it was not **worse than** the beer that came with it.
7. The speakers were **louder,** but their sound quality was **worse.**
8. In some outlet stores, the prices are not **cheaper than** in normal stores.
9. Even though the opera star did not sing very **well,** the audience applauded **loudly** after she had finished her aria.
10. He texted **faster** than his sister, but she spelled **more correctly.**

Pages 41–42:

A.

2. subjects: actors
   verb: are
   conjunctions: but
   subject: most
   verb: win
3. subject: musicians
   verb: are
   subject: most
   verb: become, earn
   conjunction: and, or
4. subject: Aisha
   verb: did like
   subject: she
   verb: did enjoy
   conjunction: nor

5. subject: John
   verb: did enjoy
   subject: he
   verb: ordered
   conjunctions: so, and

B.

7. but, yet
8. and
9. for
10. so

Page 43:

2. for, from
3. under, with
4. about, like
5. During, of, at, of

Pages 44–45:

A.

2. Prep   Obj
   (from a popular drinking song)

3. Prep   Obj
   (of Fort McHenry)
   Prep Obj
   (in 1814)

4. Prep   Obj
   (by the sight)
   Prep   Obj
   (of the American flag)
   Prep   Obj
   (over the fort)

5. Prep   Obj
   (During the attack)
   Prep   Obj
   (of "The Star-Spangled Banner")
   Prep   Obj
   (on the back)
   Prep   Obj
   (of an envelope)

6. Prep   Obj
   (with a tune)
   Prep   Obj
   (in many taverns)

7. Prep Obj
   (in Heaven)
   Prep   Obj
   (by John Stafford Smith)
   Prep Obj
   (in 1780)

8. Prep   Obj Obj Obj   Obj
   (about wine, song, love, and revelry)

9. Prep   Obj
   (at official ceremonies)
   Prep   Obj
   (for many years)

10. Prep   Obj
    (In spite of its popularity)
    Prep   Obj
    (until March 3, 1931)

Page 54:

1. The rock star was standing outside the bar.
2. The **aging** rock start was standing outside the bar
3. The aging rock star **in a tuxedo** was standing outside the bar.
4. The aging rock star in a **glittering** tuxedo was standing outside the bar.
5. The aging rock star in a glittering tuxedo was standing **tiredly** outside the bar.

Chapter Two

Pages 83–84:

2. SC
3. MC
4. SC
5. MC
6. SC
7. SC
8. N
9. SC
10. SC

Page 84:

2. PP
3. SC
4. PP
5. SC
6. PP
7. SC
8. SC
9. PP
10. PP

Pages 84–85:

2. Lewis Carroll created the word *chortle*, (which) is a combination of two other words.

3. After the battle in the lake, Beowulf returned to the hall.

4. Puck gave the potion to Titania, (who) was sleeping.

5. (Even though) I have seen *Hugo* seven times, you should still go with me.

6. A reformed slave trader wrote "Amazing Grace," (which) is played at police officers' funerals.

7. Michelle decided not to visit Saudi Arabia (because) Saudi culture is so hard on women.

8. My math teacher, (who) otherwise seemed sane, wore an *Angry Birds* hat everywhere.

9. I am going to complain (if) I have to see that Budweiser commercial one more time.

10. The Battle of Bull Run was the place (where) the first real engagement of the Civil War occurred.

Page 86:

2. (Whenever) Deborah wants a snack, she eats an apple.

3. (Because) she was wandering in an isolated part of the mountains, Ruth dressed warmly.

4. (Although) he suffered greatly, Dr. Urbino delayed his marriage to his beloved Fiorentino.

5. James Barrie was inspired to write *Peter Pan* (after) he told stories of Peter to the children of a friend.

Page 86:

Answers will vary. Here are some possible ones:

2. After the Civil War had ended, Robert E. Lee was appointed president of a college.
3. Colin always waits until spring before he plants new flowers.
4. Pooh was happy to see the swarm of bees since it meant honey was not far away.
5. Because he thought he was wearing clothing, the emperor walked naked into the village.

Page 87:

2. A cello player (whom) the owner knew led the house band.

3. The next player hired was a pianist (who) was the wife of the cellist.

4. Rum Adagio, (which) is my favorite drink, is always served in a bright red glass.

5. A Persian cat (that) everyone calls Ludwig begs for treats on the bar.

Page 88:

Answers will vary. Here are some possible ones.

1. Ludwig, who is picky, has her own special dish by the back door.
2. *Game of Thrones*, which is a popular HBO series, features a beautiful blonde woman.
3. Many people who were out driving that afternoon reported sighting a blue whale off the coast of Pismo Beach.
4. Bill, whom Jack would have lunch with every week, wanted to go to Tennessee to talk to a native of the Cherokee nation.
5. Elephants, which are noted for their long memories, do not have special places for graveyards.

Pages 88–89:

2. Lady Gaga gets attention <u>wherever she goes</u>. (Adv)

3. Manuel was looking for someone <u>who would go fishing with him</u>. (Adj)

4. <u>Although Ireland had become prosperous</u>, Fergal would not return. (Adv)

5. The carousel <u>that is near Balboa Park</u> is Katie's favorite place. (Adj)

Page 89:

Answers will vary. Here are some possible ones.

2. *Rescue Me* was a series about a group of firefighters <u>who lived and worked in New York City</u>. (Adj)
3. <u>Because they had devoted their lives to assisting the poor</u>, the nuns cared for homeless people. (Adv)
4. Prometheus warmed his hands by the fire <u>as he made plans to help humanity</u>. (Adv)
5. Microsoft, <u>which was founded by Bill Gates</u>, has developed some controversial software. (Adj)

Pages 97–98:

Answers will vary. Here are some possible ones.

2. A tired old man walked into the street
3. There stands the last living human.
4. Go to your room.
5. Lucinda and Matt walked into the diner and looked at the menu.

Page 99:

Answers will vary. Here are some possible ones.

2. General Washington stood in the boat; I was one of the rowers.
3. It was a long, hard row; therefore, I was quite tired.
4. Califia was shy, yet she wanted to join the others.
5. I was sick of Bradley's strange eating habits; however, I enjoyed his company.

Page 100:

2. compound:	S: Sumerians	V:	needed
	S: they	V:	made
3. simple:	S: pictures	V:	were
4. compound:	S: tablets	V:	were baked
	S: thousands	V:	have lasted
5. compound:	S: pictures	V:	were created
	S: type	V:	is called
6. simple:	S: pictures	V:	came
7. simple:	S: Egyptians	V:	recorded
8. compound:	S: material	V:	was
	S: it	V:	came
9. simple:	S: inventor	V:	made
10. compound:	S: books	V:	were written
	S: knowledge	V:	did reach

Page 101:

Answers will vary. Here are some possible ones.

2. Tomas liked it best when the sun set behind his ranch.
3. A 1965 Mustang, which is my brother's favorite classic car, is parked in his driveway.
4. Until she had found a birthday gift for her son, Sarah refused to go home.
5. We decided to visit Las Vegas, where we stayed for two weeks.

Pages 102–103:

Answers will vary. Here are some possible ones.

2. John will join us at the play, or he will see us at dinner after he has visited his mother.
3. The Padres, who play baseball in San Diego, were in last place almost all season; however, they finally moved out of the cellar.
4. When he went on his date, Armando borrowed Luis's car, but Luis did not mind because they were good friends.
5. The Padres might stay out of last place, or they might drop back into it because the team is so weak.

Page 103:

2. compound:	S: versions	V: are
	S: stories	V: do give
3. complex:	S: slippers	V: appeared
	S: version	V: was translated
4. simple:	S: shoes	V: were made
5. compound-complex:	S: story	V: used
	S: word	V: was
	S: that	V: meant
	S: that	V: meant
6. complex:	S: Charles Perrault	V: was
	S: who	V: translated
7. simple:	S: versions	V: depict
8. compound:	S: Cinderella	V: is helped
	S: versions	V: use
9. compound-complex:	S: mother	V: is
	S: she	V: appears
	S: she	V: takes
10. compound:	S: cows, goats	V: assist
	S: mice	V: come

Pages 113–114:

Answers will vary. Here are some possible ones.

2. *fragment:* <u>The cat that was trapped in the tree</u>
   possible correction: The cat that was trapped in the tree was saved by the firefighter.
3. *fragment:* <u>Because the Red Hot Chili Peppers were appearing in the Hollywood Bowl.</u>
   possible correction: Because the Red Hot Chili Peppers were appearing in the Hollywood Bowl, the tickets were sold out.
4. *fragment:* <u>To punish her for staying out so late.</u>
   possible correction: Amy's mother refused to let her go to the party to punish her for staying out so late.
5. *fragment:* <u>When Amy's 6'10" boyfriend arrived.</u>
   possible correction: <u>When Amy's 6'10" boyfriend arrived</u>, her mother dialed 911.
6. *fragment:* <u>That were in the Paris train station.</u>
   possible correction: Hugo liked working on the clocks that were in the Paris train station.

7. *fragments:* <u>As the election neared.</u> <u>Which irritated Brandy.</u>
   possible correction: As the election neared, the candidates started mentioning religion, which irritated Brandy.
8. *fragment:* <u>Wearing his usual outlandish costume.</u>
   possible correction: Elton John appeared at my church wearing his usual outlandish costume.
9. *fragment:* <u>To see the cranes that were nesting on my roof.</u>
   possible correction: Shawna wanted to see the cranes that were nesting on my roof.
10. *fragment:* <u>If you want to go to Rome.</u>
    possible correction: <u>You must finish the final exam if you want to go to Rome.</u>

Pages 117–118:

Answers may vary. Here are some possible ones.

2. F   The line for buying one of the new Cannibal surfboards was extremely long; we were sure they would sell out.
3. CS   When the political candidate tried to skip up the stairs, he tripped and broke his wrist.
4. CS   Barbara thinks *Grey's Anatomy* has been on too long; on the other hand, Horst hopes it runs forever.
5. F   The city installed a new skateboard park that was twelve yards from my house.
6. C
7. F   Eeyore saw the swarm of honey bees, but he did not want to follow it with the others.
8. CS   Everything at the wedding was perfect; therefore, the organizer received a huge tip.
9. C
10. CS When Mr. Nosferatu came over for dinner last night, he kept staring at my fiancée's neck.

Chapter Three

Pages 155–156:

2. <u>Reading the instructions closely,</u>(he) was still unable to figure out all the functions on his new smartphone.

3. <u>Eating with determination,</u>(he) would not allow three slices of New York cheesecake to defeat him.

4. I drove to San Francisco with a (car) <u>made in Germany.</u>

5. The (firefighter) <u>standing in the large library,</u> knew that 451 degrees Fahrenheit was the temperature at which paper ignites, and he hesitated.

6. The (woman) <u>dressed in a blue gown</u> attracted attention when she began to speak.

7. <u>Surprised by the Book-of-the-Month Club's decision,</u> (Richard Wright) knew that many more people would read his novel.

8. <u>Writing a book by candlelight,</u> (Cervantes) could not have realized that people would still know of him hundreds of years later.

9. <u>Looking at the river,</u> (Lao Tzu) understood that words could never fully describe reality.

10. Goose (liver) <u>produced through a harsh process,</u> is disliked by people who are concerned about cruelty against animals.

Page 157:

2. Hiding his criticism with irony, Moliére hoped he would not get into trouble with the king.

3. Constructed all over Central America, magnificent but empty Maya cities impress many visitors today.

4. Without the ability to support an ever-growing population, the Maya left their cities before the Europeans arrived.

5. The most recent actor to appear on *Dancing with the Stars* hoped his performance would reinvigorate his career.

6. Expecting no profit from his action, the business owner contributed an enormous amount of money to the politician's campaign.

7. The first person to contribute to the politician's campaign hoped that he would be rewarded in the future.

8. Shocked by the sudden attention, the texting student did not know the answer to the question.

9. Picasso made an appointment to visit an African art exhibit.

10. Impressed by what he had seen, Picasso changed his style.

Page 166:

2. *Beowulf*, which is an Old English epic poem, was written about 1000 AD.

3. Someone who is not presently looking at the professor is texting furiously.

4. Hurling, which is a sport played primarily in Ireland, is being considered for future Olympics.

5. Maurice Ravel, who was a famous French composer, wrote *Bolero*, which became one of the most popular concert pieces of the twentieth century.

6. She could not immediately remember the name of her classmate whom she had not seen in ten years.

7. Maurice Ravel asked Toots Thielemans, who is a famous harmonica player, to perform *Bolero* for the crowd.

8. The women who were arguing about the baby decided to ask Solomon for advice.

9. The plane that Chelsea had jumped from was circling 13,500 feet above Chula Vista, where she went to high school.

10. Wolf Moonglow, who was an exceptionally hirsute man, was telling us about the time when he first began to study lycanthropy.

Pages 167–168:

2. Gothic cathedrals are often ornamented with gargoyles, grotesque sculptures of evil spirits.

3. Remus and Romulus, the mythical founders of Rome, survived their infancy by being suckled by a wolf.

4. John Brown, a man devoted to ending slavery, was hanged for attacking a weapons arsenal in Harpers Ferry, Virginia.

5. (Istanbul) <u>a famous city in Turkey</u>, was once called Constantinople.

6. (Jules Verne) author of *Twenty Thousand Leagues under the Sea* and *A Journey to the Center of the Earth*, predicted a number of technological developments in some of his science fiction novels.

7. Martin recently introduced me to (Emma and Scott) <u>physicians from Rhode Island</u>.

8. The (djembe,) <u>a West African drum</u>, can produce many different tones.

9. Miles Davis's (*Kind of Blue,*) <u>perhaps the most famous jazz album</u>, has just been re-issued in a box that contains a tee shirt showing Miles.

10. Two thousand Cleveland teenagers demonstrated for a (skate park,) <u>a necessity for any practicing skateboarder</u>.

Pages 168–169:

Answers will vary. Here are some possible ones.

2. Indira Gandhi, <u>who was a woman from India</u>, Golda Meir, and Angela Merkel all were leaders of their countries.
3. In the 1980s, Prince and Michael Jackson produced a lot of popular dance music <u>that was constantly played in clubs and on the radio.</u>
4. Jeremy asked Diane to pass him another hot dog <u>that was wrapped in bacon.</u>
5. The wolf asked Romulus and Remus, <u>the mythical founders of Rome,</u> to take turns.
6. Chinese and Irish laborers, <u>who were often paid very little,</u> laid a lot of railroad track.
7. Johnny Cash, <u>who wore black clothes much of the time</u>, was born in Arkansas, but he later moved to Nashville.
8. Among the Navajo, <u>a southwestern Native American nation,</u> paintings made with sand could be produced only by medicine men.
9. In Hinduism, <u>which is a religion practiced mainly but not only in India,</u> the god Ganesh is depicted as having the head of an elephant.
10. In 1869, <u>four years after the Civil War,</u> the Cincinnati Red Stockings became the first professional baseball team.

Pages 179–180:

2. The gamer staring at his computer <u>sadly</u> noticed that his results were not improving.
   The gamer staring sadly at his computer noticed that his results were not improving. (Other answers are possible.)
3. Correct
4. The sinister-looking man who had been sitting in the corner <u>silently</u> got up and left the room.
   The sinister-looking man who had been sitting silently in the corner got up and left the room.
   (Other answers are possible.)
5. When Fidel Castro and Che Guevara landed in Cuba, they <u>almost</u> had no chance of succeeding in their attempt to overthrow the Batista government.
   When Fidel Castro and Che Guevara landed in Cuba, they had almost no chance of succeeding in their attempt to overthrow the Batista government.
6. Many soft drinks <u>nearly</u> contain enough sugar to be used as hummingbird food.
   Many soft drinks contain nearly enough sugar to be used as hummingbird food.
7. South Korea <u>just</u> had a low per-capita income in the 1950s, not in the decades after that.
   South Korea had a low per-capita income just in the 1950s, not in the decades after that.
8. Because she was worried about her health, Shawna asked Fernando <u>frequently</u> to take her to the gym.
   Because she was worried about her health, Shawna frequently asked Fernando to take her to the gym. (Other answers are possible.)
9. The world-famous prevaricator would <u>only</u> invite the gullible to his dinner.
   The world-famous prevaricator would invite only the gullible to his dinner.
10. She had <u>almost</u> tried everything to convince him to attend the demolition derby.
    She had tried almost everything to convince him to attend the demolition derby.

Pages 181–182:

2. Marco Polo presented the golden chest to the pope <u>filled with exotic spices</u>.
Marco Polo presented the golden chest filled with exotic spices to the pope.

3. Desperate to make an impression, the singer failed to convince the judges <u>reaching for a high note</u>.
Desperate to make an impression, the singer reaching for a high note failed to convince the judges.

4. The astronauts were monitored by personnel at NASA <u>who were sitting in a space rover on the surface of Mars</u>.
The astronauts who were sitting in a space rover on the surface of Mars were monitored by personnel at NASA.

5. Sitting at his desk, Natsume sensed that his cat would try to interrupt his writing, which <u>had a tendency to scratch</u>.
Sitting at his desk, Natsume sensed that his cat, which had a tendency to scratch, would try to interrupt his writing.

6. Alisha noticed that she had left her favorite novel at her friend's house down the street <u>with many handwritten comments in it.</u>
Alisha noticed that she had left her favorite novel with many handwritten comments in it at her friend's house down the street.

7. Naomi was sure she had left her wallet in the restaurant <u>thinking back over her day.</u>
Thinking back over her day, Naomi was sure she had left her wallet in the restaurant.
(Other answers are possible.)

8. The alien mothership crashed from the sky, <u>which was disabled by a computer virus.</u>
The alien mothership, which was disabled by a computer virus, crashed from the sky.

9. My mother loved the film *Milk*, but my uncle did not, <u>praising its honest handling of the life of a brave man.</u>
Praising its honest handling of the life of a brave man. my mother loved the film *Milk*, but my uncle did not.
(Other answers are possible.)

10. The Lewis and Clark expedition finally arrived at the Pacific Ocean, <u>which had been gone for months.</u>
The Lewis and Clark expedition, which had been gone for months, finally arrived at the Pacific Ocean.

Page 183:

2. C
3. D
4. D
5. D

Pages 184–185:

2. <u>Disappointed by his 3,098th failure,</u> the rock of Sisyphus rolled back down the hill.
Disappointed by his 3,098th failure, Sisyphus watched the rock roll back down the hill.
(Other correct answers are possible.)

3. <u>After drinking the magic potion</u>, his expectations were disappointed.
After he drank the magic potion, he was disappointed.
(Other correct answers are possible.)

4. Correct

5. <u>Examining their hearts,</u> the lives of the newly dead were judged by Osiris.
Examining their hearts, Osiris judged the lives of the newly dead.
(Other correct answers are possible.)

6. <u>Concerned about missing the bus,</u> Fatima's running speed increased considerably.
Concerned about missing the bus, Fatima ran faster.
(Other correct answers are possible.)

7. <u>To balance the stone at the top of the hill,</u> it was secured with duct tape by Sisyphus.
To balance the stone at the top of the hill, Sisyphus secured it with duct tape.
(Other correct answers are possible.)

8. <u>Huffing and puffing up the stairs,</u> the Eiffel Tower still seemed high.
Huffing and puffing up the stairs, Martin climbed to the top of the Eiffel Tower.
(Other correct answers are possible.)

9. <u>Orbited by sixty-two moons</u>, the speed of wind on Saturn can be as fast as 1,100 miles per hour.
   Saturn is orbited by sixty-two moons, and it has wind speeds as fast as 1,100 miles per hour.
   (Other correct answers are possible.)
10. <u>To survive in the Kalahari Desert</u>, ostrich egg shells were used by the San people as water containers.
   To survive in the Kalahari Desert, the San people used ostrich egg shells as water containers.
   (Other correct answers are possible.)

Chapter Four

Pages 222–223:

2. The toy poodles escape from the yard nearly every day.
3. The goalies always block my shots.
4. Tim's text messages infuriate his teachers every time.
5. Ahmed's answer is usually thoughtful.

Pages 224–225:

2. The marine always (enjoy <u>enjoys</u>) the packages that he receives from his mother. [S]
3. Every firefighter and police officer in the city (<u>has</u> have) brought an item to the auction. [S S]
4. My professor and his assistant from the graduate school usually (<u>arrive</u> arrives) at the same time. [S S]
5. All of the sailors and officers in the submarine (was <u>were</u>) rescued. [S]
6. Each glass bottle and plastic container (<u>was</u> were) recovered from the trash and recycled. [S S]
7. Somebody from one of our local schools (<u>has</u> have) won the prestigious Peacock scholarship. [S]
8. The war's length and cost (<u>have</u> has) worried the citizens of that country. [S S]
9. A squirrel with two cats chasing it (<u>was</u> were) running down the street. [S]
10. Few of the ants ever (<u>escape</u> escapes) that aardvark. [S]

Page 226:

2. A squad of soldiers (<u>has</u> have) entered the village. [S]
3. Rory is one of the dogs that (plays <u>play</u>) Frisbee in the park every Sunday. [S S]
4. Neither Angelina nor her cousins (knows <u>know</u>) that Madonna plans to adopt a child. [S S S]
5. Her long wait for a raise or benefits (<u>frustrates</u> frustrate) Josefina. [S]
6. That crowd of people at the end of the pier (<u>belongs</u> belong) to the Polar Bear Club. [S]

          S   S

7. That citizen from Liberty is the only person who gladly (pay <u>pays</u>) taxes each year.

                   S   S

8. (<u>Does</u> Do) Guinevere or Galahad regret what the two of them have done?

                     S   S

9. The speeches that Senator Cassius makes (<u>impress</u> impresses) the people each time.

         S

10. Carlos, among all of the other sailors, (<u>was</u> were) chosen to find the left-handed pipe wrench.

Pages 227–228:

          S

2. Ten ounces of sugar (<u>is</u> are) usually enough for a lemon icebox pie.

          S

3. The subject of Miles's dissertation (<u>was</u> were) three obscure Croatian poets.

          S

4. The news of Demeter's missing daughter (<u>has</u> have) cast a shadow across the land.

            S

5. (<u>Does</u> Do) gymnastics interest Antonio as much as competitive ice fishing?

            S

6. The committee for the abolishment of dangling modifiers (meet <u>meets</u>) Fridays.

            S

7. Twenty-five dollars (<u>is</u> are) too much to pay for a bacon and cheese hamburger.

                                                       S   S

8. Here, alive and well fed, (is <u>are</u>) the two-headed horned toad and the legless lizard from the pet store down the street.

               S

9. Esther's favorite hobby (<u>requires</u> require) paperclips and pots of glue.

         S

10. Ten miles of unpaved road (<u>lies</u> lie) between my house and the beach.

Page 234:

2. Many students feel anxious when facing **their** first orientation.

3. A student coming to a large campus for the first time should bring a parent or a friend if **he or she wants** help registering.

4. When my daughter left home for her first class, **I** could see she was worried.

5. In a very short time, **she** will find that the campus becomes familiar.

Page 236:

2. Somebody in one of the nearby condominiums plays **his or her** (or "**a**") trumpet late into the evenings.

3. When parents read a story by the Brothers Grimm, **they** might scare **their** children.

4. The school with the Native American mascot was worried about having to change **its** team name.

5. Neither Galileo nor Copernicus could keep **his** eyes focused on the ground.

6. Someone with gray hair wants to read **his** (or **her**) poetry at the department meeting.

7. correct

8. When a visitor plans to visit Yellowstone, **he or she** should check on the schedule for Old Faithful.

9. correct

10. One group of indigenous people in New Guinea burns all of **its** possessions at a certain time each year.

Pages 238–239:

Answers will vary. Here are some possible ones.

2. When Abbott was trying to explain to Costello the positions of the baseball players, Costello became very confused.
3. As Peyton Manning was showing the equipment manager how his uniform should be fitted, the manager seemed impatient.
4. When Jennifer Aniston discussed her new film with Meg Ryan, Meg offered her some good advice.
5. The famous archer shot an arrow through the apple on his son's head and then sold the apple on eBay.

Page 240:

Answers will vary. Here are some possible ones.

2. The king shepherd barked all night when our neighbors were having a party, so I called the police.
3. There were many pieces of glass on the kitchen floor, but Ibrahim had not broken any of the dishes.
4. Rafiki was looking forward to watching the Padres play the Angels, but the game was rained out.
5. Our plans were ruined when it rained all day Friday and then cleared up on Saturday.

Page 242:

2. Lorenzo, a misanthrope, prefers to spend his days by **himself**.
3. Several members of the congregation enjoyed **themselves** as they discussed *The Hunger Games*.
4. Whenever Fergal and **I** have time, we meet for lunch at the Market Street Café.
5. In Europe we entertained **ourselves** by listening to the music of Miles and Thelonious.

Page 242:

2. Fergal wondered if his fellow teacher and **he** should return to Galway this summer.
3. My accountant filled in my tax return in pencil, and he took a large deduction for jelly doughnuts. **This tax deduction** made the IRS suspicious. (Other correct answers are possible.)
4. Jose Luis apologized to his brother, but **his brother** (or **Jose Luis**) was still angry. (Other correct answers are possible.)
5. correct
6. She wanted to show her new painting in the gallery, but **the gallery** (or **the painting**) was not ready.
7. I did not enjoy Robert Hughes's review of the paintings by David Hockney and Patti Smith. (Other correct answers are possible.)
8. The pope and one of the Vatican cardinals recently watched *The DaVinci Code,* but **the pope** (or **the cardinal**) did not appreciate it.
9. Bean stuck a peppermint stick in his nose and broke **the stick** (or **his nose**). (Other correct answers are possible.)
10. Charlotte Brontë told Emily that Anne's new novel was not as well written as **Emily's** (or **Charlotte's**). (Other correct answers are possible.)

Page 249:

2. obj	7. obj
3. sub	8. obj
4. obj	9. sub
5. obj	10. obj
6. sub	

Page 251:

2. me	7. him
3. her	8. she
4. he	9. she
5. me	10. he
6. her	

Page 252:

2. whom
3. whom
4. whoever
5. who

Page 252:

2. me
3. he
4. she
5. me

Page 253:

2. I
3. he
4. her
5. I

Pages 253–254:

2. I
3. its, it's
4. she
5. whomever
6. him
7. him
8. her
9. whom
10. she

Chapter Five

Page 283:

2. The jetliner crash-landed in the Hudson River, but everyone was rescued.
3. correct
4. The giraffes would not come up to be fed, for the Wild Animal Park had changed their feeding location.
5. One giraffe started toward the feeding station, so the children cheered.

Page 284:

2. My red-beans-and-rice dish contains red beans, a ham hock, cayenne pepper, tomato sauce, and many other secret ingredients found only in New Orleans.
3. Martin finished the ninety-five items, grabbed a hammer, and nailed them to the church door.
4. The historical, exciting opening of the London Olympics impressed millions of people from around the world.
5. Everyone is looking forward to New Year's Day, for a holographic presentation of a Beatles concert is going to be shown.
6. The redesigned, rebuilt football stadium has been chosen as the site of the 2016 Super Bowl.
7. correct
8. You may embrace a geocentric view of the universe if you wish, or you may accept the heliocentric model.
9. Sam called Bill, loaded his pickup with fishing gear, went by Starbucks, and headed for the lake.
10. The courageous, proud Cherokee Chief Tsali surrendered to save the rest of his people in the Smoky Mountains.

Page 286:

2. On board the *Santa Maria* in 1492, Columbus and his crew were relieved to find that the world is not flat.
3. Waiting for a day and a half, Chet finally boarded his jet out of Afghanistan.
4. While he was processing the transaction for the iPhone, the Apple salesperson asked Gates for a picture identification.
5. Yes, Freud named some of his psychological observations after people in Greek myths.
6. Walking down the aisle, Barbara slowed and then unexpectedly stopped at the halfway mark.
7. As the artist looked up at the ceiling, he hoped the pope would like it.
8. When learning how to parallel park, try to avoid busy city streets.
9. In order to create a romantic atmosphere, Juliet played Louis Armstrong's "A Kiss to Build a Dream On" for Romeo.
10. To determine whether to forgive Sir Lancelot, King Arthur flipped a coin.

Page 287:

2. Wynton Marsalis, on the other hand, knows more about jazz than any other living person I know.
3. Marsalis went to Juilliard School of Music and plays trumpet; moreover, he plays both classical and jazz trumpet excellently.
4. Wynton, incidentally, has a father who plays jazz piano, a brother who plays saxophone, and another brother who plays percussion.
5. Miles Davis loved playing his trumpet; for instance, I once saw him keep playing in a rainstorm even though his trumpet had an electrical connection on it.

Pages 288–289:

2. Aspirin, which is not considered a performance-enhancing drug, is used even by archery competitors.
3. Claudius, who was the brother of the murdered King Hamlet, met an ironic death.
4. correct
5. Odysseus, who is the hero of the *Iliad*, did not know how to defeat the huge monster with one eye.

Page 289:

2. correct
3. Rosa Parks, determined not to sit at the back of the bus, was instrumental in beginning the civil rights movement.
4. The Ultradome, lying in the path of the tsunami, was almost completely destroyed.
5. correct

Page 290:

2. Lupita drove to the grocery store to buy a rib-eye steak, her husband's favorite cut of beef.
3. Eros, the son of the goddess Aphrodite, plays all sorts of tricks on mortals.
4. On his way to Sacramento, Matthew stopped in Fresno, the home of many well-known poets.
5. The cat in our backyard, an orange-and-white tabby, is stalking a robin.

Page 291:

2. The computer that was mailed on October 21, 2013, from Cupertino, California, arrived in Santa Fe, New Mexico, the next day.
3. Each of the presidential candidates smiled and said, "I will make your life better."
4. The multicolored togas arrived at The Debauchery, 415 Cicero Street, Rome, Arkansas, on the day before Saturnalia began.
5. Hit the road, Jack.

Page 292:

2. A misanthrope, who is a person who dislikes other people, is usually not well liked.
3. *The Tell-Tale Tart,* a novel by Dulcinea Baker, will soon be a movie.
4. Christine, how effective do you think the newly elected president will be?
5. This year Easter occurs on April 20, 2014, which is the first Sunday after the first full moon after the vernal equinox.
6. The missing coprolite was found on August 10, 1954, in Rome, Georgia.
7. Clare Danes, playing a CIA agent, stars in the series *Homeland*.
8. "The spiders have arrived," said Harker, "and I'm ready."
9. Steven Spielberg, for example, directed *E.T.*
10. Clark, please tell Scarlett, who is a sensitive Southern belle, that you apologize for using the word *damn*.

Pages 299–300:

2. Have you tasted the dessert?
3. The whole Atlantic coast is under attack!
4. The pitcher asked his catcher if he should throw a curve.
5. Has Ceres been waiting long for her daughter?
6. How do you know it is an atom?
7. Stop being stubborn.
8. Michael received his Ph.D. from Arizona State University.
9. Why did they leave the game so early?
10. After five days the fish wondered if it had worn out its welcome.

Page 301:

2. The aspiring star did the following to prepare for his audition: got disturbing tattoos all over his body, dyed his hair extravagant colors, and learned two chords on the guitar.
3. The child touched the burner on the stove; however, she did not react.
4. correct
5. There was one thing I really looked forward to when I visited my grandparents: exploring the creek that ran by their house.

Pages 302–303:

2. Batman was afraid of losing his significant other to the district attorney; moreover, he had lately developed a fear of heights.
3. Who was it who said, "The truth is rarely pure and never simple"?
4. My favorite Mae West quotation is this one: "When I'm good, I'm very good, but when I'm bad, I'm better."
5. Coltrane looked at Davis and said, "Tell me a few of my favorite things."
6. "For whom does the bell toll?" asked the tourist.
7. Was it Mark Twain who said, "I believe that our Heavenly Father invented man because he was disappointed in the monkey"?
8. Daedalus screamed, "Deploy your parachute!"
9. Humpty fell off the wall and broke; he could not understand why all the king's men were calling for Super Glue.
10. Bill Clinton once said, "It's the economy, stupid."

Page 304:

2. Mr. Lewis's sense of propriety was bothered by Mr. Clark's rude remarks.
3. Have you seen Rumpelstiltskin's scissors?
4. Constance was given three months' wages when she was terminated.
5. Popeye's can opener wasn't working, so he went to Walmart.

6. It's strange that Natasha won't write in anything but short, simple sentences.
7. We'll applaud when we hear something that's worthwhile.
8. He had one week's free stay at his father-in-law's hotel.
9. Staring over the rim of Sylvia's soup bowl was a cockroach.
10. The children's favorite bedtime story was the one about the man with the hatchet.

Page 305:

Answers will vary. Here are some possible ones.

2. Thomas's chance of being named chief justice seemed slim.
3. Kalie thought it was strange to be asked to judge her brother-in-law's behavior.
4. The basketball players' wives met them at the airport.
5. Mr. Lewis's German shepherd didn't know what to do once it had leaped over the fence.

Page 311:

2. In Langston Hughes's short story "Salvation," a boy ironically loses his faith while participating in church services.
3. Robert Frost's poem "The Road Not Taken" is one of his most well-known works.
4. After Hester put down the magazine *Popular Sewing,* she mended Pearl's stockings.
5. The movie *Battleship* earned only a quarter of what it cost to film it.

Page 313:

2. Mitt Romney received a signed copy of John Banville's latest novel *The Sea.*
3. Born in Lorain, Ohio, Ms. Morrison has been on the cover of many magazines, including *Time.*
4. Uncle Elvis was playing Bruce Springsteen's song "Born in the U.S.A." when I told him John Updike had died.
5. A number of men and women from Carlsbad, New Mexico, participated in the Iraq war and are now continuing to fight in the war in Afghanistan.
6. During the Christmas holidays, one can see beautiful decorations in Santa Fe and Albuquerque.
7. The online newspaper *The Huffington Post* recently published an article titled "Colorado Wildfires."
8. On my iPad, I bought the play *Waiting for Godot* by Samuel Beckett.
9. Charlie showed Marisa his collection of *T.V. Guide* magazines.
10. The Barnes and Noble bookstore on Grand Avenue is closing by the end of winter.

Page 315:

2. One never knows when all five members of Jim's jazz band will show up; it could be at 9:15 or at 12:45.
3. For the retirement party, Charlie brought 15 pastries, Blair brought 1 Clark Bar, Barbara brought 115 pounds of fresh tuna, and Deborah brought 3 chocolate cheesecakes.

or

For the retirement party, Charlie brought fifteen pastries, Blair brought one Clark Bar, Barbara brought one hundred fifteen pounds of fresh tuna, and Deborah brought three chocolate cheesecakes.
4. The inauguration ceremony on January 21, 2013, featured Barack Obama, who had defeated Mitt Romney.
5. correct

Appendix

Page 362:

2. bookshelves
3. outcomes
4. noncount
5. noncount
6. systems
7. noncount
8. governments
9. years
10. noncount

Page 363:

2. Aisha experienced nervousness because she was going to a job interview.
3. He is a vegetarian, so he doesn't eat meat.
4. Ahmed and Brigitte were planning on attending a concert.
5. As long as there is hope, there still is a chance.

Page 364:

2. Generosity is a quality that many of us could use more of.
3. correct
4. The psychiatrist in the next office specializes in treating insomnia.
5. My car does not use gasoline in its diesel engine.

Page 365:

2. Cerberus is the name of the dog that won the Most Beautiful Pet contest.
3. To tell the truth about one's character flaws requires courage or recklessness.
4. When Bill sees a homeless person, he always offers to buy him a meal.
5. The traveler who went to Kuala Lumpur on a cruise ship told many tales of his wonderful experiences.
6. Resentment was the only personal characteristic that Marie would not give up.
7. When she was asked to pronounce her name for the third time, Suprava experienced a bout of restlessness.
8. The surgeon was surprised by what she saw when she performed surgery on the baseball player's stomach.
9. Next year John will take a trip to Manila, the capital of the Philippines.
10. Marissa eats doughnuts every day because they give her a sense of happiness.

Pages 366–367:

2. Prometheus was chained to a rock.
3. Sohini wanted to return to India because she missed her family.
4. Although we were all hungry, the fish was too spoiled to eat.
5. My friend called and said he is playing soccer tomorrow.
6. When Moussa returned to Dakar, he wanted to eat some Jollof rice immediately.
7. My wife's parents were happy to see me last year.
8. It is too hot to wear a long-sleeved shirt today.
9. After the party had ended, everyone left Ensenada and drove home.
10. Confucius taught that studying was very important and that one should be respectful to parents.

Page 369:

2. He had trained hard, but he did not run fast enough to win the marathon.
3. Diego was waiting for the bus when he saw a man who had fallen on the street.
4. The suspect said the bag of money was given to him by someone else.
5. Did Maribel talk to her neighbor during class?
6. Benjamin's son does not want any of his good advice.
7. When Maurice walked home alone after the horror movie, he was scared but did not want to admit it.
8. My neighbor Zaira has worked hard all her life to support her children.
9. Please be quiet because I am concentrating on my homework.
10. If you are traveling to other countries, you must show your passport.

Pages 371–372:

Answers will vary. Here are some possible ones.

2. After two hours of discussion, we still could not figure out what to do.
3. Let's drop off the kids at your brother's house.
4. I don't want to wait for the package to arrive any longer than I have to.
5. He consistently interferes with whatever I try to do.
6. Lucinda did not approve of her sister's decision to tattoo her entire back.
7. I need to think it over for a few minutes before I make my decision.
8. Sean was furious when he learned that his son had made up the entire story.
9. I'll try on the shirt, even though I hate the color of it.
10. Will you look up his cell phone number in your contacts list?

Page 373:

2. his torn leather jacket
3. four large gray elephants
4. an expensive Chinese restaurant
5. this unimpressive plastic watch
6. my father's favorite family tradition
7. a recent modern art exhibit
8. this famous old vinyl record
9. several well-known championship tennis players
10. these five enormous blue beach balls

Index